This is vintage Denise Ackermann. A [...] her theology perceptive and challenging, and her spirituality profound and caring. The reader could not ask for more. But there is more. Denise brings to her reflections a creative freedom and conviction that is only possible for someone who has lived what she now writes, and is able to write what she has embodied and taught with courage and compassion. Denise always tells me that she does not need to quote too many sources and have loads of footnotes. But "Ordinary Blessings" is a goldmine of apt quotations from a boggling range of sources, well-chosen and always appropriate. The reader will be grateful for her many explanatory comments and directions for further reading. Thank you, Denise, for putting your soul into yet another, and hopefully not your last, book. Blessed are those who write with clarity and passion, for they shall be remembered with gratitude.

John de Gruchy, a Hulsean Lecturer at Cambridge and chair at Robert Selby Taylor Chair of Christian Studies

Denise Ackermann wrote a surprising book. Theology and spirituality are for her two sides of one coin, the coin I compare to the drachma, the woman of Lucas 15 verse 8 sought and found. Out of her immense erudition she digs for treasures: key words like faith, love, hope, prayer, blessing, silence, mystery, "God", words that became faded and somewhat rusty by too much traditional use. Denise holds them again to the light, polishes them with her everyday experiences till they sparkle. Reading, applying it to our own circumstances, we are lead to answers to the core question of this book: how can I, here and now and tomorrow, live a meaningful faithful life? Her touchstone is the man Jesus, his life and words. A joyfully inspiring book.

Riet Bons-Storm, Emeritus Professor of Women Studies and Pastoral Theology and Care, Groningen University, the Netherlands

The scholarly can often be abrasive and intimidating. In this book, Denise Ackerman is erudite and yet alluring and gentle. The reader imagines a gentle smile playing round her lips while she exposes the absurdities of the many facets of male chauvinism and the injustice in the treatment of those who are not heterosexual. She a formidable and yes a charming adversary.

Archbishop Desmond Tutu

Finding the blessings of the ordinary is the gift that Denise Ackermann shares with us from a lifetime of deep seeing, quiet listening, and faithful engagement with the sorrows and wonders of our world. Through the weaving of personal and scriptural narrative with social and theological analysis that characterizes her theology, she explores pathways of spirituality that can sustain faith and praxis for anyone open to being surprised by the man on the borrowed donkey.

Prof. Francine Cardman, Boston College School of Theology and Ministry

Not shying away from life's painful realities, this book conjures up a deep sense of wonder regarding the ordinary blessings that may surprise us when we least expect it. Structured around some profound contemporary beatitudes, this book, which is rooted in Denise Ackermann's years of doing theology in the midst of the complexities of the South African context, will speak in a fresh way to anyone who is struggling to make sense of the paradoxes and perils of life. A wise and truly beautifully written book!

L. Juliana Claassens, Associate Professor of Old Testament, Faculty of Theology, Stellenbosch

In *Surprised by the Man on the Borrowed Donkey: Ordinary Blessings* Denise Ackermann continues her memoir of reflecting on the question "What makes life worth living?" This book is grounded in the context of Ackermann's lived experiences as she combines personal witness and theological erudition with a refreshingly engaging style. It is a brilliantly personal, honest analysis of what it means to be blessed when the contradictions, paradoxes, ambiguities and incongruities of life are embraced. The reader is drawn into an experience of wonder, surprise and mystery of faith with gratitude for ordinary blessings and, is also challenged to act on her/his faith in God in ways that promote justice in everyday contexts of greed and abuse of power. I enthusiastically recommend it to theologians – academics, clergy and lay persons.

Dr. Miranda Pillay, University of the Western Cape

Joan,   1 January 2017
Baie geluk!
     Liefde Pa

Surprised by the Man on the Borrowed Donkey

ORDINARY BLESSINGS

DENISE M. ACKERMANN

LUX VERBI

Surprised by the man on the borrowed donkey: Ordinary blessings

Published by Lux Verbi
an imprint of NB Publishers
a division of Media24 Books (Pty) Ltd
40 Heerengracht, Cape Town 8001
P.O. Box 551, Cape Town 8000
www.luxverbi.co.za

Edited by Denise Fourie, Sandra Cattich and Glynne Newlands
Cover and layout by Marthie Steenkamp
Printed and bound by Paarl Media Paarl,
15 Jan van Riebeeck Drive, Paarl, South Africa

First edition, first print 2014

ISBN: 978-0-7963-1799-5 (soft cover)
ISBN: 978-0-7963-1800-8 (epub)
ISBN: 978-0-7963-1801-5 (mobi)

First print-on-demand edition, first print 2015
Printed and bound by Mega Digital cc,
5 Koets Street, Parow, South Africa

For Rebecca, Anna, Jo, Rachel and Seth

and

for Luke Stubbs (05.09.1960–20.07.2009)
who started it all

CONTENTS

FOREWORD

Some of us in South Africa have chosen to call our reflections "contextual theology", but few of us, if any, have been as thoroughly and painstakingly contextual as Denise Ackermann. She does not make use of labels like "contextual theology", but she is deeply aware at all times of the historical, political, social and economic context of her theology, as well as the personal and biographical circumstances and experiences that have shaped her thinking. This makes for a theology that is thoroughly concrete, experiential and spiritual.

In a way all theology is contextual. The difference is between those who are aware of this and those who are not. The classical definition of theology is "faith seeking understanding", and we seek understanding by asking questions and searching for answers. Genuine faith questions, however, vary enormously from place to place, time to time and person to person. The questions arise out of our context and experience of life.

Today most theologians are fully aware of this. Too often in the past, though, and sometimes in the present too, theologians have persisted with answering questions other people asked at other times and in other places as if they were the only questions people may grapple with in theology. Those who formulated these questions many years ago were often white clerical males who lived in monasteries, seminaries and universities. They knew nothing of the questions and experiences of women, of black people, of lay people or of the poor, let alone the questions and problems of the world as it is today. The theology of the past had a context, but it is not *our* context.

A theology that is fully aware of its context and how that is different from other contexts is what we call a contextual theology. Thus feminist theology, black theology and liberation theology, for example, are consciously contextual theologies.

Nor is it only the *questions* that arise out of our context. The *answers* are also shaped by the context in which we live and by our biographical experiences. That is not to say that contextual theology is totally subjective and arbitrary. Any Christian theology has to find its answers in Jesus as the incarnate Word of God. However, our particular context and experience of life can give each of us a particular perspective on the meaning of Jesus' life and death. This perspective can open our eyes to what is already present implicitly in the Word of God. It can provide us with new insights.

The theology of Denise Ackermann's book is deeply and consciously contextual. And yet it is at every point a book about Jesus, about her honest and personal experience and struggle with faith in Jesus. It is her "biography of faith" – faith in "the man on the borrowed donkey" as she calls him.

Of course, if we are honest, we will discover that there are few, if any, easy answers to the questions that arise for us today. Denise is painfully aware of that. She faces the contradictions, the paradoxes and the mystery of it all. She faces her own experience of being diagnosed with cancer and her more recent experience of macular degeneration with its threat of eventual blindness. She writes about the questions that these experiences raise for her and about her search for answers. It is clear that her faith has enabled her to live fruitfully with unanswered questions.

The result is an amazing number of valuable insights into the meaning of holiness, secularism, spirituality, freedom, death, gratitude, listening, greed, sharing and humour, as well as the wonder of God's creation, especially in the awesome beauty of birds. Looking at her life, her experience and her context with the eyes of faith enables her to see above all else a history of blessings, many blessings. Hence the subtitle of the book: Ordinary blessings.

Albert Nolan
Johannesburg
4 February 2012

INTRODUCTION

I believe that all theology is contextual and therefore, in a sense, autobiographical. A theologian's experience of place, time, culture, history, relationships, and her experience of despair, grace and hope are all interwoven in her life of faith. As circumstances change, beliefs are reshaped, perspectives revisited. My life is no exception. The experience of looking back and sifting out that which has meaning from the trivia of life is a privilege of age. Having faith, reflecting on what this means, and then trying to speak about it can never be done in a vacuum. Furthermore, it is an ongoing task, in which we reflect upon our lives within specific communities and relationships, and this shapes our theologies.

Trying to work out what is meaningful in the life of faith is much the same as the trying to answer the question "What makes life worth living?" This question was central to *After the Locusts,* a previous book in which I wrote letters to those close to me about my attempts to live out my faith in South Africa after apartheid. But what do I mean by "the life of faith"? I am reminded of a humorous little poem by American poet Emily Dickinson (1830–1886):

"Faith" is a fine invention
When Gentlemen can *see* –
But *Microscopes* are prudent
In an Emergency.

The life of faith is not wholly without microscopes. A greater intensity of seeing oneself in the world and finding joy in the small things are fruits of faith. Faith infuses life with significance, and with a surprising depth and abundance of experiences in which love, hope and peace surface. Awareness of the ever-present blessing of grace brings a sense of awe and moments of profound fulfilment. While I marvel at the riches of faith, I cannot claim to be a person who always feels fulfilled, and who is able to sail through life with impunity. Above my desk I have a framed verse: "I believe, help my unbelief!" (Mk 9:24). I do believe. I also wrestle with the contradictions in the life of faith, and with moments of abandonment. The question "What makes life worth living?" continues to gnaw at me. This book is a further attempt to find answers as I continue to mull over it.

I also wonder whether there is something like a theological identity? The older I get, the greater my unease with labels, yet at the same time I cannot avoid them. I am a woman, a Christian, a wife, mother and grandmother, a friend, a feminist, a theologian, a news junkie, a lover of icons and sushi, and much, much more, all at the same time. According to our latest census, I am a white South African of European (mostly French) descent. The irony is that my DNA proves that I am originally a native of East Africa! I also come from a mixed cultural background, am a social democrat by conviction, a cultural hybrid, an amateur "greenie", a bird watcher, walker – the list goes on. The point is that, like every other human being, my complexities of identity are endless. I belong to diverse categories simultaneously and, depending on the circumstances, one or other category will emerge and engage me. I treasure all my labels. Some of them provide a view from the margins where all the contradictions of life bump up against one another. I prefer this view; it is less stifling, and more open to paradox and contradiction.

As a theologian I have labelled myself a "feminist theologian of praxis": "Feminist" because of a lifelong concern with the dignity and equality of women; "praxis" because the only valid test of beliefs is how they translate into actions that promote love and justice. These concerns remain central to my theology and continue to shape my perspective from the edge. But they are not the whole story. More recently I further qualified my identity as a theologian by calling myself "a ragbag theologian". Why? Women know that ragbags are filled with an odd assortment of cloths that are useful the second time around. I came to theology later in life than many of my colleagues and, as I play catch-up, I cannot resist digressions, particularly when I am not sure where they will take me. So ragbag theology is second-time-around theology – a revisiting of familiar themes from a different experience of life.

Being a ragbag theologian is, in my case, not surprising. Not only do multiple identities reflect multiple affinities but, looking back on themes I have written about, it is clear that my theology does not constitute a neat corpus of concerns. The themes I have tackled are decidedly eclectic. Nevertheless, throughout I write from the critical experience of being a woman, bolstered by my view that our beliefs and actions should be held in creative tension with one another. This book reflects some of the different colours and textures of cloth in my ragbag – a pick-and-choose collection of interests with one binding conviction: my faith in the man who borrowed a donkey all those years ago, and whose life and teaching is found in the gospels.

The drawstring of my ragbag is spirituality, a testament to my belief that theology and our spirituality are inseparable. A profound longing for an ever-closer encounter with God has prompted all the byways I have pursued. In this quest, I have been filled with wonder at how my view from the margins has consistently drawn me to Jesus, the central figure of my faith. The widely divergent themes in this book represent issues that have challenged my attempts to live out my faith in a world that is increasingly unsettled, often violent, filled with poverty and human need, and yet awash with beauty and goodness.

I avoid calling myself religious. It smacks too much of something set in institutions, ritualised, consoling instead of transforming. The word "religion" is, in the main, useful when referring in general to the different religions in the world. Christian faith, however, is about an encounter with a person, not a religion. Jesus did not call us to a new religion, but to life. I prefer the vulnerability of the word "faith" – just that and nothing more. I have faith in Jesus Christ and my faith is expressed and nurtured by my spirituality. Unavoidably, this work is deeply personal for it is about what blessing has meant in my life. Because I also believe that conduct is more convincing than words, theology should focus on right actions, an emphasis that will be apparent throughout.

I write in a time when faith perspectives are often subjected to ridicule as self-deceiving, irrational, even deluded, and motivated by a deep fear of death. The woes of the world are often ascribed to religious beliefs and practices. In the case of Christianity, the Crusades, the Inquisition, and the unseemly behaviour and ridiculous claims of fundamentalists are often mentioned. The God of the Old Testament is a tyrant, and discrimination against women and homosexual people proves the intolerance of Christian beliefs and practices. Moreover, the development of science, Darwinism, new insights by cosmologists and physicists who probe our enigmatic universe and make us aware of that mysterious phenomenon called dark matter, or neuro-psychology's revelations of the working of the human mind accordingly prove how primitive faith perspectives are in the modern world.

Of course Christianity has done itself no credit when its adherents are intolerant, warlike, arrogant, unjust, unloving and unable to accept difference. Our history is muddied with dreadful, even barbarous acts in the name of Jesus Christ. Furthermore, scientists are offering new explanations of our world, and uncovering new ways of understanding the complexities of the cosmos and our place in it. All this is exhilarating and to be celebrated.

But people who find the discoveries of science riveting, while at the same time continue to believe in God are, with monotonous regularity, treated with what contemporary American writer Marilynne Robinson calls "a hermeneutics of condescension". Self-appointed guardians of "scientific truth" pronounce judgment on the maturity and the intelligence of these believers. We do not seem able to allow others to be different, to be who they are without apology. We all make our choices. Thus any condescension on the part of Christians towards agnostics or atheists is equally unacceptable. I enjoy my untutored reading of *Scientific American*, while at the same time I accept Gregory of Nyssa's (d.385/6) description of who God is: "That which is without quality cannot be measured, the invisible cannot be examined, the incorporeal cannot be weighed, the limitless cannot be compared, the incomprehensible does not admit of more or less."

Those who dismiss faith perspectives as simply a matter of false rituals and a need for social bonding must be somewhat dismayed by the persistence of the ancient and global truth that such perspectives give meaning to people's lives that they do not find elsewhere.

This book is not an apology for having faith. It is an exploration of the fruits of having faith in one woman's life. Human beings have the unique ability to ask questions of themselves and others, questions that matter and that can change our understanding. My theological reflections are prompted by questions. My bias is clear. It agrees with Robinson when she writes: "The voices that have said, 'There is something more, knowledge to be had beyond and other than this knowledge' have always been right." My questions are about that "something more".

I do not think that faith in God is diminishing because of the advance of science or because of the "death of God" theologies. However, I agree with Robinson that malaise in terms of faith can be caused when the "felt life of the mind" is excluded. This exclusion, she says, is attributed to "[...] accounts of reality proposed by the oddly authoritative and deeply influential 'parascientific literature' that has long associated itself with intellectual progress and the exclusion of felt life from the varieties of thought and art that reflect the influence of these accounts". A cursory walk down the aisle of a bookshop affirms the popularity of "parascientific literature", the authors of which may or may not be scientists. This kind of literature is a genre of political or social theory that makes a case by using the science of the moment to arrive at a set of general conclusions about the nature of the human being, from the beginning to the present, and draws political, social or anthropological inferences from such conclusions.

As the years pass, I am learning that the human mind is infinitely more complex than I can imagine; that human beings have the capacity to wonder as well as to comprehend beyond a positivist view of self and reality; that there is a longing for the beyond that will not easily leave us; that being human is not an argument but an experience; that our knowledge of the world is accelerating as is the universe itself, and that the learning of science is adding to our knowledge as it questions and probes. The source of this book is in what Robinson calls the "felt life of my mind" – the place where experience and reason meet.

For me, the one enduring certainty is the truth I find in the life and teaching of Jesus. I have no answers to questions of eternity: I know my limits; humankind is ultimately a mystery. I am happy to leave the exploration of our tiny planet, so fragile and blue in a universe that looks like a wavy compact disc dotted with exploding stars and quasars, to the scientists. I wonder at the discovery of dark matter, that mysterious substance that neither emits nor absorbs light. I cannot comprehend what it means that the Hubble telescope has captured some ten thousand galaxies in an area the size of the full moon. Now that the Higgs Boson particle, the so-called "God particle", has been found, I am told it is the "glue" of the universe. What this all means I cannot comprehend. But I am happy that scientists affirm my belief that God is the glue that holds all together! I have only my experience of inexplicable encounters to guide my questions and to temper any assumptions of "knowing it all".

This book is a further chapter in my biography of faith and my continuing surprise at its fruits. It is composed of nine chapters, each on a different topic. Although they can be read separately, there is a certain order in their sequence that makes sense to me and hopefully to the reader. The first, "Surprised and blessed", seeks to explain the title and the role of Jesus in my reflections, and what it means to be blessed. The second and longest deals with the central truth of the gospel: in order to live the life of faith we have to embrace paradox and contradiction, and learn to live fruitfully with the questions. This is followed by the third chapter, which examines what the call to holiness means in the life of faith. The gospel promises us freedom. The fourth chapter looks at the meaning of freedom and is followed by a chapter that reflects on the indispensable character of discernment in Christian spirituality. Chapter Six focuses on the discovery that gratitude is indeed a blessing. Thereafter, I attempt to deal with what it means to live with "enough" in a world of want. This is followed by the unlikely theme of incongruity and laughter in the life of faith. It reverts back to the chapter on paradox – our beliefs, when laid bare by realities, are a kind of holy foolishness. We need to be able to chuckle at the unsettling and disruptive nature of our faith in a world that is often unreceptive to the idea that to be wise is to be foolish. The book ends with a short postscript on the blessing of birds.

While I write, I call to mind the many women with whom I have done Bible study in different places over more than forty years. I hope that this book may also be of interest to, among others, students of theology, members of churches, those outside the church who may wonder about those of us who sit in pews on Sundays, and anyone else who may want to read about the blessings of a long life. I cannot help agreeing with a well-known Protestant theologian of the twentieth century, Karl Barth (1886–1968), who remarked: "The angels will laugh when they read my theology." Doubtlessly this book will give the angels cause for laughter, while I hope that it will make theology palatable for interested readers. Throughout I am aware of two pressing needs in our times: the first is a political and social need for a more just and equitable society; the second is more inward and personal – it is a yearning for a deeper spiritual awareness. I believe that the God question is the same as the human question. All faiths have their origins in the human heart and in contexts that are at times overwhelming. I cannot separate these two intertwined needs.

The phrase "the church" is fraught. Can any institution fully represent the man we know as Jesus? There is no one church, one tradition, one set of practices and characteristics. The use of the phrase "the church" is therefore rather sloppy, but it is intended to cover all denominations that are considered mainline. I am a member of the Anglican Church in South Africa. However, my experience of many different churches in different parts of the world has shown me that cultures, contexts, local traditions, personal tastes and desires all contribute towards a multitude of "flavours" even within churches with more formal frameworks. Institutions by their very nature have rules and regulations to ensure order. Churches have structures with which they operate, and within these structures hierarchies of authority are quickly formed. When I allow myself to dream of what the community of believers should be like, I know that I am in for disappointment. I understand the church as a place of plurality and inclusiveness, a place where people of all kinds are welcome and at home, because it is a place that is accepting, loving, serving, and exists by the grace of God in Jesus Christ alone.

The ideas in this book do not purport to be original. It is impossible for me to say where they all come from. Throughout, I am in conversation with selected theologians, writers and thinkers across time, many of whom I acknowledge and often elaborate on in notes at the end of each chapter. Dates are given when a specific deceased person is mentioned for the first time in order to place her or him in an historical context. Contemporary writers and thinkers are not dated. The notes at the end of each chapter also flesh out borrowings mentioned in the text. Not every quotation is referenced. However, each chapter concludes with a list of works consulted, in the hope that some readers may find topics of interest to pursue further.

I am not a biblical scholar, though I am aware of the pitfalls in using scripture to bolster arguments. My use of scripture throughout has been prompted rather by the way in which it is read in my Bible study group than by a more scholarly academic reading. All biblical quotations are taken from *The New Annotated Oxford Bible*, the Revised Standard Version (Oxford: Oxford University Press, 1991).

I owe thanks to a number of friends: Geoff Quinlan, retired bishop for reading my manuscript and making many useful suggestions on how to improve it; Karen Sporre, professor of theological education at Umeå University in northern Sweden, who cast a critical and helpful eye on the structure of the book and the themes raised; Francine Cardman, professor of early church history at Boston College, for her incisive reading, her innumerable valued suggestions and for endless encouragement; Albert Nolan for agreeing to write the foreword despite a busy schedule; Denise Fourie for her many helpful suggestions and meticulous editing; and lastly, the women with whom I have done Bible study over many years. Unknowingly they have been my conversation partners throughout.

Last, but certainly not least, to Laurie – my partner for fifty-six years – my thanks for your patient editing of many different versions of this work. If you had not on your retirement started writing your book, this one would not have happened. The book is dedicated to my five grandchildren for whom I pray for a better world, and in memory of friend and priest Luke Stubbs, who started me off on this project but did not live to see its completion.

WORKS CONSULTED

Ackermann, Denise M., "Found Wanting and Left Untried? Confessions of a Ragbag Theologian." In *Ragbag Theologies: Essays in Honour of Denise M. Ackermann, Feminist Theologian of Praxis*, edited by M. Pillay, S. Nadar and C. le Bruyns, 267-284. Stellenbosch: Sun Press, 2009.

Dickinson, Emily. *The Complete Poems of Emily Dickinson*. Edited by T. H. Johnson. New York: Little, Brown, 1960.

Goldberg, Michael. *Theology and Narrative: A Critical Introduction*. Philadelphia: Trinity Press International, 1991.

Pillay, Miranda, Saroini Nadar and Clint le Bruyns, eds. *Ragbag Theologies: Essays in Honour of Denise M. Ackermann, Feminist Theologian of Praxis*. Stellenbosch: Sun Press, 2009.

Robinson, Marilynne. *Absence of Mind: The Dispelling of Inwardness from the Modern Myth of the Self*. New Haven: Yale University Press, 2010.

Sen, Amartya. *Identity and Violence: The Illusion of Destiny*. London: Penguin Books, 2006.

CHAPTER ONE

Surprised and blessed

I remember that morning all too vividly. Sitting at the very end of the nave near the high altar of Canterbury Cathedral, I watched the bishops of the Anglican Communion enter and take their seats under the soaring, ribbed Gothic ceiling of that historic building. Clothed in robes of brocade, silk and even gold lamé, embroidered with indigenous themes, mitres on heads, among them a handful of women, they entered the cathedral with measured tread. I found myself straining forward as the doors closed slowly behind the Archbishop of Canterbury. What was I hoping to see? Then I realised and was surprised by the image that popped into my head. I was looking for "the man on the borrowed donkey"! Where, amidst all this pomp, was Jesus whom I had come to know and love, and who had changed my life?

It was 1998 and I was accompanying Archbishop Njongonkulu Ndungane to the Lambeth Conference of the Anglican Church as a theological advisor. The phrase "the man on the borrowed donkey" has since that time been pivotal to my relationship with Jesus. It is an expression that has a touch of the comical, and that is laced with paradox and incongruity when it is used for the central figure of my faith. Jesus, whom Christians attest is the incarnation of the living God, had nowhere to lay his head, washed the feet of his disciples, and had to borrow a donkey for a bitter-sweet ride that ended on a cross. Jesus, who rode that donkey to a criminal's death, appeared to his disciples three days later. The paradox of humility and power exemplified in his life calls me to account when I confront my own inconsistencies and wispy faith. It becomes my tool for understanding my life and for assessing my own conduct. It holds before me incomprehensible, all-encompassing love. It gives me hope. It never ceases to surprise me. It is the reality of grace at work in the world. And, as such, it has everything to do with being blessed.

I first encountered Jesus as an historical person in a women's weekly Bible study that I joined out of no more than a passing whim. Previously he had been a remote figure, largely limited to religious paintings and the illustrations in a children's Bible – which I did not read. In the Bible study he came alive as we read the gospel stories together. As African New Testament scholar Teresa Okure points out, "The Bible is essentially a community book, written for people living in communities of faith […]. We need to read together to be able to help one another see with a new eye." And this is what happened. In this group of very disparate women I could question, debate and ponder the relevance for my life of what I was reading. I could not fault Jesus, despite trying to. The more I read, the more I was drawn to the man at the centre of these biblical tales. I found that Jesus then is Jesus now. I was, and still am, challenged by his actions and by his relationships with those who crossed his path.

I had read somewhere that C. S. Lewis (1898–1963), literary critic, essayist and Christian apologist, once said: "Jesus is either a liar, a lunatic or Lord" and so, about two years later, I decided to give Jesus a try. Perhaps he was Lord. This was no more than a sort of show-me-who-you-really-are move. And he did. Despite my feeble, conditional and ungracious overture, my life changed. Looking back, I am deeply grateful that I encountered Jesus, largely unencumbered by the stuff of our traditions, or by different interpretations and claims. I met the man and liked him very much. The freshness of this meeting has stayed with me through the years and has never wilted, notwithstanding my theological studies and teaching. For me Jesus has never been a dogma. Through his *life* he showed me what it means to be a human being. He left no written testament. He left a life, a life personified in his words: "I give you a new commandment, that you love one another. Just as I have loved you, you should love one another" (Jn 13:34). Okure makes the point by quoting Ignatius of Antioch (born c.35-50–died d.107): "Whenever they tell me 'It is not written in the book', I tell them, 'Oh yes, it is written, because our book is a person, Jesus of Nazareth.' "

In this book I want to reflect on the surprises I have encountered along the way as I struggle to keep my eyes on the man who borrowed a donkey. I have been surprised by how this struggle, that has been one of "the felt life of the mind", has morphed into blessings. I am surprised because the richness of blessing is always unexpected; I remain astonished at how often a sense of blessedness happens in the most unlikely, mundane, daily occurrences. The man on the borrowed donkey has, in some mysterious way, given me new spectacles through which to view life, spectacles that I have to clean regularly when they become fogged up with the junk of "self", yet spectacles that I can no longer live without. In other words, I am finding grace that is both ordinary and extraordinary, but more about this later.

Giving Jesus "a try" was the beginning of a bouquet of surprises. To begin with I was filled with wonder at just how very human the man on the borrowed donkey was. He taught, healed and suffered as a human being. He got tired, exasperated, hungry and thirsty. He probably had times of feeling unwell. He shed tears and he could get angry. I saw that to deny his full humanity would be to deny what his life, his teaching, his compassion and courage offer us. It is difficult to imagine what an impression he made in an age when conformity was the test of truth and virtue. The great learning of the scribes did not impress him. He did not hesitate to question tradition, and no authority was too important to be contradicted. He did not act like a person who rebelled for rebellion's sake; he appeared to bear no grudges against the world, but he was not afraid to lose his reputation and even his life. I saw that to deprive this man of his humanity was to deprive him of his greatness.

What struck me next were the kind of people who claimed Jesus' attention: the poor, the hungry, the miserable, the oppressed and marginalised, lepers, cripples, the blind and the sick, children and those possessed, social outcasts, tax collectors, disreputable people and women from both inside and outside Jewish society. This ragtag band of people seldom allowed him time to be alone. These were people with no rights, people who lived at the bottom of the social structure with no remedies for their needs. It struck me too that the people Jesus chose to be with were, in fact, like the majority of people in my country. He himself came from the artisan classes, although by birth and upbringing he was not one of the very poor. He may, however, have suffered a slight disadvantage of coming from Galilee, since the Jews in Jerusalem tended to look down on Galileans.

When I realised that Jesus was a radical, I loved his freedom to break conventional barriers in his relationships with a variety of women. He was courageous and unbowed by the powerful religious and political forces that opposed him: he enjoyed being with all kinds of people, and combined remarkable humility with true authority. He spoke for himself, and emerges as a man of extraordinary independence and unparalleled authenticity – a man whose insight defies explanation. I was surprised and then hooked. This was someone I wanted to know – understand, fathom, plumb – more closely.

This longing to "know" led me to become aware of the grace of blessing. As I pursued my quest, Jesus' promise of abundant life (Jn 10:10) became more real. I found a new intensity to my life. I felt blessed. I am aware that claiming to feel blessed has an overtly pious ring. As I wrote of the blessings that follow in this book, I struggled to find similar words that sounded less "religious", words like "happy", "privileged", "favoured", and so on. However, in the end I decided that "blessed" actually says it all, but does need decoding. To explore blessing is in essence to find out what it means to be a fully free human being. Feeling blessed is not an uninterrupted good feeling. It is not financial security, nor physical well-being. It is not lasting pleasure, nor happiness, nor an unendingly cheerful mood. Being blessed is not some abstract faith concept of spiritual well-being. Being blessed does not mean that life becomes an easy ride. A sense of blessedness is challenged by the exigencies of life. Can one feel blessed if one is in a wheelchair, if poverty or oppression are daily realities, or if one has known depression? I cannot speak for others, though I do know human beings who have risen above pretty awful circumstances and still felt blessed.

The wonder is that by being blessed we are offered the possibility of being like Jesus. I am struck by the well-known words of Irenaeus of Lyon (late second century) that "[t]he glory of God is the human person fully alive". I have found that when I keep my eyes on the man who borrowed a donkey, I taste something of being "fully alive".

Being blessed is not an abstract theological concept. It is a practice, a way of living, not an esoteric truth. There is nothing majestic or mysterious about being blessed. It is about living in a way that makes the promise of abundant life possible, even in daunting circumstances. Being blessed is expressed practically in prosaic matters such as affirming another with a loving word, feeding the hungry, giving water to the thirsty, welcoming the stranger and caring for those in need as Jesus told us to do (Mt 25:34-46). Terry Eagleton, the Marxist Christian critic writes:

> Eternity is not in a grain of sand but in a glass of water. The cosmos revolves on comforting the sick. When you act in this way, you are sharing in the love which built the stars. To live in this way is not just to have life, but to have it in abundance.

As we look to the man on the borrowed donkey, hear and obey his words, our prayers and our deeds dissolve into one another and we know blessing. There is nothing glamorous about this rock-solid sense of blessing; "Just go and do as I tell you," Jesus says. The more I try to respond to this, the more I find new purpose, and discover a point of reference by which to measure my actions and desires. Stirred, sometimes fulfilled, sometimes failing, yet always invited to a new way of being truly human, I have found ways to deal with my persistent question: "What makes life worth living?" In the life and teaching of Jesus I am learning about love and finding the courage to hope. In this I am blessed.

I can think of nothing more appealing that Jesus' promise of "abundant life". The phrase itself is fulsome, affirming and redolent with promise. My understanding of abundant life comes from my experience of a relationship with Jesus and is encapsulated in three words – compassion, love and hope. Jesus lived out compassion because he loved and his acts of love gave hope to those whose lives he touched. Jesus then is Jesus now, offering this triad of compassion, love and hope to us today. This is cause for wonder.

Why did Jesus spend his earthly ministry with those not of his class, and become an outcast by choice? The answer in the gospels is quite simple: compassion. Matthew 14:14 tells how Jesus tried to be by himself, but the crowds stuck by him "[…] and he had compassion for them and cured their sick". He did not begrudge their intrusion on his need to be alone. He was moved by compassion for the plight of the widow of Nain. "Do not weep," he said to her (Lk 7:13) He had compassion ("moved with pity") for a leper desperate for healing (Mk 1:41). The word "compassion" comes from two Latin words, "suffer" and "with". To show compassion means to suffer with someone, to enter into a person's situation and become involved in that person's suffering. But this is almost too tame an understanding of the feeling that moved Jesus. The Greek word for compassion describes an emotion that comes from the intestines, the bowels, the entrails or the heart. It is a word that describes a welling up from the gut – a gut reaction. Expressions like "he felt sorry" or "he was moved with pity" do not capture the deep physical and emotional flavour of the Greek word. Only the deepest compassion could have moved Jesus on the cross to pray for his persecutors: "Father forgive them for they know not what they do."

Compassion is never a theoretical attitude. It is about doing, not just thinking or saying. It is more than the mere desire to relieve a person's suffering; it is expressed in actions to do so. Compassion is practical. Compassion moves us to alleviate suffering and to oppose injustice, because we are able to stand in the shoes of another.

Compassion is concerned with the dignity and worth of all people without exception. It is by *doing* that we seek justice, equity and respect, and it is by *doing* that we express love. Jesus, the man, lived a life of supreme compassion. He showed us the way by doing. There is no doubt that his actions were very unsettling to the authorities, that his actions broke barriers, and that his acts of compassion, immersed in love, changed lives. They changed mine. I now know that love and hope are real and cannot be defeated.

I cannot separate compassion from love. Sagely, the Dalai Lama commented: "Love and compassion are necessities, not luxuries. Without them humanity cannot survive." I agree, yet when Paul writes in his first letter to the Corinthians (16:14) "[l]et all that you do be done in love", I quake. This is a pretty tall order. Is it possible to do everything in love? I fear I cannot meet this demand, but does my falling short negate being blessed? I think not. Paul seems to be setting a goal and in striving to reach it he uncovers a wondrous truth: when we stumble, God's patience and forgiveness are endless. There is no condemnation.

The truth is we are able to love because God first loved us. The Taizé refrain: *Ubi caritas et amor, Deus ubi est* (Where charity and love are, there is God) affirms the truth that God is love. The foundation of love is God's love freely given. We are loved and this awakens our ability to love in return. To be loved is to experience ourselves as affirmed, desired and accepted. I often wonder why this central truth about our relationship with God is missing from our creeds. We affirm our faith in a litany of events without a single word about the central truth of our faith – God loves us.

Love or *agape* is not about feelings of affection, or the erotic, or personal intimacies, or specific preferences, as valid as such feelings are. Love (like hope) is a practice or a way of life, often fraught with difficulties, sacrifice, frustrations and the like. In Eagleton's words, it is "[…] far removed from some beaming bovine contentment".

In Jesus' actions, love of God and love of neighbour converge. He is unconditionally committed to the well-being of others; he does not discriminate between people, and his love culminates in self-sacrifice – truly a hard act to follow. After relating the parable of the Good Samaritan, Jesus says to the lawyer, "Go and do likewise." So the practice of *agape* is mandatory, while at the same time it is a gift from God, who first loved us. *Agape* is for the flourishing of creation – all of it. It is part of living as a moral person, and is expressed in our actions and their relational consequences. God's love is not only faithful but also forgiving; all that we have to do is accept this truth. If this were not so, there would be no hope of love covering our "multitude of sins" and forgiving them.

Sadly, "love" is an overused word. "I love chocolate" or "I love Ella Fitzgerald's singing" are hardly what Paul has in mind when he says: "And now faith, hope and love abide […] and the greatest of these is love" (1 Cor 13:13). Love is easily corrupted when we lose Dante's vision of that "love which moves the sun and the other stars" and settle for paltry substitutes. Our unwillingness to let go of our selfish needs, our greed and arrogance make for a pretty miserable world. But it can be different. To love another person means loving another not as an object, but as a subject. As a woman, I know about the struggle for subjectivity. I know that considering "the other" as a subject means loving others for who they are, and not simply for what they are to us. It is also a corrupt form of love to love only those we deem worthy of love. This is not Jesus' way. For him all humanity is worthy of love. Another pitiful subterfuge is to think that loving Christ is unrelated to loving our neighbour. We end up trying to love Christ instead of our neighbour, and not Christ in our neighbour.

I can understand love only in terms of the relational. Love is about how I relate to God, others, myself and to the world in which I live. To love is to risk trust and commitment. Love means creating space for another in which she can flourish, while at the same time she does the same for me. This is love that is mutual – my desire for the well-being of the other is related to her desire for my well-being. Her fulfilment is my fulfilment. When love for the other is taken to the point of sacrifice, it is truly a human achievement. In Old Testament times, neighbour usually meant those who shared one's religion. Jesus, however, broadens the meaning of neighbour. In the tale of the Good Samaritan, one's neighbour is no longer simply the person who shares one's religion, culture or nationality, but is the stranger one meets along the way. A further tweak is added to the practice of love when we are also told "[…] to love your neighbour as yourself" (Mk 12:31). Loving oneself is particularly stringent for it means that we should treat others as we would want to be treated ourselves.

In the face of these formidable demands, I like to think that we are made with the need to love and be loved; that it is in our divine DNA that stamps us as made in the image of God, enabling us to love God, others and ourselves. "Religious experience at its roots is experience of an unconditional and unrestricted being in love. But what we are in love with remains something that we have to find out," says Jesuit philosopher and theologian Bernard Lonergan. The process of finding out leads us into strange places that are not found on religious maps or in theological tomes. Early in the Gospel of John (1:38) Jesus asks prospective disciples, Andrew and Simon, "What are you looking for?" They respond: "Rabbi … where are you staying?" Jesus replies: "Come and see." We enter unknown territory, brimming with surprises, because we want to "come and see".

Our vocation to be daughters and sons of God means that we have to learn to love as God in Christ loves. Love is our only salvation. The love of God gave Christ to the world. The love of the Son for humanity, and our response to this love, is our salvation from meaninglessness. Love is the key to our existence. Love gives meaning to God's entire creation. Dante's vision is our call – to participate in that cosmic love that moves "the sun and the other stars".

In Trappist monk and writer Thomas Merton's (1915–1968) words: "To say that I am made in the image of God is to say that love is the reason for my existence, for God is love. Love is my true identity. Selflessness is my true self. Love is my true character. Love is my name." I am perpetually surprised by moments when I feel drenched with that love that knows no end and enables me to love in ways I would not have thought possible. Paul knew this: "God's love has been poured into our hearts through the Holy Spirit that has been given to us" (Rom 5:5). In the words of the classical statement of Christian faith, we no longer live but Christ lives in us.

To have faith is to have hope. Yet this statement is often taken to mean hoping for the end times when all will be made new. Hope, however, is a lived reality in the life of faith, here and now. It is not easy to hope in a world that appears increasingly to be on the cusp of implosion. While I was writing this book, the United Nations hosted yet another large gathering to debate what can be done about climate change. The world's economy is in dire straits. Hunger, violence and disease are decimating the lives of millions on our continent. What does it mean to hope in today's world?

Through the countless dark moments of apartheid I had hope. I believed it would end and that justice and equality would eventually prevail. I devoured the banned writings of Steve Biko and Nelson Mandela; I chose to oppose the injustice of apartheid mainly through Christian institutions. I found a home in the Christian Institute, the Institute for Contextual Theology and later in the secular Black Sash. At no time did I feel completely without hope. Right would prevail. I learnt the power of political and social analysis; I embraced liberation theologies and I focused on the connections between oppressive modes, such as sexism, racism and homophobia. Those times shaped my story – a story of hybridity because of my mixed cultural origins, and a growing sense of marginalisation in parts of my own community, contrasted with a deepening involvement with the story of Jesus of Nazareth and what it meant in my context. I hoped because of him. And I learnt about what hope is and is not.

I learnt that to hope is never to surrender our power to imagine a better world, that present unjust arrangements are provisional and precarious, and do not require acceptance. I also leant to be cautious about a false sense of fulfilment that believes that all is well, that promises have been kept and gifts received. If we so believe, we merely hold on mutely to what we have and lose our desire for something better. Just keeping life manageable on our terms is not hope. I saw that refusing to bow to such civility is an act of hope, for it is not satisfied with crumbs. I learnt that to lament injustice is an expression of hope for it calls God to account and rests on the unshakable belief that God will act.

To my surprise, I find that today there are times when I struggle to hope. Racism in many guises continues to flourish, inequality in our country becomes more entrenched as the gap widens between those who have and those who do not. Violent crime casts a dark shadow over the lives of all South Africans. Crude materialism permeates our society: it is encouraged in our media, visible in the lives of our leaders, and imitated in the desires of the young. I want to hope for a better world for my grandchildren. I know that there is no faith without hope. Chastened, I find that I once again need to remember in whom I hope, what I learnt about hope in the "bad old days" and how to live with hope, no matter the circumstances. Emily Dickinson wrote:

Hope is the thing with feathers
That perches on the soul,
And sings the tune without the word,
And never stops at all.

The song remains. Hope does not stop. True hope is the oxygen of faith. So I remind myself that:

Hope is not optimism. It is not that blithe sense that all will end well (*alles sal regkom*), because human progress is guaranteed. In the face of dreadful human need and the ever-increasing fragility of the earth, the belief in human progress is at best insubstantial. Neither is hope vested in naïve, upbeat, popular ideologies, which, according to Eagleton, "[…] tend to mistake a hubristic cult of can-do-ery for the virtue of hope". Hope is not magic, or living "as if", or projecting what we hope for onto some nebulous future.

Hope is not vested in some future victory. We must guard against the unattractive nature of Christian triumphalism as embodied in the apocalyptic that abandons historical realities while trumpeting exclusive insights into how God will in future break into history to bring about God's purposes. This kind of triumphalism is no more than a pie-in-the-sky-when-I-die exclusive claim that all will be well with me one day, rather than Julian of Norwich's universal vision that "All will be well, all manner of things will be well". Theologian Flora Keshgegian comments: "Once-and-for-all thinking privileges the end over the means; it turns visions into utopias, transforms imagination into wish fulfilment and hope into the eternal embodiment of desire." This so-called hope robs us of our ability to understand the workings of power entangled in structural injustice, and our roles in perpetuating what is wrong now. It prevents us from coming to grips with our fallibility and the fragility of our world. It chokes true lived hope.

Hope is to be lived. The way I hope should be the way I live. To live out my hope is to try to make that which I hope for come about – sooner rather than later. Not surprisingly, hope is usually associated with the future. Christian hope is too often garbed in language about the end times – we hope in the resurrection of the body and the life everlasting. Certainly hope has future dimensions. We do hope in a future with God, we hold to the coming vision of the fullness of God's reign on earth. Hope is both present and future. Brazilian theologian and philosopher Ruben Alves says: "Hope is hearing the melody of the future. Faith is to dance it." I am afraid that I cannot comprehend hope beyond history. I do hope that this world will be redeemed, but my dance of faith happens now. The hope that I find is a hope anchored in the history and presence of the person who at the same time is my hope for the future of all creation.

Hope is risky. It has no guarantees. German Reformed theologian Jürgen Moltmann speaks of "the experiment of hope" because it can lead to disappointment, danger, as well as surprise. "Hope is an experiment with God, with oneself, and with history," he writes. Twenty years ago I wrote:

To choose life is to choose risk. As disappointment follows disappointment, we risk losing our vision, we are tempted to despair. The challenge is to dare to hope, and in this daring to wrestle with all that seeks to deprive us of hope or disempower us. Wrestling is risky. Our strength may fail us or we may emerge wounded and scarred. Reminding ourselves that God's creation was the greatest risk ever taken, we as partners in this venture will have to risk in order to claim our rightful place as agents of history, seeking liberation for the groaning creation.

I have no reason to add anything more today.

Hope recognises the tragic in history. This book describes the blessing of being able to deal with the incongruities of life with humour. This does not mean that I do not honour the tragic in life. Hope must recognise the tragic in history to avoid blind optimism. No happy endings are ensured. History repeats itself with a monotony that would be boring were it not so tragic. The tragic demands that we remember. We acknowledge absence and loss, pain and fear, and that nothing present on earth is either past or finished. We live with the ambiguity of hope: hope for a better life and the stark reality of shattered hopes. When roads fork we are forced to make choices and have no way of knowing what will follow. Tragedy cannot be avoided. God's presence is found in the compassion that prevents suffering from having the last word, and in resilience that continues unabated. This active hope refuses to be defeated. To inhabit hope despite woeful circumstances is to offer a counter-story that dares us to become involved in making that which we hope for come about.

Hope is learning to wait. Hope requires patience and endurance, and is the opposite of resignation. Hope is expectant, open to being surprised, and willing to ride out the long wait. It is fuelled by a passion for the possible that is realistic because hope cannot be assuaged by instant gratification. Samuel Beckett's well-known play *Waiting for Godot* is about two characters who wait endlessly and in vain for Godot to appear. The play depicts the meaninglessness of life. Expectant waiting, unlike waiting for Godot, dares to remind us of the One in whom we hope, of promises made, of assurances given, of unending love and mercy. There is an element of resistance in our waiting because it resists the void of hopelessness, and the derision of a world that wants instant answers.

Hope is nurtured by prayer and community. Prayer is our greatest tool for holding onto hope. Conversing with God about our hopes, lamenting before God about those that are shattered, confessing impatience and moments of hopelessness, petitioning for what seems impossible, and meditating on God's faithfulness are Spirit-led moments that nurture hope. Whether our prayers are part of our rituals or whether they are spontaneous, whether they are uttered in solitary silence or among a group of believers, they ground our hopes and strengthen our faith in the God who made us. My hope is also sustained and shared within the community of faith. It is nurtured in communal relationships and our common faith in God who acts in history.

God is the ground of our hope. I know in whom I vest my hope. I trust in the God whose truth is found in the man on the borrowed donkey. Eagleton affirms the role of trust: "The virtue of hope for Christianity equally involves a kind of certainty: it is a matter of an assured trust, not of keeping one's fingers crossed." My trust is not in some abstract God in the heavens pulling strings on which we dangle as puppets, or some judge doling out favours to the faithful, but a living God who is present in human history and whose divine energy continues to woo us into the fullness of life, now and beyond. Our story with God has no end because it is a story of unending grace.

I have been surprised by the paradox of grace in the life of faith – it is both ordinary and extraordinary. The word "ordinary" here means "in the order of things"; it does not mean something mundane or unimportant. The *Oxford Shorter Dictionary* uses the words "regular and usual" to qualify what is ordinary. These words accurately describe what is meant by "ordinary grace" – it is in the order of things, because it is a commonplace reality, flooding the world, there for all, from the beginning of time. But, because paradox runs throughout every attempt to speak about God's presence and care for this world, grace is also extraordinary. It is extraordinary because it cannot be earned, it is unmerited and utterly abundant, and while it permeates the world, we may also ask for it. However, the very fact that it is all-pervasive also makes it "in the order of things" – ordained by God for all, thus commonplace. To say: "Blessed are those" is to acknowledge the working of God's grace in our lives.

Tagging grace as "ordinary" will, I anticipate, raise immediate objections. Lutheran pastor and theologian Dietrich Bonhoeffer (1906–1945) in his acclaimed work, *The Cost of Discipleship*, writes: "Cheap grace is the deadly enemy of our Church. We are fighting today for costly grace." He continues in scathing fashion:

Cheap grace means grace sold on the market like a cheapjack's wares. The sacraments, the forgiveness of sins and the consolations of religion are thrown away at cut prices. Grace is represented as the Church's inexhaustible treasury [...] Grace without price; grace without cost! [...] Cheap grace means grace as a doctrine, a principle, a system [...] Cheap grace means the justification of sin without the justification of the sinner. Grace alone does everything, they say, and so everything remains as it was before.

In contrast, costly grace, according to Bonhoeffer is "[...] a treasure hidden in a field [...] [that] must be sought again and again [...] asked for." He continues:

Costly grace is the sanctuary of God; it has to be protected from the world, and not thrown to the dogs. It is therefore, the living word, the Word of God, which he speaks as it pleases him. Costly grace confronts us as a gracious call to follow Jesus, it comes as a word of forgiveness to the broken spirit and the contrite heart.

Where does this leave "ordinary" grace? Is it cheap? Bonhoeffer is right. We can cheapen grace. If we trade on God's goodness and generosity, we cheapen the notion of grace. If we claim the fruits of grace without being willing to acknowledge their source with gratitude, we cheapen grace. If we refuse grace's call to discipleship, says Bonhoeffer, we cheapen it. Why would we cheapen grace? The simple answer is that we are alienated creatures who choose to reject any dependence on Ultimate Reality. We deny our finitude and alienate ourselves from one another, from nature, from history and, in the end, from ourselves, as American Catholic theologian David Tracy warns. Grace is both a gift and a painful revelation of who we are. The story is familiar – we are made from and for God. We are also made to be in relationship with God and one another. The truth is we have become estranged from each other, endangering our existence together. Despite this, God sustains us because, although we are faithless, God is faithful. God speaks a word of forgiveness in Christ that is free, pure, fresh, unmerited, and is effective grace.

But cheap grace is not what I mean by grace being "in the order of things". I have described grace as ordinary because I have been overwhelmed with surprise at just how prevalent it is, pervading my reality. It is as ordinary as the air I breathe. And I have also been surprised by my inability to have known this truth sooner. But as I said, what is ordinary is also extraordinary. Christians can speak of God's relationship with human beings only through a constant awareness of the free grace of God, given once and for all in Jesus Christ. What could be more ordinary and extraordinary than a man borrowing a donkey, a man who is Emmanuel – God with us?

Do I recognise the working of grace in my life? At times I do, and at others I am oblivious to its presence, for grace is both simple to see and not obvious. We recognise a grace-filled life when we see it, and we will know moments when grace overwhelms us. However, the very ordinariness of grace defies explanation and tends to cause us to overlook its presence. Trying to describe a plume of smoke drifting through the air to a blind person is as difficult as seeking to encapsulate grace in words. Tracy describes the nature of grace:

Grace is a word Christians use to name this extraordinary process: a power erupting in one's life as a gift revealing that Ultimate Reality can be trusted as the God who is Pure, Unbounded Love; a power interrupting our constant temptations to delude ourselves at a level more fundamental than any conscious error; a power gradually but really transforming old habits.

In my attempts at making sense of this "extraordinary" process I have found that:

God's grace is unfathomable and unmerited. Being a recipient of grace does not require perfection or high ethical standards. Grace takes no regard of who and how we are: the schemers, the thieves, the liars, the charitable, those who bargain with God, those who stumble and try again, believers and non-believers are all within the contours of God's grace. American essayist and poet Kathleen Norris in her book, *Amazing Grace,* reminds us of the indiscriminate nature of God's grace. Jacob is a man who has "just deceived his father and cheated his brother out of an inheritance". God does not punish him. Jacob is dealt with (through his even more scheming father-in-law) so that God can use him for grace-filled purposes. After wrestling through the night with the unknown man, he can say: "For I have seen God face to face, and yet my life is preserved" (Gen 32:30). God saw the potential in Jacob beyond his scheming ways and made of him a nation. David is both a murderer and an adulterer, yet he is blessed by God. In the story of Jonah the prophet, God calls Jonah to proclaim judgment on Nineveh. This political allegory tells how Jonah absconds – as one of my children's books said, by "taking a ship that went the other way". Yet ultimately the story confirms his efficacy in the conversion of all who lived in Nineveh.

Peter's record as a follower of Jesus is one of continuous ups and downs. Matthew 16:18 recounts how Jesus names Peter's calling: "And I tell you, you are Peter, and on this rock I will build my church." Jesus has barely uttered these words when Peter rebukes him for disclosing his suffering, to the extent that Jesus says: "Get behind me Satan! You are a stumbling block to me …" (Mt 16:23). Later we know that Peter denies Jesus three times in a courtyard during Jesus' hearing before the high priest: "I do not know this man" (Mt 26:74). Yet, according to the Book of Acts, Peter sets about accomplishing the task assigned to him by Jesus with devotion. Saul persecutes Christians with unseemly zeal. He does not seem a likely candidate for establishing the church in Asia Minor. But we know that Saul becomes Paul who sets about this task with dedication and courage. Evidence for the unfathomable, unmerited nature of grace is found when God chooses Isaac not Ishmael, Jacob not Esau, David not Paul, reluctant Jonah, and Peter to be the rock for the founding of the church, with Saul as its first great missionary. Is this not surprising?

God's grace is for all creation. God's choices recounted in the scriptures do not imply a lack of grace in the lives of those who are not chosen for special tasks. Scripture tells the stories of leaders. The contributions of millions upon millions of ordinary people responding to grace in the history of our faith remain hidden. Grace is universal, shed on all humanity indiscriminately. Karl Barth describes grace as that "[…] from which the pagan lives, and also the indifferent, the atheist, and he who hates his fellow man whether they know it or not. It is the universal truth, not a 'religious truth.'" The very fact that we breathe, that the earth continues to spin on its axis, that the seasons follow one another, that communities are kept alive by uncountable, unnoticed, simple acts of generosity and kindness are due to God's grace, shed upon all creation. It is true that God's grace resides in Jesus, but not exclusively, for Jesus calls a few to follow him, and the few become many, and the many will eventually become all.

God's grace pursues us. God's grace woos us because God loves us and longs for us to wake up to the wonder of godly grace in this world. We cannot escape grace. We may ignore it or deny it, but in the end it will envelop us. As Norris says: "God will find us and bless us, even when we feel most alone, unsure we will survive the night. God will find a way to let us know that he is with us *in this place*, wherever we are, however far we think we can run." Fortunately grace is not limited to the church or any religious institution. By permeating the world, grace beckons all unceasingly to an awareness of how it awakens the longing for relationship with the Source of all life.

God's grace is free, extravagant and transforming. The Barmen Declaration of 1934 (the manifesto or confession of what came to be known as the Confessing Church in Germany) speaks of "the proclamation of God's free grace". According to Barth, this does not mean anything other than what Romans 1:1 calls "the gospel of God". He points out that God's grace is not some godly property. "No, God's free grace is God Himself, His most inner and essential nature, God Himself as He is. That is God's secret, as it is now already revealed in Jesus Christ," he explains. God gives Godself freely, abundantly and conclusively in Jesus – this makes us God's business. God does not sweep our concerns, cares and needs under a carpet, but, through Jesus, takes them up and they are transformed. Jesus does not ask who we are, or what we have to offer. He simply accepts us. Acceptance is transforming. Such is the extravagance of free grace. As Rowan Williams, former Archbishop of Canterbury, explains: grace is found "[…] in terms of compassionate acceptance, the refusal of condemnation, the assurance of an abiding relationship of healing love".

God's grace enables us to respond to God in Christ. Grace enables us to answer Jesus' call to "Follow me". Jesus is the paradigm of a "graced" relationship with God. This cannot be taken for granted. Nothing hindered the Christ event from taking place, but we can resist its demands on us. Our personal perceptions and conditions can render the acceptance of grace difficult, even impede it, but nothing can make its coming impossible. Grace can prepare its own way, and make the impossible possible. Paul's conversion illustrates this truth. Grace sanctions the forgiveness of sins, restores relationship, and enables love and hope.

I cannot claim to have an uninterrupted awareness of the grace that surrounds us. When the presence of grace does strike me, I am taken aback, surprised at how unaware I have been, and grateful for the sense of being held and cared for. I understand something of what French Jesuit priest and philosopher Teilhard de Chardin

(1881–1955) meant when he wrote: "Throughout my whole life, during every minute of it, the world has been gradually lighting up and blazing before my eyes until it has come to surround me, entirely lit up from within." The extravagant, indiscriminate spilling of grace on the world makes me feel blessed.

Blessings

Daring to write of blessings could be seen as an exercise in *chutzpah.* After all Jesus Christ, the founder of my faith, gave a sermon to his followers that contained a number of blessings (the beatitudes) that have stood as a moral beacon for all times. Sitting down to speak to his followers on a hill some two thousand years ago, Jesus set out an ethical code in what Augustine (354–430) subsequently called the Sermon on the Mount (Mt 5:1-11; Lk 6:20-26). In his work entitled *The Lord's Sermon on the Mount,* he wrote: "If anyone piously and soberly considers the sermon which our Lord Jesus Christ preached on the mount, as we read it in the Gospel according to Matthew, I think that he will find in it, as regards the highest morals, the perfect message of the Christian life."

Precise yet comprehensive, the beatitudes contain a complete précis of Jesus' teaching. Their insight into the human spirit is penetrating and full of wisdom. No wonder Mahatma Gandhi (1869–1948) expressed his delight with this sermon when he said: "It went straight to my heart." He considered it second only to the *Bhagavad-Gita.* This sermon changed the life of the great Russian writer Leo Tolstoy (1828–1910). In *My Religion* he wrote: "As I read these rules, it seemed to me that they had special reference to me and demanded that I, if no one else, should execute them." However, German philosopher Friedrich Nietzsche (1844–1900) commented acerbically that the Sermon encouraged a "slave morality"!

Throughout the ages, Christians have turned to this text as the embodiment of Christ's teachings. There are no teachings in the whole of the scriptures that demand more of us than the beatitudes. The exhortations of the prophets, the cautions of the leaders of Israel, the counsel of the psalms or the concealed truths of the parables, as powerful and insightful as they are, cannot strike quite the same chord in the depths of a believer as the beatitudes. All that I have ever wanted to evade, put off, or disregard, because it quite simply asks too much, is found in these blessings.

Is my attempt to write about blessings no more than an exercise in personal hubris? I know that the beatitudes Jesus left us are unequalled in their completeness. I believe that they are intended to guide us on how to live freely and fully. I have responded to their all-encompassing demands on my life in different ways, often with monumental failures along the way, but equally with a sense of being blessed because God's love and patience are inexhaustible. My attempt to describe different experiences of blessing is merely a further chapter in exploring what has made life worth living, not an attempt to trump the Sermon on the Mount.

What does it mean to be blessed? The *Oxford Shorter Dictionary* defines being blessed as: "Enjoying supreme felicity, [being] fortunate, happily endowed". The idea of being blessed is certainly an ancient one. In the Hebrew scriptures, "blessedness" denotes personal trust in God and obedience to God's will. The desire for blessedness occurs frequently in the psalms and is, in fact, the very first word of the Psalter. "Blessed are those who do not follow the advice of the wicked" (Ps1:1). The idea of being blessed is also familiar in wisdom literature: in the Greek world of those early times, a blessed person was one in harmony with society and the world.

It is, however, difficult to capture the meaning of the Greek word *makarios* in translation. As I have said, it means more than being fortunate or happy. It includes a sense of being privileged with divine favour, of being holy, hallowed. It means experiencing gratitude at receiving unmerited grace. It is about a sense of well-being because the goodness of life is affirmed and upheld against the odds. It asserts certainty at God's presence, mercy and care. God wants to bless us. All that is required from us is to do our best to love God and one another. Then we will be blessed, for God's love can do no other.

If this sounds easy, we need reminding that it is both simple and challenging. We live, as Williams puts it, in "[t]he disturbing presence of grace and vulnerability within the world of human relationships". What I have attempted here is to strike the italics key in my life by telling the story of certain blessings that have surprised me along the way. I have been taken aback by both their very ordinariness and their supreme extraordinariness. There is nothing spectacular about listening, feeling grateful, curbing my greed and having a good laugh. I am equally amazed by the extraordinariness of finding promise in paradox, of being confronted with the truth that I am holy, and that freedom from fear is possible even when confronted with mortality. I shall settle for God's grace being "in the order of things", because this is God's world, we are God's people and grace declares God's love – and God can be no other than loving. This, the man on the borrowed donkey shows me.

NOTES

My encounter with Jesus as an historical person simply describes the person who entered history at a particular time as related in the gospels. The historical Jesus is, of course, someone we never really encounter, as little is really known about the history of Jesus. Jesus as depicted in the gospels is the Jesus in whom the early Christians placed their faith.

Albert Nolan's *Jesus Before Christianity* (Maryknoll: Orbis Books, 1986) remains one of the most readable and theologically sound accounts of Jesus the human being before he became enshrined in dogma and ritual.

There was a tendency, rather than a dogma, in the early church that considered the humanity and suffering of Jesus as apparent and not real. This is known as Docetism from the Greek *dokesis* for "appearance" or "semblance", and amounted to a denial of Jesus' humanity but not his divinity, as might be expected. To claim that God walked the earth in human form did not cause a stir in the ancient world. Ancient mythologies were full of gods taking on human form. The Docetists accepted the cross, but on their terms. According to them, Jesus the Messiah could not really have died; what is divine cannot really suffer.

Compassion, condensed in the golden rule, "Do unto others as you would have done unto yourself", is a fairly common concept in the majority of world religions. When writer Karen Armstrong sought to create and propagate a Charter for Compassion, she found that "[t]housands of people from all over the world contributed to a draft chapter on a multilingual website in Hebrew, Arabic, Urdu, Spanish and English." She continues: "The Charter was launched on 12 November 2009 in sixty different locations throughout the world; it was enshrined in synagogues, mosques, temples and churches as well as in secular institutions."

The Taizé community is an ecumenical monastic order that was founded in Burgundy, France, in 1940 by Protestant Brother Roger Schutz. It is composed of some one hundred brothers, representing the Protestant, Catholic and Eastern Orthodox traditions, from about thirty different countries. Today it has become one of the world's most popular places of Christian pilgrimage, and over one hundred thousand young people come to Taizé each year to live in community, worship together and commit themselves to prayer, Bible study and communal work. *Ubi caritas* is taken from the antiphon sung during the foot-washing ceremony on Maundy Thursday. Early manuscripts contain a slightly different version: *Ubi caritas est vera* … (Where charity is true), which has now been incorporated into a recent Roman missal.

Agape is the New Testament Greek word for God's unending love for all human beings, as well as for our love for one another.

The quotation of Bernard Lonergan is taken from William Johnston, *Being in Love: The Practice of Christian Prayer* (London: HarperCollins, 1989), 12.

The phrase "love your neighbour as yourself" occurs in Matthew 19:19, Mark 12:31, Luke 10:27; Romans 12:10; Galatians 5:14 and James 2:8.

Thomas Merton was born in France in 1915. His father was from New Zealand and his mother, an American, died when he was six years old. After schooling in France and in England, he attended Columbia University, New York, where he graduated with an M.A. degree in literature. After converting to Catholicism, he entered Our Lady of Gethsemani Monastery in Kentucky in 1941. His spiritual autobiography, *The Seven Storey Mountain* (London: Burns and Oates, 2002) in which he chronicles his early years and the impulses that led him to join the Order of Cistercians of the Strict Observance (known as Trappists) where he spent the next twenty-seven years until his untimely death in 1968, became a bestseller. His prodigious corpus of work includes books (some seventy), letters, poems, monographs and journal articles that range from the popular to the scholarly. Today he is considered one of the most important twentieth century Catholic writers on spirituality.

The Christian Institute of Southern Africa was founded in 1963, prompted by the disastrous conclusion of the Cottesloe Consultation in 1960. Delegates from the World Council of Churches (WCC) met with some eighty members of South African churches at Cottesloe and resolved to reject race as a basis for excluding some people from membership of certain churches. It also approved the right of people to own land and to have a say in how they are governed. In other words, it rejected apartheid. The Dutch Reformed Church could not agree to these resolutions and left the WCC in 1961. A deep rift remained between the Afrikaans and English-speaking churches in South Africa for the next thirty years. The Christian Institute aimed to promote dialogue and to critique apartheid. Beyers Naudé was its first national director and the *Pro Veritate* newsletter was its mouthpiece. This newsletter was banned in 1977. See John W. de Gruchy with Steve de Gruchy, *The Church Struggle in South Africa,* 25th Anniversary ed. (Minneapolis: Fortress Press, 2005), for a comprehensive account of recent church history in South Africa. (Also see note on Beyers Naudé in chapter 3 about Holiness, page 109.)

The Black Sash was founded in 1955 when six women met one morning in May at a suburban home in Johannesburg. They shared a sense of outrage at the planned removal of the coloured (the recognised name for people of mixed racial origins in South Africa) people from the voters' role in the Cape Province of South Africa. This resulted in an organised protest march, and a petition signed by nearly a hundred thousand people – but to no avail. After losing this battle, this band of white women decided to continue as a voluntary human rights organisation in resistance to apartheid. Their name came from the black sashes that were worn as a sign of mourning at injustice whenever they appeared in public protests. Until 1994, they campaigned against the pass laws, monitored court proceedings, set up advice offices to help black people deal with the pass laws, and conducted silent standing protests whenever further excesses were perpetrated by the apartheid rulers. When Nelson Mandela made his first speech as a free man, he called the Black Sash (together with the National Union of South African Students) "the conscience of the white nation". The Black Sash was reconstituted in 1995 as non-racial humanitarian organisation and continues to act on behalf of the needy in our society.

Alles sal regkom is a commonly used Afrikaans saying for "everything will be fine".

The prophet Jeremiah (12:1) raises the famous question that echoes down the ages: "Why does the way of the guilty prosper? Why do all who are treacherous thrive?" I struggled with the theodicy question in a previous book, *After the Locusts: Letter from a Landscape of Faith* (Grand Rapids: Eerdmans, 2001), in chapter 4 on the need to lament. We are challenged to hope in situations that give rise to despair. The language of lament is a way of dealing with Jeremiah's cry – we lament our situation to God in language that is direct, truthful and unafraid. The ancient Hebrews held onto prophetic hope, hope that enabled the prophet Micah (4:3) to say: "And they shall beat their swords into ploughshares and their spears into pruning hooks."

The quote from Teilhard de Chardin is taken from Annie Dillard, *For the Time Being* (New York: Vintage Books, 2000), 13.

Augustine (born c.354–died c.430), philosopher, theologian and Bishop of Hippo in Roman North Africa (present-day Algeria), was the most influential thinker in early Western Christianity. His contemporary, Jerome, described Augustine as the person who "established anew the ancient faith". After reading an account of the life of Anthony of the Desert, Augustine gave up teaching rhetoric in Milan and devoted his life to ministry in the church. He was a prolific writer and his works comprise tomes on Christian doctrine (e.g. *On Christian Doctrine, On the Trinity,* and *The City of God*), commentaries on the psalms, Genesis and Romans, letters and sermons. His *Confessions* give a personal account of his early life and his conversion to Christianity. See Peter Brown, *Augustine of Hippo: A Biography* (London: Faber and Faber, 1967).

For the last section entitled *Blessings,* refer also to Denise Ackermann, "Christian ideals laid bare by two beatitudes", in *Faith in Action*, ed. Sarah Rowland Jones.157-176 (Wellington: Lux Verbi, 2008).

WORKS CONSULTED

A Book of Hope. Cape Town: David Philip, 1992.

Ackermann, Denise M., "Christian Ideals Laid Bare by Two Beatitudes." In *Faith in Action*, edited by S.R. Jones, 157-176. Wellington: Lux Verbi, 2008.

Ackermann, Denise M., "The Alchemy of Hope." In *A Book of Hope*, 28-30. Cape Town: David Phillip, 1992.

Alves, Ruben. *Tomorrow's Child: Imagination, Creativity and the Rebirth of Culture*. New York: Harper and Row, 1972.

Armstrong, Karen. *Twelve Steps to a Compassionate Life*. London: The Bodley Head, 2011.

Barth, Karl. *God Here and Now*. Translated by P. M. van Buren. London: Routledge, 2009.

Bonhoeffer, Dietrich. *The Cost of Discipleship*. London: SCM Press, 1959.

Bonhoeffer, Dietrich. *Ethics*. Edited by E. Bethge. Translated by N. H. Smith. London: SCM Press, 1971.

Braaten, Carl E. *The Future of God: The Revolutionary Dynamics of Hope*. New York: Harper and Row, 1969.

Brown, Peter. *Augustine of Hippo: A Biography*. London: Faber and Faber, 1967.

Brueggemann, Walter. *Hope within History*. Atlanta: John Knox Press, 1987.

Gaybba, Brian. "Love as the Lamp of Theology." *Journal of Theology for Southern Africa*, no. 65 (1988), 27-37.

De Gruchy, John W., ed. *Dietrich Bonhoeffer*. Cambridge Companions to Religion Series. Cambridge: Cambridge University Press, 1999.

De Gruchy, John W., & Steve de Gruchy. *The Church Struggle in South Africa*. 25th Anniversary ed. Minneapolis: Fortress Press, 2005.

Dickinson, Emily. *The Complete Poems of Emily Dickinson*. Edited by T. H. Johnson. New York: Little, Brown and Co., 1960.

Dillard, Anne. *For the Time Being*. New York: Vintage Books, 2000.

Eagleton, Terry. *The Meaning of Life*. Oxford: Oxford University Press, 2007.

Eagleton, Terry. *Reason, Faith and Revolution: Reflections on the God Debate*. New Haven: Yale University Press, 2009.

Galilea, Sergio. *Spirituality of Hope*. Translated by T. Cambias. Maryknoll: Orbis Books, 1988.

Jackson, Timothy P. *Love Disconsoled: Meditations on Christian Charity*. Cambridge: Cambridge University Press, 1999.

Johnston, William. *Being in Love: The Practice of Christian Prayer*. London: HarperCollins, 1989.

Jones, Sarah Rowland, ed. *Faith in Action, Njongonkulu Ndungane, Archbishop for the Church and the World*. Wellington: Lux Verbi, 2008.

Keshgegian, Flora A. *Time for Hope: Practices for Living in Today's World*. New York: Continuum, 2006.

Kissinger, Warren S. *The Sermon on the Mount: A History of Interpretation and Bibliography*. Metuchen, NJ: Scarecrow Press, 1975.

Merton, Thomas. *New Seeds of Contemplation*. London: Burns and Oates, 2002.

Merton, Thomas. *The Seven Storey Mountain*. London: Burns and Oates, 2002.

Moltmann, Jürgen. *The Experiment of Hope*. London: SCM Press, 1975.

Nolan, Albert. *Hope in an Age of Despair and Other Talks and Writings.* Edited by S. Muyebe. Maryknoll: Orbis Books, 2010.

Nolan, Albert. *Jesus Before Christianity*. Maryknoll: Orbis Books, 1986.

Norris, Kathleen. *Amazing Grace: A Vocabulary of Faith*. New York: Riverhead Press, 1998.

Okure, Teresa. "What is Truth?" *Anglican Theological Review,* vol. 93, no. 3 (2011): 405-422.

Patte, Daniel. *The Challenge of Discipleship: A Critical Study of the Sermon on the Mount as Scripture*. Harrisburg: Trinity Press, 1999.

Rahner, Karl. *Foundations of Christian Faith: An Introduction to the Idea of Christianity*. New York: Seabury Press, 1978.

Tinder, Glenn. *The Fabric of Hope: An Essay*. Atlanta: Scholars Press, 1999.

Tracy, David. *Plurality and Ambiguity: Hermeneutics, Religion, Hope*. Chicago: University of Chicago Press, 1987.

Williams, Rowan. *On Christian Theology*. Oxford: Blackwell, 2000.

Willmer, Haddon. "Costly Discipleship." In *Dietrich Bonhoeffer*, edited by J. W. de Gruchy, 173-189. Cambridge Companions to Religion Series. Cambridge: Cambridge University Press, 1999.

CHAPTER TWO

Blessed are those who embrace contradiction, for they will find promise in paradox

Why, one may ask, do I place this blessing before all others? Why does embracing contradiction hold promise? What is this promise? What is the difference between contradiction and paradox? Surely the life of faith is about certainty? As the questions multiply, I find myself wondering whether there is not a profound contradiction in what I am doing. A book about being blessed says: "This and that *are* sources of blessing ..." It implies certainty. The injunctions to live out one's holiness, know gratitude, embrace freedom and one will be blessed seem to have little to do with contradiction and paradox. Yet this work begins with a plea for an awareness of the centrality of contradiction and paradox in the life of faith. This needs unpacking.

"Contradiction" and "paradox" are convenient words to deal with aspects of the inexplicable. The life of faith defies neat explanations. I have found that embracing the inexplicable, the unknowable, the enigmatic mystery that is God lies at the heart of my faith. I am learning that the way into this godly embrace is to affirm the mystery that is myself, the unpredictable, contradictory and paradoxical mixture of me – order and disorder, faith and doubt, light and darkness. Holding together opposing realities and allowing them room in my inner home means keeping the doors open and being less interested in answers and more concerned about questions. Accepting the contradictions within myself will help me to do so elsewhere. Then life becomes abundantly worth living. To explain this requires retracing elements of my faith story.

When I encountered the Christian faith as an adult, my guides were the writings of Anglican priests and theologians John Stott (1921–2011), Michael Green, writer C. S. Lewis and others who today could be described as evangelicals, though I dislike labels of this kind. I cannot but be grateful for their contribution to making the beliefs of the Christian faith accessible to me and to many others. In my weekly Bible study group I found a place where I, brimming with doubts and frustrations, could air my questions. I began to see that some of my questions had no conclusive answers, that they might never have, and that something other than intellectual certainty was required of me. That "something other" was a commitment to a different way of living and a trust in the One I could not name and did not know. But I wanted to find out. The first step was a move from my head to the involvement of the will and the heart. However, that was only the first step. What "the heart" meant was still a mystery.

A while later, in my mid-forties, I went off to acquire a diploma in theology, got hooked, and ended up with four degrees. This was all head stuff. My mind was fully engaged, extended and enthralled. I was entranced by systematic theology. The doctrines of God, sin, salvation and the hereafter were endlessly absorbing. I eventually majored in practical theology because the reality of contradiction in my own life began to creep up on me. What I believed and how I acted upon my beliefs were often at odds, and I struggled to hold them together. I saw that I was not alone in this. Such dissonance remains a trial in the life of faith. It is not something I can pretend to have solved, but how I live with this profound contradiction has changed over the years.

Something happened when I allowed my deepest longing – something that had been with me from the beginning of my seeking – to become the focus of my life. What was I longing for and from where did this longing come? All the head stuff I had absorbed could not deal with it; something else was needed. As I read more theology, I found myself attracted to those theologians who allowed ambiguity, paradox and uncertainty to pervade their writings. At the same time I wondered about and questioned the certainties of other theologians on the nature of God, the human condition, creation and the hereafter. My efforts to grasp the connection between the ineffable otherness of God and the concrete reality of the person of Jesus Christ whom I encountered in the gospels itself constituted a prodigious paradox. This led me to examine the different traditions of spirituality in Christianity. I longed to encounter God other than through what had been written about the Holy One. I soon realised that God, who far exceeds the categories and consciousness of my finite subjectivity, cannot be encountered on demand and that to explain my longing confronted me with the ambiguity of presence and absence, of knowing and not knowing. I realised too that encountering the Divine Presence was largely incommunicable.

I continued to explore the nature of my longing. If, as Augustine says, God is nearer to us than we are to ourselves, indeed is in our very midst, would I be able to find God in myself? Is any kind of "knowing" of the One who is wholly indescribable and unknowable possible? Is John Calvin (1509–1564) right to say that wisdom consists of two parts: knowledge of God and knowledge of self? Calvin believes that self-knowledge can lead to knowledge of God, but adds that there are limits to self-knowledge and the proper way to start is to seek knowledge of the Divine. "In the first place, no one can look upon himself without immediately turning his thoughts to the contemplation of God, in whom he 'lives and moves'" (Acts17:28), writes Calvin. We will never attain this self-knowledge until we first "[…] look upon God's face, and then descend from contemplating him to scrutinise [ourselves]". Looking inward is to discover God. I identified my longing as wanting to "know" God more and more intimately. This required looking inward.

But the deeper I plumbed my inward longing, the more contradictory and paradoxical things became. I knew only that I wanted to "[…] fall into the hands of the living God" (Heb 10:31). I suspected that this would be a place of surprise and utter vulnerability.

It was; but I was ravished by joy. God touched me. In an ineffable, fleeting, never-to-be-forgotten moment, I knew the Presence. My longing was met and my life changed. In the midst of paradox I saw truth. The Unknowable was momentarily known; and then became unknown again.

Now I am learning to live with the questions, ambiguities, contradictions and paradoxes of having faith. I can only wonder as questioning teaches me to trust God more and leads me ever deeper into the mystery that is so deeply part of the life of faith. In fact, this blessing could also read: "Blessed are those who learn to live with the questions!" Denying that the life of faith is full of questions simply because we think that we *know* all the truth, or that we *should* know the whole truth, or that living with questions and ambiguities implies doubt, and that doubt and faith are incompatible is to deny the reality of paradox in all of life. This blessing comes first in this book for it is foundational to all else that follows. It is my innermost truth, my continual tutelage in trusting God, my freedom in faith. It is the promise of a deepening faith and an ongoing call to greater humility. Parker Palmer is right when he says that if we refuse to flee from the tensions in the life of faith, "[…] we may receive one of the great gifts of the spiritual life, *the transformation of contradiction into paradox*".

I cannot walk on the often unmarked path of faith only in my head or even by trying to live a more exemplary life. It takes something more – what Franciscan monk Richard Rohr describes as agreeing to "[…] bear the mystery of God: God's suffering for the world and God's ecstasy in the world at the same time". I agree with Rohr that when Christianity stopped teaching us to contemplate and embrace mystery some four to five hundred years ago "[…] we lost the capacity to deal with paradox, inconsistency and human imperfection. Instead, it became winners take all and losers lose all […]" Adult spirituality begins when you start learning to live with ambiguity, rather than insisting on absolute certitude every step of the way. Why do we call it "faith"? Nevertheless, we continue to search for predictability because we long for certainty and think that it can be attained only when we are in control.

Thomas Merton, one of my spiritual guides along the way, said that he found himself like Jonah, "travelling toward my destiny in the belly of a paradox". Away with dubious certainties! He goes on to say: "[…] the creative opportunities are boundless. Resist that fact, and life can get brutal. Embrace it, and life becomes one whale of a ride!" I am on an exhilarating and, at times, unnerving ride, navigating with questions as markers on my inadequate chart, in perpetual wonder at the treasures in the deeper waters.

How is contradiction different to paradox? According to the *New Shorter Oxford Dictionary*, a contradiction is "a statement containing elements logically at variance with one another". Paradox, however, is "a statement that seems self-contradictory or absurd but in reality expresses a possible truth". So paradox promises that apparent opposites can come together in our lives and that we can replace either/or thinking with something that is closer to both/and.

I now know that contradiction and paradox are part of human nature and of our circumstances. They are not due to human ineptitude, but are woven into the fabric of life. It is, therefore, important to be aware that holding the tensions of opposites (either/or) in our lives can open doors to a new acceptance of things the way they are (both/and). This is liberating. It may not always be easy or comfortable, but finding the promise in paradox means knowing that two realities, though apparently contradictory, may be equally true and need to be held together. Balancing the claims of differing realities, such as needing to be alone but also with others, and needing to pray alone and with others is living with the knowledge that all is held together in what writer on Benedictine spirituality Esther de Waal calls "a hidden wholeness". All is related – life and death, light and dark, head and heart. How we respond to the contradictions and paradoxes is pivotal to our spiritual lives. When we are prepared to live with the questions, we meet and reckon with contradiction and paradox in our own dilemmas. Then we invariably arrive at a turning point where we either evade God or meet God. In his poem "Auguries of Innocence", William Blake (1757–1827) writes:

> Joy and woe are woven fine,
> A clothing for the soul divine,
> Under every grief and pine
> Runs a joy with silken twine
> It is right it should be so;
> Man was made for joy and woe;
> And when this we rightly know,
> Through the world we safely go.

I know that our traditions and practices are shot through with contradiction. Think, for example, of the contradiction of traditions that over millennia have upheld the dignity and worth of all human beings as created in the image of God, and yet have denied women the full exercise of their gifts in all aspects of ministry while perpetuating all-male hierarchies as divinely ordained by God. Take the psalms, whose enduring nature expresses just how complex and contradictory life can be. They are both intensely personal but also universal; they lament and they praise, almost in one breath. Take the Eucharist whose very symbols are paradoxes. Bread is the staff of life, yet it has to be broken in a world of want. Wine is a symbol of celebration to be enjoyed with friends, yet it is also the cup of blood signifying death.

Is there then no certainty in the life of faith? "Uncertainty," I have written elsewhere "[…] is a code word for the acceptance that all of life is lived within the tension between what we think we know and what we do not know, and that mystery and paradox are inherent to the life of faith." There is danger in unreflected certainty, because it rests uneasily alongside the riches of the Christian tradition that has a deep sense of mystery, paradox, uncertainty, ambiguity and contradiction. Unreflected certainty is also the foundation for fundamentalism. But more about that presently.

What is considered certain is a matter of faith. My certainties are: God is mystery. God is both known and unknown. God is totally trustworthy. God wants every single human being to live abundantly and fully. God in Christ defines what love is, and God is merciful and compassionate. Like my theologian friend Jaap Durand, I too believe that there is "[…] one metaphor that cannot and will not be replaced, the cross". My credo rests on these certainties. I am not trying to prove these convictions – they are simply the tenets of my faith. I could tell of instances when this faith has been affirmed in my life. I know that others give similar testimonies. However, this is not an essay on Christian apologetics. It is my effort to wrestle with contradiction and paradox in the life of faith, and how I cope with living in the tension between certainty and uncertainty.

It will become clear throughout this book that I often find Augustine a perspicacious guide as I struggle to express what I have found to be true. The following wisdom is attributed to him:

Let us, you and I, lay aside all arrogance
Let neither of us pretend to have found the truth
Let us seek it as something unknown to both of us
Then we may seek it with love and sincerity
When neither of us has the rashness
nor the presumption to believe that he already possesses it …
I do not pretend to understand.

The phrase "I do not pretend to understand" is one I hold on to. Life is predictable and unpredictable, ordered and random, exclusive and inclusive. To accept paradox calls for humility, one of the most formidable and exacting requirements for the life of faith. Paradox and contradiction are sublime tutors in testing and, perhaps briefly, tasting humility. Against these background remarks, I want now to look at the following topics: fundamentalism, how we interpret our texts, how we use language when speaking about God and faith, the contribution of metaphor in naming God, and the role of the mystical in exploring contradiction and paradox.

Contradiction and paradox deal with uncertainty, with questioning, with the unexpected. Life is fluid, open to surprise and new discovery. By contrast, fundamentalist views eschew questioning and operate in closed, rigid systems of argument and thought. Fundamentalist views are found in every field of human endeavour, from science to religion, from confronting political ideologies to the economics of market fundamentalism. Fundamentalism can even occur in confrontations between the fans of opposing football or rugby teams! I have heard Jungians oppose Freudians with fundamentalist fervour. And what about the fundamentalists at wine and food tastings! Religious fundamentalism is here to stay as long as we find reasons to fear change, to be wary of technological progress, to fear pluralism because it signifies loss of identity and as long as we cling to our beliefs, traditions and customs "because it has always been like this".

Today, fundamentalism as a religious force is a major source of conflict in our world. Whether it is Hindu, Jewish, Christian or Islamic, it is the opposite of being willing to live with the questions. Writer on religion Karen Armstrong, who has grappled with fundamentalist movements, says: "Every single fundamentalist movement I have studied – whether Christian, Jewish or Muslim – is rooted in a profound fear that modern society wants to wipe out religion." In her view, fundamentalism is an embattled form of spirituality that has emerged as a response to a perceived crisis – the destruction of religious life. Secularism is viewed as a modern heresy. Fuelled by conspiracy theories, the world out there is hostile and conflict is often referred to as apocalyptic. Fundamentalists are generally sympathetic to nationalist causes, practise religious exclusivism and thus resist dealing with difference. Women's rights are viewed with suspicion and usually denied, while patriarchy is embraced as a God-given social construct. Fundamentalism thrives on an inerrant, literal understanding of its chosen texts that are interpreted factually.

Analysing certain characteristics of fundamentalism, Anglican priest Kenneth Leech finds that its views are, in the first instance, unintelligent. It does not allow for the honest struggle of mind and heart in which truth is revealed. The relationship between scripture and disciple is that of master and slave. Second, it is the religion of a crusading mind rather than of a crucified mind. "True spirituality involves a dimension of listening, of abandonment, of silent brooding, features which are conspicuously absent in most fundamentalist worship and life. Third, it is selective. It chooses parts of Scripture that fit in with its ideological framework. So, for example, it often focuses more on issues such as homosexuality and abortion, on which the Bible says little or nothing, and ignores issues such as poverty and wealth on which it says a great deal," writes Leech.

According to Lutheran scholar of religion Martin Marty, religious fundamentalisms are generally speaking "[…] movements that in a direct and self-conscious way fashion a response to modernity". He describes how secular rationalists who decry religious beliefs as outmoded, irrelevant and unrespectable fuel the intentions of fundamentalists. "The smug assumption of the Enlightenment regarding religion's fate has been manifestly proven wrong by the twentieth century dynamism of fundamentalism. Religion did not 'go away' […]" writes Marty. Today many people still "believe". Some, however, believe that religion has to be rescued and defended at all costs from secularism spawned by Enlightenment thinking.

Ironically, fundamentalists do not entirely reject the benefits of modernity. Its products are employed with skill and delight – rapid transport, telecommunications, radio, television, the Internet, medical science and so on – while at the same time they are wary of the values that accompany technological marvels. Some fundamentalists are, of course, genuinely concerned about the dehumanising effects of materialism and the displacement of religion in their contexts. Is fundamentalism then motivated by some altruistic programme to restore things to "what they were"? Analysing the motives for fundamentalist beliefs is not easy because human motivations are interwoven and complex.

It is true that some fundamentalists seek power to change society and believe that they will make a better job of running matters. I do, however, find the desire for political power and for absolute authority over the lives of people disturbing. Worse still is the increasing proclivity of some fundamentalists to use terror tactics as a means of effecting change. Fundamentalists do not suffer contradiction and paradox. To be so certain of the rightness of one's views on the nature of faith and God renders questions anathema. Unquestioning certainty is the fundamentalist's hallmark. Even God does not escape this certainty. When religion wants to define God completely, it enters the realms of fundamentalism. To control God is to be able to manage God. God then becomes nothing more than human ideas. Once God is named and tamed, God must at all costs be defended against the onslaughts of secularism. It is arrogant and vain to think that God needs to be defended, to assume that God cannot cope. This fills me with foreboding. My God escapes all definition; my God is always greater, always new, and ever surprising. My God can cope with all that we can come up with because my God knows the human heart and what it is capable of – in its entirety.

Sadly, today, we are seeing a crude pathological condition of Christianity in which the Bible is misused to reinforce homophobia, gender discrimination, oppression, violence and injustice in the powerful interests of mostly dominant social classes and groups. Furthermore, when Christians in the United States urge the government of Uganda to impose the death penalty on homosexual people, fundamentalism becomes obscene. Fundamentalism of this aggressive, crusading type is essentially hostile to spiritual progress. It is quite simply a barrier to the development of a mature spirituality. Not surprisingly, it has provided fuel for those who seek to ridicule faith perspectives such as evolutionary biologist Richard Dawkins and the late Christopher Hitchens (1949–2011).

It is, of course, easy to take a swipe at fundamentalists and scoff at their beliefs and actions. But fundamentalisms themselves differ and do not all take on the same guise. I can understand the resentments that many of their adherents harbour in their desire to uphold the integrity of their religious views in the face of creeping secularism and the very problematic social contexts in which many of them live. Appalling social conditions and the dangers inherent in failed states fuel some fundamentalisms against the background of poverty, unemployment, lack of expectation, hopelessness and the rigid stratification of some societies. As I struggle to find understanding and tolerance I remind myself that God is One, all-loving and forgiving.

The truth is that we cannot know all about God or dictate how God will or will not be present. Fundamentalism does not allow room for mystery or for living with paradox in the life of faith. Thus the spirituality of fundamentalism is in danger of being dogmatic, uncritical and unreflective. Once we think we know how things really are, we live out of a naïve certainty that struggles to deal with the vicissitudes of life. In contrast, if we do not dodge a critical and questioning consciousness when wrestling with the ups and downs of life, we may begin to embrace the freedom of not knowing, and thus trust all to God. Faith that is conscious of the profound mystery of life and takes responsibility for living creatively with what we do not know or understand enables us to go on, no matter how problematic life may become.

The Bible is a document of great diversity representing different genres of writing composed at different times, in different contexts, read in hugely diverse times and situations, from Greenland to the equatorial forests of Africa, from the monasteries of Europe to the camps of the Gulag. It is a mixture of compositions, styles and mediums: prose narrative both allegorical and historical, legal codes, proverbs, prayers and moral maxims, prophesy, hymns, correspondence, as well as lyrical and dramatic poetry. The Bible is a library, not a dictionary. It is a classic text that is the source book of our faith. It is a startling history of goodness, love and courage, but also of repulsive cruelty, vengefulness and injustice. The Bible can be profoundly ambiguous. Yet, at the same time, the great themes of love and justice are played out in the relationship between God and human beings throughout its pages.

How we read and understand the Bible differs widely depending on our circumstances, our history, values, communities and our hopes. As we read we interpret. All understanding is based on interpreting. I have a high regard for scripture. I believe that I am in conversation with the text, that I am open to new meaning, and to the fact that other conversations are also taking place. Our personal conversations with the text have limits because we interpret what we read differently. What I regard as truth is the result of my best interpretation, arrived at through my membership of my community of faith, my studies of the Bible and my interaction with other scholars. It is not a closed reading, but rather one that is continuously open to new insights and ongoing revelation.

A literal use of scripture is impossible to sustain. I do not have to be a biblical scholar to know that I should not condone slavery, or stoning as punishment for adultery, or be compelled to marry my husband's brother when my husband dies. It gets trickier when I decide (on shaky scholarly grounds) that the few texts that purport to refer to homosexuality are so authoritative that they warrant dividing my church, and yet ignore the authority of the thousands of other texts that inveigh against human greed and exploitation of the poor. Why we choose some texts as authoritative and others as time bound and not relevant to our lives today remains the challenge to fundamentalist interpretations of the Bible. It would be more modest to read its texts with some understanding of the times in which they were written and allow the great biblical themes of love and justice to interpret the texts themselves.

The Bible has a wondrous ability to critique itself. It is also a very flexible source. Luke and Acts appeal to different groups in different ways: charismatics call on the role of the Spirit in these texts, while liberation and political theologians claim the preferential option for the poor. John's Gospel will always appeal to contemplative mindsets, mystics and theologians of all Christian traditions, yet it has been received in different ways. This is what is called the history of reception. Texts are received and interpreted – a process that takes place in particular contexts, situations and historical traditions.

Male interpreters have for centuries told women what the biblical texts mean for our lives. Women biblical scholars now reject this one-sided, and often oppressive, interpretation of the Bible. When seeking wisdom and understanding for their lives, African women have identified ways of reading the scriptures that draw on story-telling, a custom that is central to African societies. Biblical scholar Musa Dube and theologian and president of the Global Fund for Women, Musimbi Kanyoro, have both promoted African women's Bible commentary from a storytelling perspective together with a postcolonial culturally rooted interpretation for readers on our continent. This method challenges current frameworks of biblical interpretation as it engages "[...] the patriarchy of African cultures, the Bible and colonial masters. It confronts the imperialism of historical and contemporary times, exposing its impact on women's lives and its link with patriarchy," writes Dube.

This type of reading encourages diversity for African women who are not a homogenous group. As Isabel Phiri, Betty Govinden and Sarojini Nadar point out, we "[...] straddle a wide spectrum of positions from active intervention or radicalism, to negotiating roles and identities, to authoritative reformist, even collaborative strategies of engagements". Thus our stories differ as they are embedded in specific cultural and historical contexts. This makes the reading of the scriptures rich and varied as our women claim our identities as truth tellers and believers.

Throughout our engagement with the Bible, the paradoxes of our faith become apparent – and they are quite wonderful! As Esther de Waal points out, Christians (and this includes fundamentalists) live with

A God who became a man
A victor who rides on a donkey in his hour of triumph
A saviour who is executed like some common thief
A king whose kingdom is not here but to come
A God who tells me "when I am weak I am strong"
A God whose promise is that "in losing my life I shall find it".

These statements are not simply contradictions. They are examples of how apparent contradictions are, in fact, full of the promise of paradox. The power in these paradoxes does not present us with a closed system, but with a series of open doors. We can choose whether to engage paradox or not. Life is riddled with conflicting claims that are not easy to live with. Why then do we shrink from those inherent in our faith? Probably because our minds fail to appreciate the full truth of paradox and contradiction – only the heart can, driven by our longing for God.

Contradiction and paradox raise the question of the language we use about our faith. Language is never innocent; this all women know, as does anyone who has experienced racism or homophobia. Language is always loaded and is more than words alone. There is power in how language is used. It expresses consciously or unconsciously held beliefs or ideologies. Naming oneself, one's reality and one's God is claiming one's identity, one's values and beliefs.

This is true of religious language as much as it is true of political speak. It is a particularly poignant truth when we speak about God. Because we are in a relationship with God of both knowing and not knowing, our language for God is never adequate. God is this, but not that. God is both this and that. We speak because speak we must, but our words are always inadequate, and at times it may be better to remain silent. Philosopher Ludwig Wittgenstein (1889–1951) affirmed this: "Whereof one cannot speak, thereof one must be silent."

But we must speak of God, so we use images and metaphors, limited by our own experiences and biases. "God" is in a sense a humanly constructed symbol. Biblically speaking, God gave Godself only one name – "I AM WHO I AM." This phrase encompasses the total incomprehensibility of God. God is beyond description. When we do not acknowledge this truth – that we both know and do not know God – I am troubled.

Our inability or unwillingness to acknowledge the paradox inherent in God-language can result in the word "God" being misunderstood, misused and even becoming irrelevant. It is true that millions of people have been tortured, killed, oppressed and discriminated against in the name of "God". It is also true that we persist in using misleading images for God: God is a tyrannical monarch who imposes *his* will on the world at all costs; God is a fierce and unrelenting judge; God is a patriarch; God is a powerful despot who sends natural disasters to punish the world, or allows innocent children to die because it is his will to do so. I continue to use the word "God" as it has a long history and I know of no more useful term. It can be redeemed from its oppressive and discriminating connotations once we understand that *all speech about God is metaphor*. No one word can describe the whole truth and the whole reality of the One we call "God". The word "God" is itself a metaphor, about which more later.

Sadly, a great deal of our speech about the Holy Other is simply hubris. Too often we label the Creator in our own image. Abandoning all caution, we highjack God into our own limited view of Ultimate Being with frightening certainty. Embracing the awe of silence as a response to the sense of the immanence of divine reality is foreign to most of us. We dare to talk about God as though we have privileged access to what theologian Ian Ramsey calls "God's private diaries". But we need to speak about the Holy One, who is *the* Reality, *the* Truth, *the* Source of our lives. The problem is that our God becomes so small, often tied to one name only. If one name only is not enough for human beings, neither is it for God. We dare not imprison what is the Sacred One in one name. That is why Dominican theologian and medieval mystic Meister Eckhart (1260–1328) said: "Therefore I pray to God that he rid me of God" – a prayer to be liberated from the prison of language that is too limited for God.

I am concerned about the use of God-language in Christian worship. We worship and pray as a community of believers, hopefully in ways that enable everyone to participate, while nurturing our spirituality. When we worship we largely jettison the mystery of the paradox that lies at the core of our God-language. At a weekly Eucharist service in my church, God is called "Father" about eighteen times in the liturgy. "Lord" occurs even more frequently – and that is when it is often clearly not referring to Jesus. So I wonder – is this all that can be said about God in prayer and worship? If "Father" is a metaphor for the finest father-child relationship, it may mirror something of the divine-human relationship, but how many father-child relationships are truly fine? How would someone who has had an abusive father feel about this metaphor? Clearly this metaphor – like all others – makes meaning through the association with human experiences of fatherhood. What has cemented this metaphor for God above all others and what might this imply for our spirituality? Where is the sense of mystery surrounding the truth of God? The danger, liturgist Brian Wren warns, arises when "[…] our naming of God is distorted, [then] our knowledge of God will be also". The God we speak of is the God we have.

In the Christian tradition, the male God has become *the* metaphor for God. Not only is the focus on God as male/father a limited model, but it also reflects a patriarchal order. Where does this leave the other half of the world's human beings who are also created in God's image? The root metaphor for Christianity is not patriarchy. It is what Jesus called "the kingdom of God" (itself a male metaphor!). God's reign offers all, women and men, freedom to be in relationship with God, ourselves, others and creation as citizens of the not-yet-but-coming reign of God on earth. This root metaphor for Christianity has everything to do with relationship. We are offered a new, living, human-divine relationship characterised by unending love and unmerited grace. We are promised freedom from *all* domination, from poverty, fear, oppression and suffering. This is a bold and contradictory claim. On the one hand, so much is at variance with this claim. On the other, the Bible teaches us that God is with those who are suffering and are marginalised, promising justice, equality, renewal and peace.

How different it could be if we spoke of God in relational categories that are both opposites but also harmonious and dynamic – present and hidden, powerful and powerless, suffering and comforting, punishing and saving. We can relate to God in a myriad ways that name our spiritual and physical needs – God as life, wisdom, being, friend, creator, nurturer, advocate, fire, light, rock, mother or father, refuge;

God who is the giver and transformer of life, the ever-merciful and compassionate one. God's unmerited and never-ending love is not meant to describe God as much as to suggest the new relationship offered to us by God.

~

I have no problem with God being called "Father". I take issue, however, when "Father" is the *only* metaphor for God when I worship. The arguments for the sole use of this metaphor are usually threefold: God the Father is biblical, it is Trinitarian, and Jesus uses it. I do not deny the truth of these claims, but I do know that too literal an understanding of naming God does not do justice to the multilayered nature of our relationship with God.

It is useful to know that the word "father" has its origins before Christianity in the myths of monarchical societies. In these myths the deity brings order out of chaos in the universe by appointing a male ruler who becomes the prototype for subsequent kings. Thus the divinely appointed king is a "son" of their god or gods and the patriarchal culture is reified. Psalm 2 reflects this reality (and is quoted in Acts 4:25–26). Yet interestingly, referring to God as Father is rare in the Hebrew scriptures and is used mainly as a metaphor for the relationship between people and their deity. The language of the Hebrew scriptures is not intended to be read literally. Neither is that of the New Testament.

Second, Augustine said that the language of the Trinity – Father, Son and Spirit – cannot fully embrace the mystery of the Godhead. The early theologians of the church wrestled with the relationship of the Creator, the Redeemer and the Sustainer. They rejected the understanding that the Son was subordinate to the Father or the Holy Spirit to the Father and the Son. By the fourth century the Trinity was affirmed: Father, Son and Spirit are of the same being, one yet distinctive, coeternal, all equally to be praised. Understanding the Trinity is tricky. It is in itself a paradox: we proclaim one God – in three! This alone should make us more humble when speaking about God!

A couple of years ago, I spent two weeks learning to "write" icons. For many years, icons seen in churches in different parts of the world moved me. The earliest icons appear to come from St Catherine's Monastery on the Sinai Peninsula. From a visit there, I shall never forget the eyes of Christ Pantocrator (Ruler of all), and the rough chiselled face of the grey-bearded apostle Peter, looking very much the former fisherman. Both date from the seventh century. To return to my theme – one of the best-known and best-loved icons was painted by Andrei Rublev (born c.1360) and is found in the Tretyakov Gallery in Moscow. It is called *The Hospitality of Abraham* and recalls the story of Genesis 18 when three angels visited Abraham by the oaks of Mamre. The icon, depicting three angels around a table with an oak tree in the background, has, according to Rowan Williams, "[…] been taken by Christians as a foreshadowing of the revelation that God is three agents sharing one agency […]The angels in the story represent, we are told, an appearance of 'the Lord'; they speak and act as one." God and the Holy Spirit could not be depicted because they had not taken on flesh. For Williams, attempting to understand the Trinity points us to the way of the Word, the way of Jesus Christ:

> We have granted that this is not a "picture" of the Trinity in any ordinary way, and that the three figures are not straightforwardly portraits of the three divine persons; rather we are looking into and following the path of the divine process of dealing with us to reveal and save. And in the centre of that is the Word […] Nothing is known of God the Trinity that does not come through the Word incarnate; this is the movement we must be drawn into so as to come fully and finally to our home in God's life.

The Eastern tradition avoided the silliness of depicting God the Father as an old man with a beard and the Holy Spirit as a white dove. What this icon shows is the insurmountable difficulty of depicting the Trinity. It leaves us with questions, with mystery, and draws us into the circle of holiness around the chalice on the table.

Third, Jesus uses the Aramaic word *abba* for God in the gospels. And yes, there are a number of texts where this occurs. There is the Lord's Prayer that uses two different ways of addressing God: "Father" in Luke 11:2 and "Father in heaven" in Matthew 6:9, which may reflect different liturgical practices. Most scholars think that Luke's version is the original, while Matthew's also appears in the *Didache*. But it is often Mark 14:36 that is central to claims about Jesus' use of *abba*. "*Abba* Father, for you all things are possible; remove this cup from me; yet, not what I want but what you want" (Mk 14:36). Jesus is in Gethsemane when he makes this prayer – a scene of desolation with no disciple present to hear his agony. New Testament scholar Mary Ann Tolbert has described this scene as an "interior monologue" – a critical moment of internal struggle about which we really know nothing. Mark's portrayal here is an acknowledgement of God's power at the very moment when Jesus is about to be handed over to the crowd with their swords and clubs. "[F]or you all things are possible" is in poignant contrast with Jesus' cry from the cross, "My God, my God, why have you forsaken me?" (Mk 15:34). These two prayers in Mark's Gospel warn readers that following Jesus means taking up the cross – the paradox of both knowing and believing that for God all things are possible, while knowing moments of God-forsakenness.

Today, Jesus' use of *abba* is often used to legitimate the dominance of "Father" in Christian worship. This contention has created some confusion and debate. The theory that Jesus' unique experience of God as *abba* is the root of the relationship of Christians to God is no longer held, as it is unclear to what extent the Jewish Christians saw *abba* as a unique, divine word or whether they were drawing on the surrounding culture that described the typical pagan head of the pantheon of gods. It is important also to note that the use of *abba* could have reflected a common practice in Mark's community, just as its use in Galatians 4:6 and Romans 8:15 reflected practices in the Pauline churches, and not necessarily the special intimacy of a child with its "Father", or the stamp of divine authority on "Father".

It is also a fact that imperial Rome was the context of Jesus' life. In some Greek and Roman texts "father" also functioned as a synonym for God. Zeus, for instance, was father of the many beings he created. In the first century, the Jews did not live under an exclusive Hebrew culture. Roman Caesar Augustus adopted *Pater patriae* (father of the fatherland) in 2 B.C.E. as one of the emperor's titles. The Jews may well have been calling into question Caesar's right to being the *Pater patriae* by addressing their God as "Father", thus staking a claim on their God's mercy, protection and providence. The words "Call no one your father on earth, for you have one Father – the one in heaven" (Mt 23:9) may well be an explicit rejection of the emperor's claims to the title "father".

Does Jesus' use of *abba* thus provide twenty-first century theology and practice with a kind of normative value? Is this sufficient to argue for the almost exclusive use of "Father" in worship? Although *abba* was certainly significant in the early Greek-speaking communities of Paul and Mark, writes New Testament scholar Mary Rose D'Angelo, "[…] where it expressed empowerment through the spirit", its use cannot be attributed to Jesus with any certainty. It appears that using "Father" for God cannot be shown to originate with Jesus, or to have been so central to his teaching that it should be the only way of addressing God. We can with assurance say the Lord's prayer and address God as "Father in heaven" provided we remember that it is not the only way of calling upon God. According to D'Angelo, Jesus may well have used "Father" in resistance to the imperial order of his day rather than as an expression of familial intimacy. A more informed reading of the complex, challenging historical realities is required.

To change liturgical practices is a monumental task. I wonder to what extent changing words will really effect change? I know that it will encounter resistance. I do not seek change for the sake of mere innovation. My concern is with the nurturing of believers' spirituality. Any change must go hand in hand with respect for people's piety. Worshippers are not guinea pigs for liturgical reform to be manipulated in the service of some or other ideological agenda. Reform must be rooted in our best traditions – they are rich and span over thousands of years. Nevertheless, to keep God safely in our childhood images is to hamper seriously our relational understanding of the One who made heaven and earth and who is intimately involved in our welfare.

The challenge is to find existing contemporary speech that does justice to the mystery of God's identity. Along the way we have lost the gender neutrality of YHWH and the I AM in the masculinity of the words "Father" and "Lord" – something most Christians find acceptable. The words of worship matter. They either stultify or nurture relationship. This is also true of the community at worship. Are we willing to be more open to mystery and paradox in our God-language? We cannot adopt a more literal approach or we shall lose our sense of wonder that, in Gail Ramshaw's words, drops "[…] the believer finally in amazement in the lap of God".

Understanding the use of metaphor in our God-language is helpful as we struggle to name the Unnameable. Once we discover the richness and variety offered by metaphorical language when speaking about God, our worship, our prayers and our spirituality are enriched. Of course we choose our metaphors according to our needs and situations. If life is experienced as unjust, God becomes the righteous judge. If enemies threaten one's life, God will become a warrior on one's behalf. If parents let a child down, God may become the good Mother or Father. Judges, warriors or parents are human descriptions of God, but they are not literal. They are only metaphors. While human judges, warriors and parents may fail us, God will not. Thus metaphors are limited. Even the most discerning cannot grasp the totality of who God is. Metaphor itself is paradoxical. It describes, ascribes and is useful; yet it is limited and incapable of telling the whole story. The truth is that all speech about God is metaphorical; theology is itself metaphor.

The *New Oxford Shorter Dictionary* defines metaphor as "a figure of speech in which a word or phrase is applied to something to which it is not literally applicable". Allowing two thoughts of two different things to come together at the same time in a word or a phrase can spell out a new meaning. Because a metaphor is not literal, it can hold contrasting elements at the same time; it is open to interpretation, and is tentative and alive to new linkages. Metaphor has a touch of the riddle about it – one either "gets" it or one does not. If metaphors are overused and commonplace, their ability to lead us to new insights can be lost.

We use metaphors daily: the sweet smell of success, the singer's velvet voice, the long arm of the law illustrate the point. Our religious language is deeply metaphorical and even Jesus' teaching in parables is, in essence, a use of metaphor. In her searching study of metaphor in religious language, philosophical theologian Janet Soskice defines metaphor as "[...] that figure of speech whereby we speak about one thing in terms which are seen to be suggestive of another". Quite rightly, Soskice remarks: "All metaphors which we use to speak of God arise from experiences of that which cannot adequately be described, of that which Jews and Christians believe to be 'He who is' ".

A root metaphor for Christians is the "reign of God" that will come in its fullness on earth "as it is in heaven". It is the central metaphor in Jesus' teaching. He is the key to the relationship that we are offered when this comes about. His life shows us how to be truly and fully relational human beings, worthy citizens of God's rule. For over two thousand years we have tried to understand what this means for the life of faith, interpreting and reinterpreting it over and over again, while knowing that no metaphor can fully capture the enigmatic nature of the God-human relationship.

The great advantage of seeing the root metaphor of Christianity in relational terms is that we are freed from inflexible interpretations of our faith. God is then not only and exclusively "Father", but this metaphor is understood as one of many for God. Our concept of God is then open to possibilities that we have not seen previously. Tertullian (born c.164–died c.220) suggested root, tree or fruit, or fountain, river or stream. Julian of Norwich named God as Maker, Lover and Keeper. Augustine wrote of the trinitarian God as the Lover, Beloved and Love. Dietrich Bonhoeffer described God as the "Great Beyond in the midst of us", a phrase that neatly captures the challenges of speaking about God in human language. It is a phrase laced with paradox – the paradox of God's immanence and transcendence.

The metaphor of God as "friend" appears in certain mystical literature as a counterbalance to parental images for God. It occurs sparingly in the Bible when, for instance, Isaiah (41:8) includes Israel as a friend of God: "But you, Israel, my servant, Jacob, whom I have chosen, the offspring of Abraham, my friend […]" Jesus refers to the "Son of Man" as the "friend" of tax collectors and sinners (Mt 11:19). However, Gregory of Nyssa, the father of Christian mysticism, writes in his *Life of Moses* that there is only one really worthwhile thing and that is to become God's friend. These are not wild words. "Thus the Lord used to speak to Moses face to face, as one speaks to a friend" in the tent at Mount Horeb (Ex 33:11), explains Gregory.

The central theme in viewing God as "friend" is relationship. It is, however, not a relationship of equality, as friends are not necessarily equals, and friendship can be offered to the outsider in our midst. As God is the source of the power and love of friendship, God's share is always primary. One of my ten-year-old twin granddaughters, Anna, said: "God is everybody's imaginary friend." I know what she means by "imaginary" – it is what we cannot see. But to her it is real. The idea of God as friend does not meet with approval of those who wrestle with the issue of how to speak of God. They find "friend" too familiar and unable to covey the otherness of divinity.

Our attempts at speaking of God remain flawed and limited. Tying God up in a box stamped "God" is unproductive, untrue and spiritually impoverishing. In contrast, embracing mystery, and being willing not to know and yet to believe, lays the foundation for a spirituality that is life giving. Augustine knew that human speech and understanding are limited when speaking about God: *Si comprehendis non est Deus* (If you comprehend what you are saying, you are not talking about God). Yet, like us, Augustine continued to speak and write about God. We are all in the belly of this paradox.

Ambiguity, contradiction and paradox lead us into the realm of mystery. There is much we do not understand, much that is uncertain, even mystifying, yet also revealing and filled with wonder. Christianity has a long and valued tradition of the mystical. I know that some of my Reformed friends shudder at the word "mysticism", a word that is so often misunderstood. I suspect that this is largely due to a misconception that mysticism is all about feelings and experience, and is not rooted in the Word of God. Mysticism has always been present in some form or other in Christian history, and we dare not lose this deeply valued tradition.

The mystical tradition is caricatured when it is hijacked by the occult and when phenomena such as parapsychology, astrology, tarot, alchemy, magic or drug-induced states of consciousness are lumped together as "mystical" in a New Age fashion. German fascism spawned a very peculiar mysticism when it embraced nationalism, militarism and nature-romanticism in a kind of Aryan mystique. Echoes of this were also found in the nationalist Afrikaner idea of *die volk* that undergirded the ideology of apartheid. Clearly this is not what is meant by the mystical here. The mystical in Christianity is different because it is rooted in the mystery of Christ in scripture and sacrament.

So what is mysticism? I do not find this easy to answer as centuries of writings on the mystical bear evidence of different experiences and understandings. What appears to be common to all is the one truth – the mystical is about a loving encounter or union with the Holy One. It is an ineffable experience of "loving knowing", initiated by God because God loves us, enabling us to love in return. Meister Eckhart, whose insights into the mystical nature of faith speak across the centuries, affirmed this. "The love by which we think we love God is actually the love by which God first loved us," he says. The mystical moves us beyond self to a humble knowing – it is about being held, rather than holding, and knowing so deeply that one can balance knowing with not knowing. I understand the mystical quite simply as "a loving encounter with God". Describing an encounter with love is really beyond words. The closest I can get is to say that *it is being touched by God where I am most truly myself.* But it is not simply a "feel-good" experience reserved for a special category of persons. It is possible for all to know those inexplicable, fleeting moments of love, peace, joy and Presence that bear fruit in greater charity and humility, and a deepening of relationship. Such encounters have profound implications for the way we live – our relationships and the justice of our practices, our works of charity, and our concern for creation and beauty in our world.

Acknowledging mystery is particularly poignant in times of suffering, loss and grief. We cry out to God, but God appears to be silent. We feel abandoned, forsaken, even angry. Hearts weep and we wonder: "Where are You, God?"At the same time we hold on to the hand of Jesus who remains our reality, our guide, and our friend in troubled times. We enter the great paradox: our God is both the God of Mount Sinai – "symbol of fierce majesty, a landscape of terror and theophany where we meet Yahweh in the darkness of unknowing" according to Belden Lane – while at the same time we know the God of Mount Tabor, the God of light revealed in Jesus to the disciples. The truth is God is both unknown and known.

The mystical is redolent with paradox. It is both ordinary and extraordinary. On the one hand, a mystical experience belongs to the realm of the extraordinary that cannot be plumbed by rational means. It is a moment when, in Augustine's well-known words: "God is utterly, deeply, closer to me than I am to myself." It also does not matter where I am – God is there, present and close, and it is in God that I live and move and have my being. All this is mystery, not something I can pretend to understand. The moment I write these words I know that they are totally inadequate. All I know is that I am loved by God in a way that is profoundly personal and yet extends to the whole human race, whether we know it or not.

On the other hand, despite the fact that the mystical is often associated with times of withdrawal, silence and solitude, an experience of the mystical envelops us in a very ordinary moment. I have felt the loving, creative presence of God surging in me in a deeply mysterious way when holding a newborn child in my arms, or watching an albatross fly, or simply looking at a landscape of great beauty. We cannot predict when we will encounter God. I remember reading C. S. Lewis's account of his mystical moment of conversion in his book *Surprised by Joy*. It is so matter of fact, almost reluctant. Yet it is also meticulously observed and highly reflective, though not without irony. It has stayed with me over the years.

> The odd thing was that before God closed in on me, I was in fact offered what now appears a moment of wholly free choice. In a sense, I was going up Headington Hill on the top of a bus. Without words and (I think) almost without images, a fact about myself was somehow presented to me. I became aware that I was holding something at bay, or shutting something out. Or, if you like, that I was wearing some stiff clothing, like corsets, or even a suit of armour, as if I were a lobster. I felt myself being, there and then, given a free choice. I could open the door or keep it shut […] Neither choice was presented as a duty; no threat or promise was attached to either, though I knew that to open the door […] meant the incalculable. The choice appeared to be momentous but it was also strangely unemotional. I was moved by no desires or fears. In a sense I was not moved by anything. I chose to open […]. I say "I chose," yet it did not really seem possible to do the opposite […]. You could argue that I was not a free agent, but I am more inclined to think that this came nearer to being a perfectly free act than most that I have ever done. Necessity may not be the opposite of freedom, and perhaps a man is most free when, instead of producing motives, he could only say: "I am what I do." Then came the repercussion on the imaginative level. I felt as if I were a man of snow at long last beginning to melt. The melting was starting in my back – drip-drip and presently trickle-trickle. I rather disliked the feeling.

God present on a British bus! What could be more ordinary – and extraordinary?

A further paradox in encountering the mystical is that it is both an experience of solitude and one of solidarity. We believe that God is love – creative, overflowing, ongoing and infinite love. We are recipients of God's love and love is experienced in communion, in relationship. So both solitude and solidarity need to be held together. The mystical is experienced in both solitary moments as well as in the profound joy of loving relationship – with a child, a lover, a friend, a stranger. Viennese Jewish philosopher Martin Buber (1878–1965) pointed out: "In the beginning is the relation, and in the relation is the power which creates the world, through us and with us and by us, you and I, you and we, and none of us alone." We receive love and are able to shed love from its overflow. We know this love by being alone with the Alone, yet we cannot help loving another because relationship with God and with one another is inseparable and reciprocal.

It is therefore dangerous to see the mystical as withdrawal from the world or as something on a higher plane, and solely for the truly enlightened and spiritually mature. Then silence, withdrawal and the contemplative lifestyle are worshipped per se, forgetting that these are merely vehicles for God to use. We become addicted to transcendence and inwardly dazzled by what Chilean poet Pablo Neruda (1904–1973) calls the "fetish of the incomprehensible".

If an encounter with loving Presence does not resonate with our theological praxis, it remains an esoteric tool for spiritual self-gratification. The mystical has everything to do with poverty, need and suffering in the world. Mysticism is eminently practical in the life of faith. An experience of the gift of love is life-changing and this means greater awareness, greater discernment and increased will-ingness for service in the cause of justice and charity and beauty in the world. We cannot nurture only our own personal joys and suffer-ings. Structural, economic, political and social injustice permeates our societies. The plight of the poor, the torture of the innocent, the agony of the dispossessed, the abused and raped, and other victims of violence are our concern. An experience of the love of Christ is love for the other, and for the world in which we find ourselves. This the life of Desmond Tutu has mirrored to me and I am very grateful for knowing him.

I have said that a mystical encounter is a moment of "loving knowing". Is this a different kind of "knowing" from that which comes from reading, reasoning and debating? Often fear of the mystical is based on the belief that reason and our capacity to think go out of the window. Perhaps our view of what it means "to know" is too restricted; perhaps we believe that "knowing" must be related to facts. I am not dismissing the importance of knowledge that is factually based and logically reasoned. What I am referring to is a more direct intuitive knowledge that is based on communion and likeness. The prophets talk about "knowing God"; Jacob and Job come to "know" God by wrestling intensely with God in the darkness. In the *Life of Moses,* Gregory of Nyssa describes how Moses entered a thick cloud and had a vision of God, but it was a dark vision. It was seeing, but not seeing, a knowledge which is ignorance. He writes: "This is the true knowledge of what is sought; this is seeing that consists in not seeing, because that which is sought transcends all knowledge, being separated on all sides by incomprehensibility as by a kind of darkness." Paradox upon paradox!

Knowledge of God means union or communion with God that enables us to become more of who we are in God. Loving knowledge of God is like W. B. Yeats's thinking "in the marrow bone".

> God guard me from those thoughts men think
> In the mind alone;
> He that sings a lasting song
> Thinks in the marrow bone.

Knowledge does not come only from the brain, but from the entire human being right down to the blood, sinew and marrow. Such is the lasting song.

I have never found it necessary to deny my ability to think while longing to "know" God more intimately. We do not find our way to mystical contemplation through reading or study, although I have found reading the works of the mystics helpful in trying to understand how to speak about what is ultimately mystery. What we do need to know is how to live in a way that will prepare us to be responsive to God. By now it should be clear that I struggle to find the right language to describe the paradoxical nature of the mystical. I resonate with Carmelite mystic Teresa of Avila (1515–1582) who prayed: "Lord, give me other words!" How do we express the inexpressible? No wonder phrases like "dark-light", "bittersweet", "silent cry", "filled emptiness" and "listening to the silence" pepper our efforts.

Turning to the medieval mystics, I find that they deal with their experience of God with great metaphorical freedom. They accept that God cannot be contained in one metaphor, and even metaphors can never appropriate the intimacy of the mystical experience of God. Often their language is radical and unconventional, original and descriptive. The Syrian monk known as Dionysius the Aerop-agite (fifth–sixth centuries) understands the Greek word *eros* as divine yearning and says that the most important name for God is "Good". He also describes God as "the darkness that outshines all re-splendence". He concludes by defining God as "Divine Eros [who] is the Good of the Good for the sake of Good". For Benedictine writer and composer Hildegard of Bingen (1098–1179), God is Divine Wisdom (*Sapientia*). Wisdom is restless until it finds its place in a fertile heart where it can grow towards its origin: the Creator of life. She says that Wisdom "is a spirit intelligent" and within Wisdom is life and healing. Anselm of Canterbury (d.1109) speaks of Jesus as Mother because God gives birth to souls and nourishes them. Cister-cian monk Bernard of Clairvaux (1090–1153) attempts to answer the question "What is God?" in a number of different ways. God is "The Beginning". God is the One of whom scripture says "from him and through him and to him are all things" (Rom 11:36). God is that of which nothing better can be thought. God is pure sim-plicity. "God is not formed; he is form." God is Trinity. For German Benedictine mystic Gertrud of Helfta (1256–1302), God is "Divine Being". English mystic Julian of Norwich also sees God as Mother: "We owe our being to him, and this is the essence of motherhood!"

The mystics do not restrict themselves to personal images of God. Often fire, oceans, springs, food and so on appear in their writing as they search to express the inexpressible. They know that God cannot really be captured in language.

In a thoughtful little book entitled *Tensions*, monk and theologian Harry Williams (1919–2006) neatly describes the "life-giving conflicts" that confront us as believers. Conflict and ambiguity produce tensions that tempt most people to think that something is wrong. While some tensions can be destructive, Williams argues that tensions in the life of faith should not be swept under the carpet. They are in reality a sign of growth. Growing pains are not comfortable "but they are the price we have to pay in order to become more richly and satisfyingly our full selves". We have no need to feel tense when we encounter contradictions in faith – they hold the promise of paradox and are deeply part of a believer's life.

Take the paradox between dependence and autonomy or independence. We are entirely dependent on God, yet we must also learn to be independent of God. Spiritual maturity is the acceptance of the paradox of being both utterly dependent on God while knowing that to become fully ourselves in all our frail humanity requires independence – a willingness to stand up and be counted for who we are. Since God is the ground of our being, our very origin, it is not surprising that the feelings we channel to God are often those of a child to a parent. Children, however, while feeling love and obedience, also know resentment, rebellion and self-assertion – in short, the bid for independence. We know that this kind of conflict is necessary for a child's progress towards maturity. And so it is in our relationship with God. One only has to read the psalms to find evidence of the struggles of God's people to grow to maturity in faith. They are full of feelings of longing, love, awe, obedience, praise, resentment, anger, rebellion, revenge and remorse.

If we believe that we cannot know God unless we know ourselves, and we have to find ourselves through becoming independent, then we are faced with letting go of what is reckoned to be "me" in order to find that the core of our total dependence is on God. Once again, paradox upon paradox! It is said that the greatest sinners make the greatest saints! We cannot save our lives unless we risk losing them. Spirituality is risky. As Harry Williams remarks:

> Respectability is not only a sociological phenomenon – suburban middle class and all that. Far more insidiously it is a spiritual phenomenon, a state of heart and soul. Whatever God wants in our relationship with Him it certainly isn't respectability. I imagine that the church in Laodicea treated God in the most respectable way. The divine reply to this treatment is invective worthy of youth at its most rebellious: "I'll spit you out."

Consider the contradiction between faith and doubt. Harry Williams points out that Paul tells us that we walk by faith, not by sight. Walking by sight stands for certainty – we know where we are going. Often people confuse sight and faith, implying that perfect faith consists of complete certainty, the absolute inability to doubt. This kind of faith is confusing because it anaesthetises our critical intelligence by putting to sleep the awkward questions. The result is a disguised form of fundamentalism about what the Bible purports to say and what the church is supposed to say, expressed with irresponsible complacency. We forget Jesus' cry on the cross – he was loyal to the totality of his experience at that moment. Truth about our doubts, feelings and experiences lies at the core of mature spirituality. This truth acknowledges the paradoxical nature of our faith.

Consider also the tension between knowing and not knowing. According to Harry Williams, there are inevitable tensions in our ways of knowing. We know only partially. In order to know we have to put ourselves into the mental frames of space and time of that which we seek to know. We then proceed to know, not the thing in itself, but the thing as it appears to us, shaped by our experiences. Our doctrines of faith are not photographs of spiritual reality; they are attempts to describe, with hints and guesses, that which is often indescribable. What does this mean for our spirituality? It means that we approach our speech about God, the *eschaton* (end times), the nature of human beings and their salvation, with greater humility, as our knowledge is always partial. Our faith symbols are the product of our creative imagination checked by our critical intelligence. When, on the one hand, critical intelligence or discursive reason is vanquished by creative imagination, people will believe anything to be literally true. Conversely, when creative imagination is entirely defeated by critical intelligence, rationalisations will flatten what is held to be truth, making it dull and even funny: Williams writes: "the five thousand are fed by everybody suddenly remembering that they have picnic baskets, an odd thing to remember when you are hungry [...]".

These examples of tensions arising from contradictions hopefully illustrate the danger of an attitude of absolutist, often bourgeois, narrow certainty on matters of faith, the arrogance of "we know the whole truth" that characterises so much of fundamentalism and, sadly, can also be found in the dogmatism of churches over the ages. The mystics and many thoughtful theologians would agree with Williams. Our task is to embrace the tension between questioning and wonder, between knowing and not knowing, and to encourage the fearsome undertaking of wrestling with God, like Jacob, in order to be blessed.

We know Jesus as the man who travelled with a band of followers, teaching, healing and working miracles, and who had to borrow a donkey to ride to his death on a hill outside Jerusalem. If Jesus were to ask us: "But who do you say I am?" (see Mk 8:29), we may answer: "You are the Son of God," or "You are Messiah," or "You are Emmanuel," or "You are my friend and companion." But the same Jesus also says: "Whoever has seen me has seen the Father" and "I am in the Father and the Father is in me" (Jn 14:9, 10). He says he will give us "[...] another Advocate to be with you for ever" (Jn 14:16). Hence we have a series of mysteries all contained in the mystery that is the Christ. This is not a mystery that escapes from the world. It is a mystery that is centred on the cross. This means that it is the mystery of the poor, the sick, the suffering, the oppressed, the deranged, the imprisoned and the dying. It is our mystery for it is the mystery of the sinful world, redeemed at the cross. Do we really understand what all this means in rational terms? The mystery of Christ is the mystery of love. The mystical in Christianity is nothing other than entering into the baffling mystery of God's love and its transforming power in Jesus Christ through the Spirit. Ultimately, it is the cross that shows us that contradiction and paradox rather than consistency or chaos lie at the heart of human experience.

Merton knew that the cross is ultimately about the power of God:

> The Cross is the sign of contradiction – destroying the seriousness of the Law, of the Empire, of the armies [...] But the magicians keep turning the cross to their own purposes. Yes, it is for them too a sign of contradiction: the awful blasphemy of the religious magician who makes the cross contradict mercy! This is of course the ultimate temptation of Christianity! To say that Christ has locked all the doors, has given one answer, settled everything and departed, leaving all life enclosed in the frightful consistency of a system outside of which there is seriousness and damnation, inside of which there is the intolerable flippancy of the saved – while nowhere is there any place left for the mystery of the freedom of divine mercy which alone is truly serious, and worthy of being taken seriously.

Of course we resist living with contradiction; we resist the tension of being torn in different directions. This is not necessarily a bad thing if our resistance generates conversation with God, because we trust God in every aspect of our lives. And yet, acceptance of the cross of contradiction is not easy, and this Jesus knew. The cross is a scandal, yet it is also what Thomas Merton describes it in *The sign of Jonas* as "mercy within mercy within mercy". In death on the cross is the promise of the fullness of life and the power of God. Artists have depicted Christ on the cross in an infinite variety of ways. When I picture his nailed arms stretching to the left and the right, I see how life pulls us in opposing directions. But, at the centre is his body where all conflicting claims converge. The cross draws us, the Body of Christ, into the Great Paradox – *in order to live we have to die.*

We cannot dismiss paradox in the life of faith. People throughout the ages have testified to the experience of God's loving presence. I know this truth. I know what it feels like to have God alive at the centre of my being. I need no proof that God exists. I cannot deny my own experience, I can only testify to it. Of course my certainty is subjective. I cannot prove God's presence – I can only bear witness to it in my life.

However, it is equally true that there are times when God seems far away, even absent. Abandonment, desolation and darkness overwhelm us. "My God, my God why have you forsaken me?" cries the psalmist (Ps 22:1). This cry Jesus echoes from the cross. Paul, in times of desolation, knows God's absence. He writes to the Corinthians (2 Cor 1:8-9) "We do not want you to be unaware, brothers and sisters, of the affliction we experienced in Asia; for we were so utterly, unbearably crushed that we despaired of life itself. Indeed, we felt that we had received the sentence of death." Paul does not hide his despair and desolation about shipwrecks and hunger and criticism from those whom he is trying to reach. Over the ages, wise figures in our tradition have counselled the despairing – stay with the darkness, do not run away and you will know God in new ways, for God is often more present in the dark times than in the good.

Finally, when we contemplate the mystery we call God, it evokes wonder, awe and bafflement. We stand utterly naked before Truth. In our frailty and finiteness, the Mystery is for us and with us, encircling us with love, despite our discord and blindness. A willingness to explore the borderlands between certainty and uncertainty reveals that contradiction and paradox are not separate entities or experiences – they are one truth. Contradiction melts into paradox. In paradox our limitations, our certainties, our dogmas and our illusions are shaken and broken open. Knowing is converted from head only to head plus heart plus spirit. This kind of exploring comes from faith held in what Marilynn Robinson calls "the felt life of the mind".

When Jesus is asked about teaching in parables, his answer is somewhat paradoxical. Those who have been given the secret of the kingdom of God will understand, but those who are "outside" will look and not perceive, listen and not understand (Mk 4:12). Emily Dickinson, who surprises and inspires me with her insights, captures the paradox of knowing, while not knowing:

> Tell all the truth
> But tell it slant
> Success in circuit lies,
> Too bright for our infirm delight,
> The truth's superb surprise
> As lighting to the children eased
> With explanation kind,
> The truth must dazzle gradually
> Or everyone be blind.

"All the truth" is not hidden; but what is "too bright for our infirm delight" should rather be told "slant". I think Jesus' parables "tell it slant". The truth's "superb surprise" needs to dazzle us gradually as we absorb its contradictions and its paradoxes. All that is required from us is to stand naked, trusting and loving the One in whom we have put our faith. God is the only one to whom we can surrender all without losing ourselves.

NOTES

Practical theology is the theological discipline that studies the relationship between what we believe (our theological theories) and our praxis (our theological actions or practices). Reflection and action are in a relationship of bipolar tension with one another, neither takes precedence over the other, and both are parts of the same endeavour. Beliefs are required to be consonant with how we act and vice versa, and when they are not, change is sought. Thus practical theologians require a knowledge of the teachings of Christianity, the scriptures and traditions of the church, and how they are translated into actions such as worship, teaching, ethics, spirituality, pastoral care and counselling, and so on.

Attempts to describe God are at best limited. In a recent article in the *Anglican Theological Review,* Old Testament scholar Walter Brueggemann suggests ways to express what is ultimately indescribable. Referring to Jewish modes of interpretation, he says that Sigmund Freud's insights into the human self are based on rabbinical ways of reading the Hebrew texts. According to Freud, "[t]he self is thick", which means that our words, images and memories are "[…] freighted with more meaning and force than any single saying can ever unpack". Furthermore, "[t]he self is layered" because we have stacked "[…] experience upon experience, hurt upon hurt, rage upon rage, and sometimes even joy upon joy". Lastly, "[t]he self is conflicted" because there is inescapable conflict between our feelings and "[…] the socially expected self, a friction that we spend our lives negotiating". Brueggemann finds that we can use Freud's insight about the modern self – as thick, layered and conflicted – when we read biblical texts. What can this mean for our efforts to speak of God? I do know that my God refuses the old Greek rationality and in Brueggemann's words "[…] continues to refuse our modernist thinness, this triune God […] refuses the old deistic flatness of monarchy". I cannot reduce God to "thin" or flat understandings. My language for God is admittedly just that – flat and inadequate. But my experience of God is more complex, layered and at times conflicted. This is similar to my experience of human beings. We who claim to be made in the image of God are complex, layered and conflicted people. My understanding of God is also complex, layered and conflicted. My attempts to decode what I experience of God is only possible through grace, that ordinary and yet extraordinary gift of God to us all.

My attempts at describing my fleeting "knowing" of the ineffable God are also found in my previous book, *After the Locusts: Letters from a Landscape of Faith* (Grand Rapids: Eerdmans, 2003).

It was Karl Marx (1818–1883), borrowing from the philosopher Georg Hegel (1770–1831), who said that contradiction is the engine of history, and that historical movements have their source in contradiction. This process is called dialectic and has three stages. The first is dominated by a thesis that describes the dominant state of affairs. When opposition arises to this state of affairs, it is called antithesis. Out of this tension something new emerges called synthesis. The synthesis then becomes a thesis, and so the process continues.

Certain passages here are drawn from my contribution "Metaphor, mystery and paradox: Orientations for Christian spirituality" in Jaap Durand's "Festschrift", *Discerning God's Justice in Church, Society and Academy*, edited by Ernst Conradie and Christo Lombard (Stellenbosch: Sun Press, 2009), 25-26.

The quotation attributed to Augustine (page 57) is taken from the website of the Society of Mary's Spiritual Ministry, Wellington, New Zealand, see www.maristmessenger.co.nz.

Before the term "fundamental" acquired an "-ism", it was not a term of opprobrium. In the early part of the twentieth century, two Protestant Christians, Milton and Lyman Stewart, sponsored a series of pamphlets entitled *The Fundamentals: A Testimony of Truth*. These were written by leading conservative American and British theologians and aimed to stop the perceived erosion of what were considered the fundamental beliefs of Protestantism: the inerrancy of the Bible; the direct creation of the world and humans *ex nihilo* by God (in contrast to Darwinian evolution); the virgin birth, and so on. The well-known Scopes trial in Tennessee in 1925 further contributed to the use of the term "fundamentalism". John Scopes, a high school biology teacher, was on trial for contravening the state's Butler Act. This Act forbade the teaching of "[…] any theory that denies the story of the Divine Creation of man as taught in the Bible, and to teach instead that man has descended from a lower order of animals". Teaching about evolution was therefore not consistent with God as revealed in the Bible. Scopes was found guilty, but the verdict was overturned on a technicality and many felt that he had won a moral victory. The term "fundamentalist" became fixed in our vocabulary. It is, however, a term that is never precisely definable as not all fundamentalisms are alike.

The kind of religiosity that peppered the speech of the former president of the United States, George W. Bush, is an example of the use of fundamentalist rhetoric for political aims. As leader of the most powerful nation in the world and the most powerful army in the world, he laced his messages with apocalyptic, moral and theological utterances: "I heard a call. I know that God wants me to run in the presidential elections" (Bush speaking to TV preacher James Robinson in 1998). "This is a national tragedy. An act of war. Liberty and democracy have been attacked […] The war that awaits us will be a monumental struggle of good versus evil […] Either you are with us, or you are with the terrorists […] God is on our side […] God bless America" (Bush after the attacks of 11 September 2001). "Anyone who is not with us is against us. We know that God is not neutral […] For many years and all around the world, we are going to have to fight evil. It is our mission, and we are sure that we will win" (Bush speaking to the military destined for Afghanistan, 21 November 2001). Mr Bush's convictions share their breathtaking certainty with the New Christian Right, the Moral Majority and other groups whose ideologies are similar to his.

Richard Dawkins, evolutionary scientist and popular science writer, held a chair at Oxford University in the Public Understanding of Science from which he retired in 2008. He is now a fellow of New College. Dawkins is well known for his views on religion, evolution and creationism. In a recent book, *The God Delusion* (London: Transworld Publishers, 2006), he caused much controversy by contending that a supernatural creator does not exist and that belief in God is the product of a deluded mind, aided by hallucinations. For a critique of this book, see John Cornwell, *Darwin's Angel: An Angelic Riposte to the God Delusion* (London: Profile Books, 2008). A Christian theological perspective on Dawkins's book can be found in Alister McGrath and Joanna Collicutt McGrath, *The Dawkins Delusion? Atheist Fundamentalism and the Denial of the Divine* (London: SPCK, 2007). For further reviews of Dawkins's *The God Delusion,* see Terry Eagleton http://www.lrb.co.uk/v28/n20/eag101_.html and H. Allen Orr in *The New York Review of Books* 2007.

Author and journalist Christopher Hitchens was identified as the champion of New Atheism. He described himself as an antitheist and held that the concept of a god or supreme being is actually a totalitarian belief that destroys individual freedom (see *God is not Great,* New York: Hachette Book Group, 1997).

No mention of women scholars on the African continent can ignore the pivotal role played by Mercy Amba Oduyoye, known as the mother of African women theologians. She has published extensively and worked tirelessly in a number of capacities to nurture African women studying theology, including establishing the Circle for Concerned African Women Theologians in Ghana in 1989. Realising that African women need to liberate ourselves, the Circle has promoted African women's writing, research and publications through its networks, conferences and local circles. To quote from its website: "We have broken the silence and we are speaking for ourselves. We must stretch our theological imagination, our reading of the Holy Scriptures to take cognisance of our presence as women of Africa. We discovered that we are heavily attached to our traditions and cultures and that we must name these as subjects of analysis and critique within the field of theology."

The common noun "god" refers to a person or object of supreme importance. Capitalising the word "God" does not add great clarity to its meaning until one comes to the era of distinguishing between many gods and the monotheism of early Judaism. The Canaanites venerated different deities including *El*, the creator. The Hebrew word for God, *Elohim*, may well be a plural form of the Canaanite *El*. Images for God were prohibited and thus we find YHWH (God most high) in Exodus 15. He is a conquering warrior, or a storm raining down terror in Psalm19 (see also in Deut 32 and 2 Sam 22). The Transjordanian word *El Shaddai* occurs in the Pentateuch, Ruth, Psalms, Isaiah, Ezekiel, Joel and repeatedly in Job; it is a word that may be used for mountain or the deity residing on the mountain. In Genesis 16 Hagar praises God as *El-Roi*, "the God who sees", and in Genesis 21 Abraham calls on YHWH as *El-Olam* "God Everlasting", and so on. We speak of the divine only in the language available to us. The more limited our metaphors, the more limited our speech about God. The move from goddesses and gods to one God was also a move to gender particularity. God became mirrored in a masculine identity. In the Christian tradition God became humanised and many of our hymns are a prime example of this truth. The interpretation of humans as being image bearers of God has contributed further to this tradition. In the Christian tradition, particularly in pre-Nicene times, the Hebrew YHWH was rendered as *Logos*. *Logos* was and is an idea, not a male or a female person. Later *Logos* was incorporated into the second person of the Trinity, as "the Son" (see Gail Ramshaw, *God beyond Gender.* Minneapolis: Fortress Press, 1995) for a detailed discussion of these issues.

John Chrysostom described speaking about God as follows (although he could not avoid the usual gender certainty): "Let us invoke him as the inexpressible God, incomprehensible, invisible and unknowable; let us know that he surpasses all power of human speech, that he eludes the grasp of human intelligence, that the angels cannot penetrate him nor the seraphim see him in full clarity, nor the cherubim fully understand him, for he is invisible to the principalities and powers, the virtues and all creatures without exception; *only the Son and the Holy Spirit know him.*"

Bishop Geoff Quinlan has drawn my attention to the fact that in the old Anglican prayer book (The Book of Common Prayer) formerly used in South Africa, God is seldom addressed as "Father". Rather, God is nearly always referred to as "Almighty God", "Lord", "God", and occasionally as "Lord Jesus Christ". "Father" became entrenched in the revised prayer book, An Anglican Prayer Book (1989).

Janet Morley's *All Desires Known* (London: SPCK, 1992) contains inclusive prayers in which addressing God is creatively dealt with, for example: God our deliverer, God our disturber, God our teacher, vulnerable God, God lover of sinners, God our mystery, God of terror and joy, unfamiliar God, God source of our longing.

I was taught that the paradox of the Trinity can be summarised as follows: the persons of the Trinity are coequal with each other; they can be distinguished from one another; they are interrelated, and they subsist in a unity of being and acting. They are one God. "Coequal" means that no one member of the Trinity is subordinate to the other. All are to be worshipped. Each one can be distinguished from the other. Yet they are one. Wrestling with this paradox Karl Rahner wrote: "There are not three consciousnesses; rather, the one consciousness subsists in a threefold way."

In recent times, women scholars have devoted a great deal of attention to the problem of language and imagery for God. Stimulated by the work of German scholar Joachim Jeremias in his *The Prayers of Jesus*, tr. J. Bowden, SBT 2nd series (Philadelphia: Fortress, 1967), the use of *abba* in the gospels has also received attention, particularly in the meticulous work of New Testament scholar Mary Rose D'Angelo (e.g. see "*Abba* and 'Father': Imperial Theology and the Jesus Traditions," *Journal of Biblical Literature*, vol 111, no. 4 (1992): 611-630. Jeremias contends that Jesus' use of *abba* was central to his teaching, that it represented a kind of intimacy and that Jesus' practice was distinct from the ways of the early church and Judaism. These arguments have been refuted in recent times as new evidence in biblical scholarship emerges (e.g. see James Barr, "*Abba* Isn't Daddy," *Journal of Theological Studies, no.* 39 (1988): 28-47. Jewish scholars, both before and after Jeremias, have seen Jesus' use of *abba* in addressing God as a testimony to the Jewish character of his teaching. According to D'Angelo, in early Jewish literature "father" firstly designates "God as the refuge of the persecuted, [...] [secondly] frequently accompanies a petition for an assurance of forgiveness, [...] [thirdly] evokes the power and providence that govern the world". The arguments related to naming God are complex, drawing on the interplay between culture, wisdom literature, redaction of the gospels, politics and the traditions of the ancient world.

The *Didache* (which means "teaching"), also known as the Teachings of the Twelve Apostles, is to date the oldest surviving piece of non-canonical literature. Dating from the late first or early second centuries, it is a handbook for Christian converts, purportedly based on instructions from Jesus himself. It contains the first written catechism, lessons on rituals such as baptism, the Eucharist and church organisation.

My thanks to Professor Francine Cardman for pointing out that the phrase *Si comprehendis non est Deus* is from Augustine's sermon 52.16 and a correct citation to this phrase is found in Benedict's *Deus caritas est*!

Scholars have spent much time in determining the origin of the word "mysticism". The Greeks used the words "mystery" and "mystical" to describe rites in their mystery religions. Early Christian writers took over these words in their unique way. William Johnson explains: "The church fathers took the noun *mystery* and the adjective *mystical* and applied them to the mystery of Christ, particularly as it appears in St Paul. Indeed, for the fathers, this Pauline mystery was a key to the understanding of the whole New Testament."

For the history and development of mysticism, see Bernard McGinn's magisterial work in four volumes: *The Foundations of Mysticism* (1991), *The Growth of Mysticism* (1994), The *Flowering of Mysticism* (1998), and *The Harvest of Mysticism* (2005), all published by Crossroads, New York. In the Introduction, McGinn cautions against separating mysticism from interpretation and failing to see it within the broader context of the historical development of the Christian faith. He discusses the term "mysticism" under three headings: as an element of religion, as a process or a way of life, and as an attempt to express one's direct consciousness of God.

For the quotation from W. B. Yeats, see "A Prayer for Old Age", *The Collected Poems of W. B. Yeats*, ed. R. J. Finneman (New York: Scribner, 1996), 282.

Meister Eckhart, German Dominican, renowned scholar, lecturer and disputant, was investigated for heresy by the Archbishop of Cologne. He had a considerable following, but laid himself open to opposition by his bold language and the novelty of his ideas, often expressed in baffling paradoxical terms. As proceedings dragged on, Eckhart appealed to Pope John XXII. While his theology was being examined by Cardinal Fournier (who became the next pope), he died. Pope John XXII then promulgated a bull with twenty-six of Eckhart's statements, of which fifteen were declared heretical. Ironically this pope was later condemned by his successor for heresy. As Peter

Hebblethwaite comments: "Thus we have a heretical Pope who denounces as a heretic Eckhart, whose work he had not read and whose defence he had not heard" (quoted from Smith, *The Way of Paradox*). Meister Eckhart said: "God never gives, nor did He ever give a gift, merely that man might have it and be content with it. No, all gifts which He ever gave in heaven or on earth, He gave with one sole purpose – to make one single gift: Himself. With all His gifts He desires only to prepare us for the one gift, which is Himself." The gift and the Giver can never be separated.

Mysticism as a way of "unknowing" that emphasises the incomprehensibility of God falls within the apophatic tradition. The term "apophatic", derived from the Greek word meaning negative, to deny, or to negate, is also known as negative theology: we know God only in terms of what we do not know about God. In contrast, kataphatic mysticism (from the Greek *kataphasis*) is the way of affirmation that uses positive statements about God – God as loving, merciful, wise, and so on. It is unnecessary to get into a knot about these distinctions. The Christian tradition embraces both the incomprehensibility of God together with what we can comprehend of God, particularly through the life and teaching of Jesus Christ. They can never be separated. We live with this paradoxical truth and accept that there are differences between the apophatic and kataphatic aspects of spirituality in terms of silence and prayer. Sometimes we employ imagination and reason in prayer – the kataphatic way. At other times, we move beyond discursive methods and simply wait upon the presence of God, beyond words and structured thoughts. Both are central to the life of faith.

Dorothee Sölle, in *The Silent Cry*, mentions four characteristics of the experience of the mystical taken from American psychologist and philosopher William James (1842–1910):

- The loss of all worry, the sense that all is ultimately well with one; the peace, the harmony and the willingness to be, even though the outer conditions should remain the same;
- The sense of perceiving truths not known before that make life's mysteries lucid;

- The objective change that the world seems to undergo, making it seem "new" and never having been seen that way before;
- The ecstasy of happiness.

James also said: "A great many people think they are thinking when they are really rearranging their prejudices!" This is a chastening warning to those of us who try to write about matters of faith, the mystical and metaphor.

WORKS CONSULTED

Ackermann, Denise. *After the Locusts: Letters from a Landscape of Faith.* Grand Rapids: Eerdmans, 2003.

Mary Rose D'Angelo (e.g. see *"Abba* and 'Father': Imperial Theology and the Jesus Traditions," *Journal of Biblical Literature,,* vol 111, no. 4 (1992): 611-630.

Anglican Prayer Book 1989. Church of the Province of Southern Africa. London: Collins Liturgical Publications, 1993.

Armstrong, Karen. *The Battle for God.* New York: Knopf, 2000.

Augustine. *On the Trinity.* Edited by G. B. Matthews. Translated by S. MacKenna. Series: Cambridge Texts on the History of Philosophy. Cambridge: Cambridge University Press, 2002.

Baggley, John. *Doors of Perception – Icons and Their Spiritual Significance.* Oxford: Mowbray, 1987.

Barr, James. "Abba Isn't Daddy" *Journal of Theological Studies,* no. 39 (1988): 28-47.

Bernhard of Clairvaux. *Selected Works.* Translated by G. R. Evans. Series: The Classic Works of Western Christianity. New York: Paulist Press, 1987.

Blake, William. *The Complete Poetry and Prose of William Blake.* Edited by D. V. Eerdman. New York: Anchor Books, 1988.

Brueggemann, Walter. "Where is the Scribe?" *Anglican Theological Review,* vol. 93, no. 3 (2011): 385-404.

Buber, Martin. *I Thou.* Translated by W. Kaufmann. New York: Charles Scriber's Sons, 1970.

Calvin, John. *The Institutes of the Christian Religion.* Translated by H. Beveridge. Grand Rapids: Eerdmans, 1989.

Chrysostom, John. *On the Incomprehensibility of the Divine Nature.* Translated by P. W. Harkins. Washington: Catholic University of America Press, 1984.

Conradie, Ernst and Christo Lombard, eds. *Discerning God's Justice in Church, Society and Academy: Festschrift for Jaap Durand.* Stellenbosch: Sun Press, 2009.

Cornwall, John. *Darwin's Angel: An Angelic Riposte to the God Delusion.* London: Profile Books, 2008.

D'Angelo, Mary Rose. "Abba and 'Father': Imperial Theology and the Jesus Traditions." *Journal of Biblical Literature,* vol. 111, no. 4 (Winter, 1992): 611-630.

Dawkins, Richard. *The God Delusion.* London: Transworld Publishers, 2006.

De Villiers, P. G. R., C. E. T. Kourie and C. J. S. Lombard, eds. *The Spirit that Empowers: Perspectives on Spirituality. Acta Theologica Supplementum 11.* Bloemfontein: University of the Free State Press, 2008.

De Waal, Esther. *Living with Contradictions: Reflections on the Rule of St Benedict.* London: Collins, 1989.

Dube, Musa W., ed. *Other Ways of Reading: African Women and the Bible.* Geneva: WCC Publications, 2001.

Duck, Ruth C. *Gender and the Name of God: The Trinitarian Baptismal Formula.* New York: Pilgrim Press, 1991.

Durand, Jaap. "Festschrift". *Discerning God's Justice in Church, Society and Academy.* Edited by E. Conradie and C. J. S. Lombard. Stellenbosch: Sun Press, 2009.

Durand, Jaap. "When Theology Becomes Metaphor." *Journal of Theology for Southern Africa,* no. 111 (2001), 12-16.

Francis, John R. "Evelyn Underhill's Developing Spiritual Theology: A Discovery of Authentic Spiritual Life and the Place of Contemplation." *Anglican Theological Review* no. 2, vol. 93 (2011): 283-300.

García, Jaume Flaquer. *Fundamentalism: Between Perplexity, Condemnation and the Attempt to Understand.* Barcelona: Christianisme i Justicia Booklets, 2005.

Gordon, Gus. *Solitude and Compassion: The Path of the Heart of the Gospel.* Maryknoll: Orbis Books, 2009.

Gregory of Nyssa. *Life of Moses.* Mahwah, NJ: Paulist Press, 1978.

Hansen, Len D. "Reformed Mysticism? Toward Transforming a Tradition via the Hermeneutics of Suspicion and Retrieval." *The Journal of Theology for Southern Africa,* no. 130 (March 2011): 110-119.

Hitchens, Christopher. *God is Not Great: How Religion Poisons Everything.* New York: Hachette Book Group, 2007.

Jeremias, Joachim. *The Prayers of Jesus.* tr. J. Bowden, SBT 2nd series. Philadelphia: Fortress, 1967.

Johnston, William. *The Mystical Way: Silent Music and the Wounded Stag.* London: HarperCollins, 1993.

Kourie, C. E. T. "Mysticism: The Way of Unknowing," In *The Spirit that Empowers: Perspectives on Spirituality. Acta Theologica Supplementum 1.* edited by De Villiers, P. G. R., C. E. T. Kourie and C. J. S. Lombard, 59-75. Bloemfontein: University of the Free State Press, 2008.

Leech, Kenneth. *Spirituality and Pastoral Care.* Eugene, OR: Wipf and Stock, 2005.

Lewis, C. S. *Surprised by Joy: The Shape of My Early Life.* London: Geoffrey Bles, 1955.

Marty, Martin E. and R. Scott Appleby. *The Glory and the Power: The Fundamentalist Challenge to the Modern World*. Boston: Beacon Press, 1992.

McFague, Sallie. *Metaphorical Theology: Models of God in Religious Language*. London: SCM Press, 1983.

McGinn, Bernard and Patricia F. McGinn. *Early Christian Mystics: The Divine Vision of the Spiritual Masters*. New York: Crossroad, 2003.

McGrath, Alister and Joanna Collicutt McGrath. *The Dawkins Delusion? Atheist Fundamentalism and the Denial of the Divine*. London: SPCK, 2007.

Merton, Thomas. *Raids on the Unspeakable*. New York: New Directions, 1964.

Merton, Thomas. *Sign of Jonas*. New York: Mariner Books, 1979.

Merton, Thomas. *Contemplative Prayer*. London: Darton, Longman and Todd, 2005.

Nolan, Albert. *Jesus Today: A Spirituality of Radical Freedom*. Cape Town: Double Storey, 2006.

Palmer, Parker J. *The Promise of Paradox: A Celebration of Contradictions in the Christian Life*. San Francisco: Jossy-Bass, 2008.

Phiri, Isabel A., Devakarsham B. Govinden and Sarojini Nadar, eds. *Her Stories: Hidden Histories of Women of Faith in Africa*. Pietermaritzburg: Cluster, 2002.

Rakoczy, Susan. *In Her Name: Women Doing Theology*. Pietermaritzburg: Cluster, 2004.

Ramshaw, Gail. *God beyond Gender*. Minneapolis: Fortress Press, 1995.

Rohr, Richard. *The Naked Now: Learning to See as the Mystics See*. New York: Crossroad, 2009.

Ruthven, Malise. *Fundamentalism: The Search for Meaning*. Oxford: Oxford University Press, 2004.

Schmitt, Miriam, Linda Kulzer and Mary M. Kaliher, eds. *Medieval Women Mystics: Wisdom's Wellsprings*. Collegeville, MN: The Liturgical Press, 1996.

Smith, Cyprian. *The Way of Paradox: Spiritual Life as Taught by Meister Eckhart*. London: Darton, Longman and Todd, 1987.

Sölle, Dorothee. *The Silent Cry: Mysticism and Resistance*. Minneapolis: Fortress Press, 2001.

Soskice, Janet Martin. *Metaphor and Religious Language*. Oxford: Clarendon Press, 1985.

Tracy, David. *Plurality and Ambiguity: Hermeneutics, Religion, Hope*. Chicago: University of Chicago Press, 1987.

Underhill, Evelyn. *Practical Mysticism: A Little Book for Normal People*. Guilford: Eagle, 1991.

Vallès, Jaume Botey. *Bush and his God: The Theological Roots of the Policies of George W. Bush*. Barcelona: Christianisme i Justicia, 2005.

Vendler, Helen. *Dickinson: Selected Poems and Commentaries*. Cambridge, MA: The Belknap Press of Harvard University Press, 2010.

Weitzmann, Kurt. *The Icon: Holy Images, Sixth to Fourteenth Century*. London: Chatto and Windus, 1978.

Williams, Harry A. *Tensions: Necessary Conflicts in Life and Love*. London: Fount Paperbacks, 1989.

Williams, Rowan. *The Dwelling of the Light: Praying with Icons of Christ*. Grand Rapids: Eerdmans, 2003.

Yeats, W. B. "A Prayer for Old Age". *The Collected Poems of W. B. Yeats*. Edited by R. J. Finneman. New York: Scribner, 1996.

CHAPTER THREE

Blessed are those who live into their holiness, for they will be surprised by wonder

In the past, any mention of holiness made me uneasy, and even now my attempts to write about what I perceive to be a truth at the heart of faith confronts me with the inadequacy of words to express the wonder of holiness. Writing about holiness is an exercise in contradiction and paradox, tinged with incongruity and surprise. Imagine being caught red-handed reading a book titled *Holiness for Dummies* or *Teach yourself Holiness*! Donald Nicholl tells of an effort every bit as comical when, during the 1930s, the Soviet government distributed thousands of pamphlets entitled *Teach yourself to be Godless*! I treasure the reality that God loves me, but the idea that I might be holy fills me with a sense of the absurd. Holiness is surely a quality found only in saints. I suspect I was afraid of being thought of as self-righteous or "holier than thou", the worst among the lexicon of vices! So, in order to sidestep the biblical injunctions to be holy, I took refuge in a sense of unworthiness that bordered on the farcical – *I* can't possibly be holy; I'm simply not up to scratch.

Eventually I could no longer escape the biblical truth that, in fact, I was holy. Denying my holiness was refusing to accept what God offers all humanity, to be what we truly are – a holy people – made in the image of the Holy One. For a Christian this means becoming a new person in Christ. I am compelled to face the truth: the call to live as a holy person is nothing more nor less than God saying to me,

"Are you brave enough to be truly Denise? If you are, be holy, as I am holy."

The truth is that we live between our holiness and our continual fall from grace. Rowan Williams explores the terrible paradox that the place where the holy is present is also the place where human wickedness is manifest.

> A human being is holy not because he or she triumphs by willpower over chaos and guilt and leads a flawless life, but because that life shows the victory of God's faithfulness in the midst of disorder and imperfection. The Church is holy [...] not because it is a gathering of the good and the well-behaved, but because it speaks of the triumph of grace in the coming together of strangers and sinners who, miraculously, trust one another enough to join in common repentance and common praise [...] Humanly speaking, holiness is always like this: God's endurance in the middle of our refusal of him, his capacity to meet every refusal with a gift of himself.

Looking back I can see that my reluctance to accept and live into my holiness was simply evasive poppycock, another case of "If I can't be perfect, I won't even try". It was refusing "Christ with us" and showed lack of courage to face failure while trusting that God would not let me go.

Defining holiness neatly or comprehensively is not easy. I am more certain of what holiness is not. Holiness is not a calling limited to the "professionals", the spiritual elite, or the elect few. It is not about knowledge that I can pick up from books, though I do not discount the wisdom some writers bring to the subject. It is not about *my* pursuit of the Holy One. It is not a state of perfection or a sense of having arrived; it therefore does not require the impossible. It is not located in some spiritual realm removed from my earthbound life, neither is it a revised and edited version of everyday life.

Holiness may be described as the entire life of a person directed towards God. It is not a part of life, nor is it part of a person – it is everything. Being made whole is to acknowledge our past, that it cannot be unmade and that we have to live with it. Then we become aware of grace at work. Living into our holiness is a process, a continual movement towards Ultimate Being that has a great deal to do with the realisation and acceptance of failure and the need for continual conversion. To live into our holiness is to go to the heart of what it means to be human and to discover just how worthy we are as people made in the image of God. To know this is to be amazed and filled with wonder.

Traditionally "the holy" refers to the sacred, to saintly devotion, and it evokes a sense of awe, even mystery. We seldom think of holiness in terms of ourselves, but rather as a property belonging to God alone. Yet for Christians, holiness is rooted in the mystery of the Incarnation – the idea of "Christ with us". This phrase is redolent with mystery. I believe "Christ with us" means that God's loving intimacy comes to us through the creative action of the Spirit. As the Spirit continues to woo us to live into our holiness, we begin to enjoy its fruits – love, joy, peace and hope. We are taught how to pray and intercede for others. "Christ with us" is quite simply being at home with ourselves. This is true for all, because God's loving action in the Spirit is ceaseless and envelops all of creation. Yet, we remain uncomfortable with the idea of holiness. The very idea of a human person being holy seems a contradiction in terms. The notion of holiness does not sit easily in today's world because it smacks of a sanctimoniousness that shuns the hurly-burly of everyday life. Speaking about holiness is decidedly incongruous in a secular society.

Ours is undeniably a secular age. Secularism has different faces and means different things in different contexts. In the United States, for example, there is a rigid separation of church and state, yet many Americans are openly religious. In Germany no such separation exists, yet many Christians there embrace a kind of secular Christianity that is largely a leftover of nineteenth century liberal Protestantism.

South Africa also is not straightforward. While a significant number of people openly adhere to one or other religion, South African society is secularising at a rapid rate. Currently, there are public voices in South Africa that use the language of religion, but only when it suits their political agendas. However, there are also the exceptions, such as the irrepressible Desmond Tutu, whose earthy brand of faith engages South Africans on issues as diverse as soccer and morality.

The roots of the present secular age vary and cover a gamut of beliefs. The rise of science coupled with the suspicion that what is considered transcendent is a threat to human progress; disillusionment with institutionalised religion and the emphasis on self-reliance together with rampant individualism are but a few of the contributing factors to present-day secularism. It is also true that many who consider themselves Christians desire "believing without belonging". Institutionalised religion fails to reach these believers, yet they hold to the basic tenets of the Christian faith. Fed up with the tendency to authoritarianism, clerical power play and materialism in the church, they remain on the periphery.

In this marginality, I detect a persistent longing for something beyond the nagging dissatisfaction with the present moral order that is not assuaged by the plethora of marketplace spiritualities. On the one hand, there is the social alienation created by the increasing power of globalised business interests and the mounting frustration with incompetent, corrupt political bureaucracies. On the other, the daily television diet of starving women, children and the elderly, wars, terrorism, droughts and natural disasters is numbing. These realities prompt the need for a world that is more truthful and just, and that enhances, rather than destroys people's quality of life.

In his work *A Secular Age*, Canadian philosopher Charles Taylor writes about how public spaces are being emptied of God. He describes secularism as the move "from a society in which it is virtually impossible not to believe, to one in which faith, even for the staunchest believer, is one possibility among others". Belief in God is no longer axiomatic. This move away from a dominant public religious voice is to be welcomed. Religion has been hijacked too often for political ends. Any alliance between church and state, any display of the trappings of power, any tendency to support or condone behaviour that is not affirming and inclusive of all humanity denies the reality of the true nature of the church – a pilgrim body of people seeking to follow Jesus, "the man on the borrowed donkey".

What then are we left with? A situation in which there is only confrontation between those who believe and those who do not (as, for instance, in the shrill naturalism of Richard Dawkins versus the deadly certitudes of religious fundamentalism) is decidedly unhelpful. A faith perspective that finds engagement with science threatening and which resorts to using God as a stopgap to knowledge is antiquated and infantile. My mother-in-law, who graduated in mathematics and chemistry in the early 1920s, was told by her minister that she would have to choose between evolution and Christ. As a person of integrity and intellectual honesty she chose evolution. "I was not prepared to commit intellectual suicide," she said. Sadly, this ridiculous kind of choice is still entertained seriously today.

Faith is about the search for God's truth. *Fides quaerens intellectum* (Faith seeking understanding) demands that we remain intellectually honest in all things, including matters of faith. The truth we seek may present us with contradictions and paradoxes. As I have already indicated in the previous chapter, an honest seeker should have no difficulty in admitting that there is much she cannot know or explain, and that there are diverse ways of experiencing reality. A secularism that allows room for different ways of understanding life makes for better communal relations and a healthier society. Accepting that we live in a pluralist world, in which many forms of belief and unbelief jostle to find a place, is simply realistic.

Not surprisingly, the idea of holiness is sometimes understood as a simile for that all-encompassing term "spirituality", a term that today has become a buzzword for almost anything associated with a search for the "beyond". This search takes on myriad guises. For some, spirituality is centred on prosperity as a blessing. For others, words like "harmony", "balance" and "individuation" are frequently found in what is little more than a search for a healthy lifestyle. "Wholeness" is preferred to holiness, though undoubtedly holiness encompasses it. "Finding oneself" or "expressing oneself" as opposed to "denying oneself" becomes the order of the day. Spirituality is then characterised as the pursuit of self-fulfilment.

For hundreds of years there have been two dominant and different understandings of spirituality in the Christian tradition. The first is that of devout humanism. Devout Christian humanists stress their belief that we are all made in the image of God. Thus we are all worthy of respect, we all have equal dignity and human worth. Our principal goal is to cultivate the love of God, and seek to trust the promptings of this love in ourselves. The opponents of devout humanism object to this view, believing that any intuitive experiences or understandings of faith are sources of self-deceit. The believer should rely solely on external sources such as scripture, tradition and the teachings of the church.

Charles Taylor maintains that, to this day, these two kinds of religious sensibility underlie people's spiritual quest. While not disputing his view, I wonder why it has to be a case of either/or? Why not listen to the promptings of God's Spirit while cultivating discernment to deal with self-deception and, at the same time, depend on scripture and communal wisdom to critique and nurture our spirituality? This seems preferable to relying solely on "experience" or attempting to nail down ultimate authority in a particular interpretation of scripture or in some papal fiat.

I understand spirituality as the nexus where our beliefs (our theology), our source (the Bible), our prayers and our daily practices come together. For me, the word "spirituality" expresses the conscious human response to God that is both personal and communal. Spirituality is embodied. This means that it is grounded in life. We live out our faith in our bodies. We pray and worship with our bodies and hopefully live out our spirituality day by day by sharing our material goods, offering hospitality, standing for justice and making relationships of friendship and trust. How these actions can be taken out of our bodily reality into some elevated sphere is beyond me. The idea that spirituality is only an inward-looking desire to achieve serenity and personal mindfulness is not tenable and at worst can be self-centred, showing scant concern for the pressing needs of our world. Living into our holiness is tested by our actions. By contrast, if spirituality is solely expressed in outward-oriented acts for justice and equality, it can be restricted only to "doing". A balanced spirituality is both contemplative and active; it is lived holiness.

Christian spirituality is embodied spirituality. God's very act of creating us, the reality of the Word who became flesh and dwelt among us, our celebration of this event by drinking wine and eating bread together, our membership of a community that calls itself the Body of Christ, the belief in the resurrection of the body, and last but not least, our very earthiness all confirm the relationship between body and spirit. All theology starts in the body. I have previously written: "Bodies are personal and private, political and public, bone, flesh, blood and spirit. Bodies are our reality." So spirituality is not some lofty ritual garment to put on and take off, depending on our whims. Our spirituality is our embodied attempt to live into our holiness. Living into our holiness is another way of saying that we discover our worth, our place and our peace in an often alien world – and we are surprised by a feeling of wonder, that unexpected sense of something beautiful, inexplicable, present and very real.

The idea that we are holy is, at times, met with the objection that, in fact, only God is holy. Once again paradox confronts us. It is true that the Old Testament tells us that God's holiness is the all-embracing, all-encompassing attribute of God. God is the ground of holiness, its source and its promise. God's holiness is radically other and not to be confused with anyone else's. No wonder Moses at the burning bush hides his face and is afraid to look at God (Ex 3:2-6). Divine holiness is experienced as a mysterious, even terrifying power. Yet, the Israelites are told that they too must be holy. "For I am the Lord your God; sanctify yourselves therefore and be holy for I am holy" (Lev 11:44). These words contain a covert warning and a clear command. "You know that I am the Holy One, the source of your life, Israel, so take care and make sure that you too reflect this holiness."

When I began to discover my holiness, this paradox puzzled me. I cannot and may not brush aside the truth that God is "wholly other". God's name is holy. Yet, this same holy God is in our midst, in relationship with you and me. Just as Israel, despite repeated betrayals, was loved and repeatedly rescued by God to live in obedience with God in a covenantal relationship of both awe and gratitude, so are we. Just as God defines what is holy, we too are called to holiness. When God tells the people of Israel "*Consecrate* yourselves therefore, and be *holy*; for I am the Lord your God" (Lev 20:7), we too are being told to consecrate ourselves for holiness. I find the word "consecrate" scary. Am I to make myself sacred? "Consecrate" is a word I associate with the Eucharist. Could this be a clue to understanding this startling idea? Could it be that the bread and the wine hold the promise of holiness? What I can see in the biblical texts is a clear directive – accept your holiness, you are sacred to me.

In Jesus, the paradoxical nature of holiness is again raised. He teaches us to say: "Our Father who is in heaven, hallowed (holy) is your name …" Holy is God's name. When the man with the unclean spirit at the synagogue in Capernaum, cries out: "I know who you are, the Holy One of God" (Mk 1:24), Jesus' holiness is recognised. Jesus is the revelation of the holy – in a manger, as a carpenter's son, as a friend of sinners and outcasts, crucified as a criminal, and appearing again to his followers. He was born and died on days that were not then holy, but were made holy by the way he lived them. From the raw material of everyday life, Jesus fashioned his holiness. Thus the apostle John calls Jesus Christ the "Holy One of God" (Jn 6:69). John also says that the Holy One of God is the One who *abides* in us (Jn 15:4). That Christ, the Holy One, abides in God and in us can mean nothing other than that we too are called to holiness. No wonder believers are called "saints", "a holy priesthood" and "partakers of the divine nature".

Paul believes that holiness is central to being a community of believers. When he addresses the Christians in Rome, he stresses, among other things, that their vocation is holiness: "Present yourselves as a living sacrifice, holy and acceptable to God which is your spiritual worship" (Rom 12:1). We confess in the Nicene Creed that holiness (together with oneness, catholicity and apostolicity) is a mark of the church in its fullness. Holiness is a prerequisite for worship that is pleasing to God. According to Paul, God's mandate for the gathering of believers is to be a holy people, "acceptable to God which is our spiritual worship". In worship we respond to God's holiness and reach out to one another, affirming that we are all holy. If this were not so, worship would be an empty, meaningless ritual, devoid of relationship with God and one another. Far better then to stay at home, read a good book, tend the garden, or walk in the veld. Worship is an embodied, heartfelt response to the beauty of God's holiness in all. We are all loved and valued, and have intrinsic worth. Holiness can be no other than an inclusive summons to all of us to be whom we truly are – people made in the image of God – "called to be saints" (1 Cor 1:2). Holiness is concerned with concrete reality and how we assume the responsibility of living in the world. It is not a topic to be researched. It is a truth by which we are all called to live in community with one another.

Writer Annie Dillard asks: "Who shall ascend into the hill of the Lord? Or who shall stand in his holy place?" Her answer is simple: "There is no one but us." She continues:

> There is no one to send, nor a clean hand, nor a pure heart on the face of the earth, but only us, a generation comforting ourselves with the notion that we have come at an awkward time, that our innocent fathers are all dead – as if innocence had ever been – and our children busy and troubled, and we ourselves unfit, not yet ready, having each of us chosen wrongly, made a false start, failed, yielded to impulse and the tangled comfort of pleasure, and grown exhausted … But there is no one but us.

For Christians "the holy" is never just the church, the chapel, the shrine, or the place set apart where only a few may enter. It is never simply a holy day, or a particular holy woman or man. Holiness is at the core of every believer's identity, both personally and as a member of the holy priesthood of believers. Holiness is not an optional extra; rather it is the whole point of creation that enables us to pray "Our Father, holy be your name". Thus holiness is not a quality we can acquire like a fit body or a certain status. It is a given. We are holy – yet too often we just do not know this truth.

Am I brave enough to live out my holiness? I know that I am not like those exceptional people who have in their own way fully heeded the call to do exactly this. I have known people who have devoted their lives to praying for the needs of others and the state of the world. They would not want to be mentioned here. There are others who have written about their struggles to live holy lives. I have my favourites. My list is idiosyncratic and incomplete. Augustine's *Confessions* (c.398) is more than a document of a man's struggle to overcome his profligate ways. It is essentially about confronting the truth about himself that leads to an experience of God's unfathomable love. "Seek for yourself, O man; search for your true self. He who seeks shall find himself in God." Unlike Augustine, Francis of Assisi (1181/2–1226) did not leave us a body of writing. His generosity, his profound faith, his devotion to God and creation, his humility and his simplicity are examples of living holiness. Theresa of Avila's insights on prayer in her *Way of Perfection* and Julian of Norwich's earthy hopefulness in her *Revelations of Divine Love* are practical guides to holy living. So too is Ignatius of Loyola (1491–1556) who taught us how to find God in all things, both in the inner life and in the every day.

In more recent times, the Catholic social activist Dorothy Day (1897–1980), who worked among the homeless and hungry in New York and founded the Catholic Worker Movement in 1933, practised what it means to live a holy life. There are two further remarkable women who have been guides for holy living: French Jewish philosopher, mystic and social activist Simone Weil (1909–1943), whose ascetic lifestyle caused her early death, and Etty Hillesum (1914–1943), a Dutch Jew whose letters and diaries were published after her death in Auschwitz in 1943. Both these women sought to live with integrity and humaneness – surely hallmarks of holiness. Dietrich Bonhoeffer is high on my list of favourite theologians. His life and his spirituality were inseparable, and he did not shrink from the ultimate sacrifice as he sought to obey the call to live out his holiness. Thomas Merton is a remarkable guide for holy living. Lastly, there are the South Africans Beyers Naudé (1915–2004) of the Christian Institute and Desmond Tutu who opened my eyes to the ordinariness and the wonder of living as holy people.

The above names are those of well-known people, people whose lives over the ages speak of holiness in very different contexts. But we are *all* challenged to live into our holiness today wherever we find ourselves. Looking back over the years, I can pinpoint moments when I have glimpsed holiness in another, when I have been aware of an unveiling of holiness in a particular moment. Suffice it to say that holiness is caught in the ordinary. I remember the patient beauty of an old *gogo* (grandmother) in a shack, holding a spoon to the mouth of a child with cerebral palsy; the loving care of friends for a little daughter with Down's syndrome; the courageous resolve in the eyes of a member of the Black Sash in the face of a police armoured vehicle in the 1980s, and the dignity accorded to homeless people by a friend who runs a night shelter. These moments radiate an everyday ordinary holiness in acts of loving grace. They are sacred moments when human beings are touched by the Spirit and lifted out of the tyranny of self into the grace of holiness.

I can also vividly recall moments when I was filled with wonder at the gift of the holy. A time of self-doubt and rejection was turned upside down when, on a retreat, I read: "Those who love me, will keep my word, and my Father will love them, and we will come to them and make our home with them" (Jn 14:23). To know that God and the Son are willing to be "at home" with me is a blinding affirmation of the gift of my holiness. My awareness of holiness has also been deeply part of my awe for the sacred in creation. Long before I called myself Christian, I was enthralled by God's creative power when my collection of tiny eggs hatched silkworms that spun golden threads around a papier mâché cross. Years later, I sat alone early one sunny morning on a cold stone among the ruins of Machu Pichu, the fifteenth century pre-Colombian holy site in the mountains above Cusco in Peru. As I looked across the tropical mountain forest to the valley of the Urubamba River below, I had a profound sense of the universality of human holiness.

I remember another sacred moment sitting on the edge of a rocky promontory off the cliff path along Walker Bay on the southeastern Cape coast. Close to the rocks a southern right whale lolled in a calm sea. It was so close that I could hear the rumbles in its stomach. For a long time the whale and I looked at one another. I knew it was aware of me with a gentle watchfulness, at ease, a bit curious, trusting the quietness between us. Human creativity in art and music can also be a conduit for the holy. A Bach chorale or the haunting tone of a cello playing Brahms rouses a sense of the sacred in me. On a visit to the Hermitage Museum in St Petersburg the holy again overwhelmed me quite unexpectedly as I gazed at Rembrandt's painting of *The Return of the Prodigal Son*. I stood transfixed and was moved to tears by the son's feet – one in a broken sandal and the other a bare sole – and the father's tender loving hands embracing the son who had been lost. For an hour or more I could not tear myself away. Through his brush Rembrandt had captured the holiness of love with incomparable art. Admittedly these moments of holiness are personal. But I do not believe that they are in any sense unique. Every living being can know matchless moments when she or he is open to wonder.

The call to holy living is not new. There is one particular response to this call in Christian history that has left me wondering whether it has something to say to us today. I am referring to the movement of people to the deserts of Upper Egypt and Syria that took place between the third and fifth centuries. The women and men who took to the desert are known as the desert mothers (*ammas*) and fathers (*abbas*). Living either as hermits or in small, flexible communities, they sought to obey Christ's call: "Follow me." Can their values, virtues and practices of faith speak to our contexts that are so very different to theirs? If so, how? These questions are worth exploring. But first – why did they take to the desert?

The reasons for this movement to the desert were varied, ranging from the desire for silence and solitude, to the need to escape from fractious communities, compromised churches and persecution. Flight to the deserts of Upper Egypt and Syria increased from about 250 when the Roman Emperor Decius issued an edict for the suppression of Christianity. Believers left their towns and villages to seek the protection of the desert. Their retreat was, however, not simply for safety from persecution; it became a quest for purity and authenticity. In a significant way it was also a rejection of the secularism of their age. After 313, when Emperor Constantine became the patron of the Christian church, there was growing disillusionment with what was perceived to be a compromised church that had taken on the trappings of privilege and power. Withdrawal to the desert as an individual quest for perfection through prayer and silence also contained elements of religious critique and a critique of the world. These women and men prayed for the church and for the world as they sought ever greater closeness to God.

They attempted to live out their holiness in the desert. The desert is a place set apart, a place of silence and solitude; it is also a place of privations – extreme temperatures, no comforts, beset with dangers. There is nothing romantic about life in the desert. The desert is inhospitable, and indifferent to the needs of humans; it is a place of terrifying silence, scorching sun, blinding sand storms, scorpions and adders, scant vegetation and continuous drought. It is a place for fasting and keeping vigils, free from everyday distractions; a place to do battle with the temptations "of the flesh" and what was understood as demonic attacks. This Jesus knew, for he too spent a taxing time in the wilderness. Living in the desert cannot therefore be viewed as an easy escape from the travails of life in the town. These desert people renounced rather than rejected their former lives, and responded to a personal vocation to pursue their call to holiness though prayer, silence and fasting, a life that was often solitary but, ironically, led to a new kind of community.

Who were these desert ascetics and what was their life like? Benedictine Lawrence Freeman describes the desert mothers and fathers as "fighters, not escapees, pilgrims not tourists". They were striking individuals of all ages, drawn from the educated and wealthy classes as well as from the peasantry and illiterate poor. They learnt from the trials of life in the inhospitable wastes of the desert and this enabled them to distil their experiences into practical wisdom and offer counsel and guidance to those who sought them out. According to Jerome (born c.340–died c.420), Paul of Thebes (died c.341) – known as the First Hermit – lived in the desert for over ninety years and was the first known of these desert dwellers. Jerome relates how Paul was visited by Anthony (born c.251–died c.356) shortly before his death at the age of one hundred and thirteen years. Anthony was profoundly moved by his encounter with this holy man. On a return visit, he found Paul dead, his body kneeling in a last act of prayer.

Reading about the lives of the desert dwellers, one is struck by two paradoxical reactions. On the one hand, their choices and experiences are so radically different from those known to readers of a book like this that they seem positively alien. They had little sleep, no baths, wore ragged clothes, had to work hard to survive, and lived celibate lives. For the most part they were simple, practical people, not given to sophisticated theology or mysticism, attempting to follow what they understood as God's way. There were, of course, exceptions like Evagrius Ponticus (345–399), a well-known classical scholar and thinker. On the other hand, a closer look at some of their sayings reveals a wisdom that has endured through the ages. Freeman makes the point: "These monastic oddballs of an unimaginably different and ancient world may indeed hold a secret for our modern world that no economist, sociologist, politician, or religious leader can match. The desert wisdom teaches rather than preaches. Its authority is experiential, not theoretical."

Evagrius said: "[…] the one who prays is a theologian and the theologian is one who prays." It would have been unthinkable for the women and men of the desert to separate theology from prayer, or thought from experience. Their attempt at holy living was a down-to-earth everyday affair, nurtured by prayer and their knowledge of the scriptures. "Holiness […] requires a degree of inner and outer peace that respects the at times conflicting, though not contradictory, demands of body, mind, and spirit. The first requirement for this peace or harmony is order in human living and a right use of time," writes Freeman. This is what the desert offered them. A great deal of what we know about the *ammas* and *abbas* is contained in the writings of John Cassian (born c.360–died c.435). As a young man he went on a visit to meet desert dwellers and stayed for twenty years. In his *Conferences of the Fathers*, he composed a collection of stories and pithy, earthy fragments of spiritual wisdom that have become part of our spiritual heritage.

We meet the desert mothers and fathers in their sayings, a rich collection of wisdom that has been handed down in the Christian tradition for millennia. Can the legacy of these people offer us wisdom for living into our holiness today? Do their values and virtues suggest clues for dealing with the contingencies of our lives? Are the differences between their age and ours, their chosen context and our modern life in cities, simply too great to bridge? Any attempt at answering these questions must avoid modernising desert traditions and practices in a shallow way. I am no church historian. My attempts to explore the relevancy of their ways can draw only on what I have read and how this relates to my experiences and my understanding of the holy life. In their sayings and stories we find that the priority of silence for prayer, nurtured by the scriptures, was central to their existence. They also prized charity, humility, hospitality, patience, self-control, and refraining from judging others.

One must appreciate that my reading of the sayings of the desert mothers and fathers takes place against the backdrop of my context:

first forty years of apartheid and now the reality of a fairly apathetic church in a time of greed, increasing corruption, violence and the degradation of the environment. During the apartheid years, I learnt that faith convictions across our differences could prompt resistance to injustice. Sadly, not all who went to synagogue, church or mosque fell into this category. But singular people like Rabbi Cyril Harris, Archbishops Denis Hurley and Desmond Tutu as well as Beyers Naudé and Faried Esack were beacons in the fight against apartheid. There were also hosts of good, concerned people who engaged in acts of resistance because they believed that what was happening was not consonant with their understanding of their faiths. Apartheid had to be resisted and resistance came, among others, from religious institutions across our different beliefs.

Today in my context the voices of resistance to present instances of injustice are muted, in particular those of the churches. Here, as in other parts of the world, the fastest growing churches are not those to whom the traditions of the desert are familiar or of interest. I cannot think of an appropriate term that includes the different emphases found in these churches as they do vary depending on their cultural and social contexts. They are known as churches that preach the "health and wealth gospel" or "the prosperity gospel" or are called the "word of faith movement". Church members are encouraged to pray for their material needs – anything from larger bank accounts to a motor car or new furniture. Accumulation of the material is seen as a gospel directive. Concern for the environment is singularly lacking. Not surprisingly, many of these churches have their origins among the poor who lack resources, who have little or no access to health care, who are often jobless and for whom life is a daily struggle to survive. Members of these churches are encouraged to give generously; interestingly their church leaders are seldom impoverished. Ironically, all this is taking place on a continent that is home to the world's largest desert in the north, the Sahara, and the beautiful deserts of the south, the Namib and the Kalahari.

I cannot find any traces of my man who rode on a borrowed donkey in this version of the gospel; neither can I find anything of the mystery that is God (when reduced to a kind of benevolent bank manager), or the paradoxes and contradictions that are deeply part of the life of faith. But individualistic materialism is not an African prerogative, and neither is the desire of the poor to climb out of poverty. It would not be fair to focus only on the beliefs of these churches as representative of my context. Our whole world is dominated by the mad rush of the wealthy to have more; by the tyranny of corporations whose only interest is an increase in profits at the expense of the environment and the needs of the workers; by the desire to ape the obscenely lavish lifestyles of the rich and famous, and by values permeated with the cheap tricks of advertising. We are all in danger of being increasingly addicted to and dependent on the brutal realities of so-called progress.

Against all these bewildering circumstances, the people of the desert seem so distant and far removed from our twenty-first century realities. Can anything from their lives, lived in circumstances so radically different from ours, speak to us across time? The answer is both a qualified "no" and a qualified "yes".

The qualified "no" refers to the truth that we are faced with living out our holiness in the twenty-first century. Our calling is to be at home in *our* world. Through every age people encounter God in the reality of their time and needs. Life is lived in a web of relationships with their own demands, and in particular political and social milieus. Our reality is different from the one in which the desert people lived. Ours is a world of instant communications, where Facebook and Twitter are a chosen way of conducting relationships, where sending messages on a cellphone is a substitute for hearing a human voice. It is not easy to live with integrity and love in our relationships in cyberspace. Is this where living into our holiness is put to the test? The idea of "Internet holiness" fills me with disquiet. There is no easy escape, for our task is to live out our holiness in the here and now.

There are still singular people who choose to give up life in the world and devote themselves to intercessory prayer. They are rare. Some are called to live out their holiness in the monastic life. Monastic communities have contributed a great deal to the nurture of

Christian spirituality, as exemplified in the recovery of contemplative prayer. Monastic life does not necessarily imply a lack of concern for what happens outside the walls of the monastery. Thomas Merton, for instance, though he lived in a Trappist community, displayed a deep knowledge and concern for the affairs of the world and their effect on people through his writings. Sadly monastic communities are shrinking in many places in the world and I wonder how some of our valued traditions will be preserved for future generations.

In what way are the desert practices relevant to our life; what can we say "yes" to in these practices? I think that there is a universal validity in certain values and practices of the desert mothers and fathers and their keen insights into the trials and tribulations of attempting to live a holy life. I long for elements of desert wisdom to find a way into both the mega-churches of today as well as the community here in Cape Town to which I belong. Perhaps one day the knowledge that age-old traditions born on this continent have validity for today will filter into our different communities, bringing hope and renewal.

What can we find in the desert values and practices that can encourage us for today? To begin with, the desert emphasised the value of *silence and solitude*. Time off from our noisy, cluttered world – from telephones, television, computers, billboards, traffic, advertising jingles, and meaningless chatter – is, quite simply, good. For the people of the desert, silence and solitude were conditions for encountering God and for encountering themselves before God. Silence can be manipulative, even destructive in relationships. But silence that is motivated by the desire to encounter God and that honestly acknowledges our frailty, distractedness and woundedness is potentially wholesome and restorative. According to a church father:

> A brother questioned a young monk, saying: "Is it better to be silent or to speak?" The young man said to him, "If words are useless, leave them alone, but if they are good, give place to the good and speak. Furthermore, even if they are good, do not prolong speech, but terminate it quickly, and you will have peace, quiet, rest."

Again and again, the desert dwellers pointed out that too much speaking can lead us astray. *Abba* Pambo (born c.303–died c.373) refused to speak to the visiting Archbishop of Alexandria saying: "If he is not edified by my silence, he will not be edified by my speech." I know the pitfalls of rushing into words. But I also know that, when I take time off for silence in solitude, something else happens. Silence then becomes simply "being fully in the moment". In silence and solitude we face ourselves. Anthony said:

> He who sits alone and is quiet has escaped from three wars: hearing, speaking, seeing, but there is one thing against which he must continually fight: that is his own heart.

We may ask whether silence and solitude are really attainable in today's noisy world. The very idea can smack of an elitism that few can afford. Yet being alone in silence is a way of meeting our longing for an encounter with the transcendent. Silence can be found in a small corner of our lives at a quiet time of the day. As *abba* Moses (330–405) said to a brother who sought advice from him: "Go and sit in your cell and your cell will teach you everything." Despite contemporary limitations, many today know the need for a quiet place for prayer and some are fortunate enough to find time for an annual retreat. Withdrawal for a short period of time is still part of Christian practice (as it is in other religious traditions). In essence, this is simply an adapted continuing legacy of these early desert dwellers. This we can learn from the ancients of the desert without embracing their way of living. Jesus achieved a balance between the values of silence and solitude, simplicity and moderation, humility and self-knowledge, and being in relationship with others as an active participant in his community. I believe God longs for us to live into our holiness in the world. There is no escape from integrating the inward and the outward in the life of faith.

I detect a growing desire for *simplicity and moderation* as a counter to the excesses of materialistic individualism today. What wisdom can the desert offer this desire? Voluntary poverty as practised by the desert dwellers seems almost bizarre in today's world. *Amma* Syncletica (died c.350) was an upper-class woman who lived as a solitary in the desert, east of Jerusalem, and who concealed her beauty so successfully that she was taken to be a eunuch monk. When she was asked if poverty was a perfect good, she replied:

> For those who are capable of it, it is a perfect good. Those who can sustain it receive suffering in the body, but rest in the soul. For just as one washes coarse clothes by trampling them underfoot and turning them about in all directions, even so the strong soul becomes much more stable thanks to voluntary poverty.

I think that the value of desert teaching on simplicity and moderation is founded on the notion of "detachment", also described as "indifference". The very word "indifference" can be confusing. It does not mean being neglectful or uncaring; neither does it denote an accommodating kind of Christianity that chooses not to speak out against the twisted values of the day. I first encountered the idea of "active indifference" in the *Spiritual Exercises* of Ignatius of Loyola, and believe that this is what the desert people meant by the term. Here "indifference" means to sort out what is important from what is not, to be detached not only from the material things of life, but also from praise, blame and the temptations of spiritual arrogance. It advocates travelling lightly through the world, free from the shackles of wanting or desiring anything other than God.

The temptations are legion. Ours is an age of needing. "Consumerism is not so much about having more as it is about having something else; that's why it is not simply buying but shopping that is the heart of consumerism," writes William Cavanaugh. We joke about "retail therapy" – the need to go down to the mall to shop, not for anything specific, but just to buy. Every few months new malls pop up around our suburbs catering for our need to have that "something else". At the same time, I am aware of a small but growing band of people who are seeking a simpler lifestyle. Perhaps the desire for simplicity and moderation is a deeper human desire than we imagine. Is this desire all that different today from what it was long ago? I suspect not. While I remain intrigued by the sayings of the desert people, I cannot pretend to emulate the action of a desert dweller who had no possessions except a gospel book that he sold in order to feed the poor. He said strikingly: "I have sold even the word that commands me to sell all and give to the poor." Such is true detachment!

Embracing moderation and "indifference" requires giving up self-interest. Relinquishing the demands of the self necessitates *humility and self-knowledge*. The idea of humility is often perverted. I know of a woman who was counselled by her priest to be humble "[…] even when you are subjected to abuse by your husband for it is God's way". That is not humility. That demands a sacrificial role from women and burdens us with self-denial in the interests of those who want to exercise power over us. True humility engenders respect, not subservience. *Amma* Syncletica, whose sayings are intriguingly full of nautical imagery, said: "A ship cannot be built without nails, and no one can be saved without humility." True humility is letting go of the tyranny of self. By bringing attentiveness and prayer together, the desert people strove for humility. This required obedience to their God. "It seems to me for those who live in monasteries, obedience is a higher virtue than chastity, however perfect. Chastity is in danger of pride; obedience has the promise of humility," said Syncletica. According to the desert people, the way to humility is through patience, endurance and fidelity – all conditions for growth and for building relationships with one another.

Benedict of Nursia in Italy (480–547) devoted a whole chapter to humility in his *Rule*. He was probably influenced by what came to him from the desert tradition. Humility for the desert people had a down-to-earth quality that bears out the derivation of the word itself: *humus* (earth). A hermit was asked, "What is humility?" He said, "It is if you forgive a brother who has wronged you before he is sorry." How different our world could be if we and those who are in positions of leadership were given to greater introspection, and developed the desire for more self-knowledge and a good dose of humility. I write this with more than a little disquiet about myself.

Self-knowledge is also *body knowledge*. How we treat our bodies is not unrelated to our quest for holiness. There is no division in reality between the spiritual and the material, and our spirituality is manifested in our treatment of matter. The people of the desert put their bodies through privations. Hunger and thirst, heat and cold, disease and all manner of bodily afflictions took their toll. Living in the desert was profoundly an experience of the body.

Let us consider our tongues – we are responsible for every single word we utter. I know that hasty words too often get me into trouble! Jesus warns us that we will be called to account for every word we waste (Mt 12:36). We are profligate with speech. It is sobering to listen to ourselves – easy speeches, glib answers, worn-out clichés. The desert mothers and fathers were economical with words. The simplicity of their sayings is born from attentive silence and the willingness of the desert people to wait. No wonder their wisdom is fresh and direct. They show us that silence gives rise to speech that comes from inner listening. Anthony's revered successor, Sisoes (born c.421), wisely said: "Our form of pilgrimage is keeping the mouth shut."

We can also consider sexuality, a matter of intense concern for the desert people who embraced chastity. Not surprisingly, they prized the virtue of self-control. It was said of *amma* Sarah (fifth century) that she was fiercely plagued by lust for thirteen years, but she never prayed that lust would leave her. Instead she said: "Lord, give me strength." Living into our holiness is to assume responsibility for all that we are and do. Self-control and responsibility are nurtured by the practice of prayer. A hermit said: "Chastity is born of tranquility and silence in inner prayer." The bodiliness of living faith requires that we value our bodies and act responsibly as creatures made in the image of God. It does not mean that all are called to a celibate life or that celibacy is the greater good. The celibate life is a deliberate choice and should never be prescribed. Our sexuality is a gift to be enjoyed responsibly.

The presence of women in the desert does raise a familiar theme. Columba Stewart points out that "the most common portrayal in non-hagiographical material is the familiar one of woman as temptress, threatening the monks' celibate way of life". The result is an absolute prohibition on any contact with women. Women relatives are also referred to as distractions and reminders of the past, while stories of prostitutes "generally relate the conversion of a woman by a monk who resists her blandishments"! The women of the desert lived in exclusively female communities and, according to Palladius (born c.361–died c.321), "[n]o one goes over to the women's monastery except the priest and deacon and they only go on Sunday". These insights show how human sexuality and holy living are unhappily entwined in the imagination of some of those early desert dwellers. In *amma* Sarah's nine recorded sayings there are a number of conversations with men, a surprising fact for someone who lived as a solitary. Pushing gender boundaries, she says to the brothers, "It is I who am a man, you who are a woman." This startling view must have been problematic in her context. Yet, it does raise the question of women becoming "male" and male identity being their frame of reference for shaping their ideals.

Living in the desert did not equate to a lack of *hospitality, communal awareness and love of neighbour.* The desert women and men saw themselves as members of the Body of Christ. These early communities wanted to reflect a different way of being Christian and witnessing to their faith. Love of neighbour was key to living in such communities, as was intercessory prayer for compassion and forgiveness. Anthony knew this: "Our life and our death is (sic) with our neighbour. If we win our brother, we win God. If we cause our brother to stumble we have sinned against God." Paradoxically, the solitary life was not a denial of the value of relationship. John the Dwarf (born c.339–died c.405) confirmed the need for relationship.

He said: "You don't build a house by starting with the roof and working down. You start with the foundation." They said, "What does that mean?" He said, "The foundation is our neighbour whom we must win. The neighbour is where we must start. Every commandment of Christ depends on this."

It is true that the ascetics of the desert often lived solitary lives, but their lives were not entirely without relationships. Brothers living in monastic communities would seek wisdom and advice on spiritual matters from an *abba*, a practice that gave rise to master-disciple relationships that were forerunners of the tradition of spiritual direction. The *abbas* themselves would, on occasion, visit one another. For some, visiting the desert fathers and the monastic communities that sprang up later could have been an early form of tourism; for others it was a sincere quest for guidance. The need to receive and practise forgiveness, and to live with compassion toward one's neighbour characterised these encounters and the teachings of the desert ascetics.

In these early communities hospitality was prized and guests were to be welcomed as Christ himself would do. No one should be turned away. This was seen as practising the love of Christ who cared for the needs of those who crossed his path. A story is told of *abba* Moses who broke the mandated fast over Lent to cook a vegetable stew for some visiting brothers. This surprised his community because Moses was known for his piety and obedience. "What is that smoke? Moses must be disobeying the order and cooking in his cell." Yet, on Easter Saturday, the clergy spoke to him before the whole congregation and said: "Moses, you have broken a commandment of men. But you have kept the commandments of God valiantly." Moses' meal confirmed the practice of Christian hospitality. We are not made to be separate persons. Growing into our holiness means growing ever more deeply into community through support, the necessary correction and a proper sense of our dependence.

Finally, the lives of the desert fathers and mothers were *acts of resistance and hope for the love of God*. Holiness resists all that seeks to detract from the love of God for the entire creation; this includes our personal lives and our present contexts. Spirituality cannot be located in some other-worldly realm. I cannot separate my spirituality from my political and social realities. Yet there are times when we find ourselves imprisoned by our circumstances, and we feel helpless as our world bludgeons us into a way of being that does not

accord with our deepest longing. As Persian Sufi mystic poet Rumi
(1207–1273) says:

Why, when God's world is so big
Do you fall asleep in a prison
Of all places?

Why indeed? Can we escape our prisons and resist the madness of
our world? Holiness demands that we resist the present inversion of
values and speak the truth; that we resist injustice and any treatment
that demeans the dignity of people; that our resistance confirms that
God cares and that God's desires for the world will not be thwarted.
Holy resistance is an act of love for the sake of Jesus. Thomas Merton
describes the kind of love that is free enough to place the welfare of
the other above self-interest. "We have to *become,* in some sense, the
person we love, and this involves a kind of death to our own being,
our own self." Holy love requires courage, and resists sentimental-
ity and possessiveness. Holy love can lead to dissent and resistance,
even civil disobedience. The Jewish philosopher Emmanuel Levinas
(1906–1995) said: "To know God means to know what has to be done."

Now I am not saying that the people of the desert were taking
part in civil disobedience as we know it today. Some were, however,
resisting what they perceived as a compromised church, and a world
whose values they did not share. A world that is founded on power,
possessions and violence needs to be resisted. Such resistance, when
fuelled by love for God and for one's neighbour, should be marked by
what German theologian Dorothee Sölle (1929–2003) calls "revolutionary patience that sets out from the experience of what has always
been good". Following the spiritual way is not cosy self-sufficiency,
but rather the willingness to be part of the risky business of building
up the reign of God on earth.

Resistance is risky and may call for sacrifice. Paul could appeal
to the Romans (12:1) "[...] present your bodies as a living sacrifice,
holy and acceptable to God" because he knew from experience that
attempting to live a holy life entails sacrifice. The very thought of

being "a living sacrifice" makes me shudder. I do not want to leave my comfort zones. Yet I know that resistance for the sake of the love of God requires sacrifice of one kind or another. Merton believed that holiness cannot escape being plunged into the mystery of suffering. I know that there is suffering that I cannot understand. I know that things are taken out of our hands and beyond what we think we can control. I know that it is only human to want to avoid suffering. Jesus hoped it could be avoided when he prayed in Gethsemane (Mk 14:36). The psalmist (119:75) declares: "I know O Lord that your judgments are right, and that in faithfulness you have humbled me." This scares me. Being humbled needs surrender of self, of my idea of who I am, of letting go and trusting that whatever happens, God is faithful. This letting go is the way to being a "living sacrifice". The cup will not pass from us and we will know the "sadness of not being a saint". But the ultimate reality is that the whole climax of creation is the completion of wholeness. Restoring harmony and order is the goal still beyond our reach. We are but beginners, trying to leave our prisons behind us by risking holiness, as did the people of the desert.

Having looked at some of the values and practices of the desert mothers and fathers, the question remains: to what extent can we draw on their wisdom for today? The Christian life has never been limited to specific physical environments. We do not need to withdraw literally to a desert. For many millions of people life in our cities today is as hazardous, as threatening, and as inhospitable as the desert was to those early dwellers long ago. Not more than five kilometres from where I live, people are trying to survive in appalling conditions. Disease ignores class, race and gender barriers, while HIV and AIDS cut a swathe of death across our population. Women struggle to rear children in single-parent families, and unemployment is growing daily, as is violent crime. In my neighbourhood, electrified fences are becoming common, creating new pockets of desert.

We know our twenty-first century desert, albeit involuntarily. There is no escape from it, but it need not be a prison. We can voluntarily embrace our desert. Then we find we are not alone. We meet others who are wounded and struggling to find meaning that will sustain us. We glimpse what the Body of Christ is called to be – a community of people, broken, self-confessed failures, stripped of all pretences, knowing only that we are loved and able to love in return. We see that throughout our tradition there have been both physical and spiritual desert experiences and that our modern-day desert contains many of the same challenges that people have faced throughout Christian history. The wisdom gleaned through experience by the desert dwellers in the early centuries of Christianity bridges time and offers us valuable clues for living into our holiness today. They distilled their experiences into an earthy wisdom with a simplicity and directness that is still fresh today. Our loss is not to heed it.

The desert is a metaphor for our existence – life and death, stasis and renewal, despair and hope. It is both a wild, untamed place, scorched and inhospitable, as well as a place of mystery, great beauty and surprises. In the Namib Naukluft Park of Namibia there is a shallow depression called Sossusvlei. It lies between the largest sand dunes in the world. When I first saw the vlei, it was dry, and the temperature hovered around fifty degrees Celsius. We could barely breathe. Despite the beauty of the coral-coloured dunes, the vastness of the landscape, and the thrill of seeing a majestic oryx appear out of nowhere looking sleek and well fed in a barren environment, all I wanted was shade and ice-cold water. On my next visit, a metamorphosis: the vlei, now a small lake, was filled with water birds – black-winged stilts, little stints, sandpipers, a couple of geese and red-billed teals. A metaphor come alive: a scorched dead landscape was now full of life and movement and sound.

The desert people went to the desert is to pray. Prayer is our tool for surviving the rigours of the desert. Theodora of Alexandria (d. 490), a prominent woman ascetic of the desert, said: "It is good to live in peace, for the wise man practises perpetual prayer." The struggle to live a holy life was not simple or straightforward then, neither is it today. It is loaded with contradictions and paradoxes – being solitary and cultivating community; resisting worldliness while embracing the world; living in total dependency on God, while accepting the responsibility of surviving in the desert. As I struggle to be brave enough to be Denise, desert wisdom helps to clear the clutter that clouds my vision. I can say no more.

A final word from the desert itself that describes how the women and men who lived there sought balance in life:

> A brother came to visit Abba Sylvanus at Mount Sinai. When he saw the brothers working hard, he said to the old man: "Do not work for the food that perishes. For Mary has chosen the good part." The old man called his disciple: "Zachary, give this brother a book and put him in an empty cell." Now when it was three o'clock, the brother kept looking at the door to see whether someone would come to call him for the meal. But nobody called him, so he got up, went to the old man, and asked: "Abba, didn't the brothers eat today?" The old man said: "Of course we did." Then he said: "Why didn't you call me?" The old man replied: "You are a spiritual person and do not need that kind of food, but since we are earthly, we want to eat, and that's why we work. Indeed, you have chosen the good part, reading all day long, and not wanting to eat earthly food." When the brother heard this, he repented and said: "Forgive me, Abba." Then the old man said to him: "Mary certainly needed Martha, and it is really by Martha's help that Mary is praised."

From the end of the fifth and into the sixth century, the pressures created by the spread of Islam led to the tapering of the desert movement. Generations of disciples of Jesus Christ have, however, pondered the wisdom of the desert people. Despite the difficulties the women and men of the deserts faced, their attempts to live holy lives gave rise to monasticism, an extraordinary phenomenon in Christian history. Although the majority of Christians did not follow this exodus to the desert, the movement and the beliefs that inspired it were to nourish the faith of Europe for centuries.

The call to withdraw from the hurly-burly of the every day and to take up a life dedicated to prayer still exists. I am reminded of a wet and misty day a couple of years ago when I rode a mule up a mountain to visit a sanctuary in Ethiopia. Eventually I was forced to dismount as the ascent grew too steep for the mule, and I continued up the very muddy path on foot. On the way, I passed a number of caves with crude wooden doors covering their entrances, some open. Inside, the floors were covered with straw on which hermits sat silently in prayer. The tradition of withdrawal, silence and solitude lives on, not only in this remote place but in a number of enclosed orders dedicated to prayer.

~

The moment we imagine that we can pursue holiness, we realise that it is, in fact, the Holy One who has initiated the pursuit. The hunter becomes the hunted. This is both a terrifying and an irresistible discovery. "It is a fearful thing to fall into the hands of the living God," says the writer to the Hebrews (10:31). But it would be more fearful to fall out of them. As terrifying as it is, there is no turning back. There is no escape, unless you do not care to meet the Holy One. It is terrifying because instinctively we know that much will be asked of us. "To know what purity is you have to be pure. To know what holiness is you have to be holy," warns Donald Nicholl. He points out that just as Jacob was left with his left hip dislocated after the night of struggle, so anyone wrestling with holiness is likely to find her or his secure existence put out of joint. "Before he arrived at Peniel (which means 'I have seen God') the son of Isaac was called 'the supplanter' (i.e. Jacob), but after being touched by the Holy One he was changed into 'the perseverer with God' (i.e. Israel). You cannot approach holiness without being changed into either a supplanter or a perserverer," says Nicholl.

Our comfort and encouragement is that our call to holiness comes from the Holy One who endows us with holiness. Opening ourselves to our holiness takes one simple step only. There is an Indian saying that "if you take one step towards God then God will take ten steps towards you". I believe that the first step is so surprisingly homely that it fills me with wonder. It begins when we seek to be attentive to the ordinary, seemingly insignificant things and happenings that crop up in everyday life. It is turning on our antennae and tuning in to what Buddhist monk Thich Nhat Hanh calls "the miracle of mindfulness". He explains: "Mindfulness is the miracle by which we master and restore ourselves [...] it is the miracle which can call back in a flash our dispersed mind and restore it to wholeness so that we can live each minute of life."

Mindfulness is the practice of awareness in every aspect of life – the bright green freshness of a basil leaf, hearing a pot sizzling on the stove, smelling seaweed on a beach. It starts with awareness that is sharpened, as if this moment of this day is the last moment of my life. A look, a word, a smile, a gesture, a passing stranger, the wind, the sun on a leaf – all noticed because the moment passes, never to be repeated. The most ordinary happenings of the day are lived every second before the face of God. For me, it started with my breath, the awareness that God is in every single breath – there is no breath without God – that God is the breath inside the breath. For Brother Lawrence (1614–1691), a lay brother who lived in a Carmelite monastery in Paris, it began with the practice of keeping his mind "on the holy presence of God" as he went about his menial tasks. He first attempted to live the solitary life as a hermit, but soon realised that he needed to live in community in submission to a common life. Assigned to cook and clean in the monastery kitchen, he practised attentiveness to the presence of God. "Is it not quicker and easier," he asked "just to do our common business wholly for the love of God?"

Attentiveness is nurtured by listening and the more intense the listening, the greater the desire for more stillness. The psalmist (46:10) who said: "Be still, and know that I am God" knew this need. Busyness is exchanged for stillness, noise for silence, and anxiety for trust. We slow down and instead of viewing continuous activity as a virtue we begin to see that there is another, more simple way of living the moment. The great Russian saint of silence, Seraphim of Sarov (1759–1833), spent thirty years living as a hermit in the great forest of Temniki. Now I am not advocating the hermit's life. But this story illustrates something of the quality of silence that can quieten our preoccupations and nurture mindfulness. A student walked four hundred miles to seek his advice. He could not find Seraphim in his hut. After walking around for about an hour he came upon a clearing in the forest. There he saw Seraphim curled up like a squirrel asleep in the thick grass. For a long time the student just stood and gazed at the sleeping man. Then he experienced a great sense of peace, and the spiritual conflict that had brought him all the way to find Seraphim disappeared. He set off on the long journey home. Seraphim's lived holiness spoke to the student without words. "Silence," said Seraphim, "is the cross on which man must crucify his ego." Matters of daily life are the material of our holiness. No experiences are wasted. Everything that happens to us can teach us holiness. It is about a way of being *in* the world.

If it is all so simple and so compelling, why are we not living holy lives? I suspect that we do not want change in any way that will rock our comfort zones. Let life remain undisturbed, no unexpected twists or interruptions. But daily life is full of obstacles, confusion and the unexpected. We are often ill equipped to deal with its vagaries. The practice of mindfulness is, in essence, an opening to the Spirit of God, jolting us into looking at what we are truly made of and having to ask: how much truth is there in me? What happens, for instance, when someone gets credit for something for which I think I should get the credit? How do I react when I hear another being praised? Am I quick to judge others? Confronting my true condition takes my breath away. Then I realise that this is the beginning of being cured of my illusions. A shift takes place – God is found in all things. Meister Eckhart once said: "Wisdom (i.e. holiness) consists of doing the next thing you have to do, doing it with your whole heart, and finding delight in doing it."

We need companions on the way. As we live in a web of relationships, our efforts to live out our holiness mean living more deeply in our relationships. Being in communion with others happens when we worship together, pray together, have a meal together, walk on the beach together, or share our experiences and our feelings. I have learnt that I need a soul-friend, one person with whom I can share the twists and turns of life and who helps to keep me from straying into the byways that divert me from finding God in all things. This I have found in the age-old tradition of spiritual direction. I cannot do without such a person.

So, yes, we can look to the enduring values of the women and men of the desert – the need for silence and solitude, humility and self-knowledge, compassion and prayer for the world, and the practice of loving one's neighbour. These are helpful markers along the way as we open ourselves to our holiness. The challenges of our times will, however, reframe the issues we face, and the ways and contexts in which we are called to live a holy life. Holiness is not for ivory towers. It is God-given and is to be lived in the messy, often perilous present.

We are told that we are made in the image of God – the *icon* of the invisible God. Nicholl points out that the Hebrew word for "image" in Genesis is *tselem*. The root meaning of *tselem* is "shadow", whereas the Greek *icon* means "image". "In the process of man's enlighten-ment, from Genesis to Christ, he moves from the shadow into being the *icon* of God, radiating light," writes Nicholl. I long to radiate light, but know that I am not the *icon* I should be. Are we accepting the responsibility of being bearers of the holy image?

Writing these words, I am filled with unease. The call to live as a holy person is either everything or nothing. It requires utter obedi-ence to God's will. Perhaps this is what Tolstoy, who struggled with his faith, meant when he said: "It is easier to write ten volumes of phi-losophy than to fulfill one of the commandments!" Yet I take heart by reminding myself once again that the Holy One who calls me makes it possible for me to respond. We are all meant to be saints, which means no more than that we become our true selves. We will all know failure. Courage will desert us. Yet holiness is not an arbitrary command. We are created in and meant for holiness. God wants to sanctify us for very practical reasons – *holiness restores harmony and order*. All we are to do is to be open to the discovery of our true identity, our true self, our holy self, which is our destiny. The discovery of our holiness is the discovery of what it means to be made in the image of God. God is love. Love is my true identity. God is holy. Holiness is my true being. To live into holiness is to live in God's love and to be God's love here in the world. The call to holiness comes from the Holy One who longs for us all to be holy as God is holy. I know that when all is said and done, *it is a simple matter that is no less than everything*. It calls for a renewing of our minds and our hearts. We must begin to think about our plans, our visions, our lives and our vocations in terms of holiness. *For such thinking is, in fact, a thinking about God.*

Nicholl points out that we may take comfort from asking ourselves: who of all the characters in the gospels was the first to recognise God's reign in the person of Jesus? It was not the "professional" religious people like the scribes and the Pharisees; neither was it the Roman authorities; nor were his disciples any more perceptive, nor the faithful women who followed Jesus.

In fact there is only one person who is recorded in the Gospels as accepting the kingdom of heaven on Jesus' own terms, and he was, like Jesus, a condemned criminal nailed to a cross. As he hung there, in his last agony, it was the 'good thief' who proclaimed Jesus to be innocent when he said "Lord, remember me when thou comest into thy kingdom". The good thief had recognized that even though he himself did not possess that purity by means of which the holy ones can "penetrate and pervade all beings", nevertheless the Holy One himself could penetrate and pervade all beings, including dying criminals such as himself […] This he (Jesus) did […] Without any preparation, the good thief, that total beginner, arrived at the end in an instant. The moment he began he was at the end.

Blessed are those who have the courage to begin, for they will be surprised by the wonder of holiness.

NOTES

The quotation from Rowan Williams on page 100 is taken from Stephen Barton's "Introduction" to *Holiness: Past and Present*. It comes from Rowan Williams, *Open to Judgment: Sermons and Addresses* (London: Darton, Longman and Todd, 1994).

According to *A Country Profile: South Africa, Religious Intelligence*, 2007–2008, South Africans identify their religious affiliations as follows: Christians, some thirty million; traditional ethnic religions, some six million; non-religious, three and one-third million; Islam and Hindusim, both approximately half a million; Judaism seventy thousand; the Bahâi faith, twenty thousand, and Buddhism/Chinese folk religion, approximately twelve thousand.

Liberal theology is open to criticism for its weak Christology. In his *Letters and Papers from Prison*, Dietrich Bonhoeffer writes that "[...] the weakness of liberal theology was that it granted the world the right to assign Christ his place in it; in the struggle between church and world, liberal theology accepted the – relatively mild – peace dictated by the world".

Francois de Sales (1567–1622) defined devout humanism simply as: "Be what you are and be that well." He was violently opposed by the Jansenists who emphasised original sin and human depravity, and the need for divine grace.

In the Old Testament, holiness and God are mutually defining. For further references see: Josh 24:19; Ps 99:3,5,9; 1 Sam 2:2, 6:20; Isa 6:3, 37:23; Lev 0:3; Ex 15:11.

Quotations from the writing of Benedictine Lawrence Freeman are taken from Rowan Williams, *Where God Happens*. See Works consulted.

Desert father Anthony, known as Anthony the Great, was born in Lower Egypt in 251 of well-to-do, landowner parents. At the age of thirty-four he gave up his possessions and went to live in the Nitrian Desert about ninety-five kilometres west of Alexandria for thirteen years. Later he lived for a further twenty years in an abandoned Roman fort on a mountain near the Nile. He suffered many privations and emerged as a prominent early figure among the desert fathers. He is remembered for his wisdom and his teaching. Athanasius of Alexandria wrote a life of Anthony around 360 AD. It remains one of the best-known biographies in the Christian world.

I cannot resist quoting the following description of Anthony from Athanasius's *Life of Anthony:*

And so for nearly twenty years he continued training himself in solitude, never going forth, and but seldom seen by any. After this, when many were eager and wishful to imitate his discipline, and his acquaintances came and began to cast down and wrench off the door by force, Anthony, as from a shrine, came forth initiated in the mysteries and filled with the Spirit of God. Then for the first time he was seen outside the fort by those who came to see him. And they, when they saw him, wondered at the sight, for he had the same habit of body as before, and was neither fat, like a man without exercise, nor lean from fasting and striving with the demons, but he was just the same as they had known him before his retirement. And again his soul was free from blemish, for it was neither contracted as if by grief, nor relaxed by pleasure, nor possessed by laughter or dejection, for he was not troubled when he beheld the crowd, nor overjoyed at being saluted by so many. But he was altogether even as being guided by reason, and abiding in a natural state. Through him the Lord healed the bodily ailments of many present, and cleansed others from evil spirits.

John Cassian, monk, Christian theologian and writer on asceticism, introduced Eastern monasticism to the West and was the founder of a complex of monasteries at Marseilles in 415. His two principal works are *Institutes*, his personal observations on monastic life in Egypt and Palestine, and *Conferences,* a record of conversations with Egyptian solitaries.

Evagrius Ponticus, Christian monk and classical scholar, was one of the most influential writers and thinkers of the fourth century church. He led an eremitical life in a community of monks in the Nitrian Desert and later at Kellia. He refused to be a bishop and later, as a supporter of Origen, he was condemned for his platonic views and his efforts to reconcile Christianity with reason.

The *Apothegmata Patrum* is a collection of over a thousand brief stories and sayings of the most prominent monks and hermits who lived in the Egyptian desert from the fifth to the sixth centuries. Some are terse aphorisms, while others sketch dramatic encounters. Often these sayings were in response to the request: "Abba give me a word that I might be saved." The sayings of the better-known ascetics were collected and repeated by their disciples. It is impossible, however, to know how accurate the attributions are, but their authenticity is widely accepted.

Palladius (born c.361–died c.431) was a bishop in Bithynia who composed an account of the women and men living in the deserts of Egypt, Palestine, Syria and Asia Minor. His *Lausiac History*, written in 420, is dedicated to a palace official in Constantinople called Lausa who asked him to record his journeys and encounters with the "saints" of the deserts. He spent nine years with them, observing and recording their lives, while drawing considerably on a preceding work by Rufinus written between 404 and 410.

Beyers Naudé was a renowned anti-apartheid activist. He came from an Afrikaner family, was ordained in the Dutch Reformed Church and joined the *Broederbond* (a secret society that furthered the interests of the Afrikaner) as a young man. The Cottesloe Consultation and the Sharpeville massacre in 1960, when sixty-nine black people were killed while protesting against restrictions on their freedom, were turning points for Naudé. He set up ecumenical contacts with the World Council of Churches, founded the Christian Institute in 1963 with the aim of working for reconciliation, lost his status as a minster and was eventually banned from 1977–1984. Nelson Mandela called him "a true humanitarian and a son of Africa".

The solitary life has been questioned by some on the grounds that it is removed from the struggle to live life in the world; see in Works consulted, Tardiff ed. *At Home in the World*, for the correspondence between Rosemary

Radford Ruether, historian, feminist theologian and social activist, and Trappist monk Thomas Merton in the late sixties. Trappists belong to the Order of Cistercians of the Strict Observance, a Roman Catholic religious order of contemplative monks who follow the Rule of St Benedict that was written in the sixth century. Contrary to popular belief, they do not take a vow of silence, but speak only when necessary and discourage idle talk.

Basil the Great (330–379), bishop of Caesarea, was known for his care of the poor and underprivileged. He liked to emphasise the practical aspects of Christianity. He tried to moderate the austerities of monasticism in his day. He warned that the law of solitude could violate the divine law of charity and thus be a danger to the soul of the solitary person. He asked: "If you live alone, whose feet will you wash?"

"The idea of *hesychia* is undoubtedly the central consideration in the prayer of the desert fathers. In its early use the term *hesychast* referred to a solitary hermit. But *hesychia* is used not only of physical solitude and quiet, but also of interior vigilance and spiritual sobriety," writes Kenneth Leech in *True God*. From those early days onwards, the tradition of the *hesychia* has been part of Eastern orthodoxy and is also associated with Mount Athos. Central to *hesychia* is the Jesus Prayer.

The Centre for Christian Spirituality in Cape Town was established in 1986 by the then Archbishop Desmond Tutu. Under the initial leadership of Dr Francis Cull, the Centre (first known as the Institute for Christian Spirituality) grew into an inter-denominational organisation with its main focus on meditation, contemplative prayer, and spiritual direction. I was privileged to work in this organisation from 1987–1990 and have remained associated with its work ever since.

Jesuits William Barry and William Connolly define spiritual direction as "[…] help given by one Christian to another which enables that person to pay attention to God's personal communication to him or her, to respond to this personally communicating God, to grow in intimacy with this God, and to live out the consequences of the relationship".

The quotations from the poet Rumi and philosopher Levinas are taken from Dorothee Sölle's work, *The Silent Cry*. See in Works consulted.

Old Testament scholar Gerhard von Rad (1901–1971), in his commentary on *Genesis*, Old Testament Library Series, (London: SCM Press, 1961), refers to "*tselem*" as predominantly an actual plastic work, an idol or a painting.

Further sources for the sayings of the desert fathers are:

Athanasius, *The Life of Anthony*, tr. R.C. Gregg (New York: Paulist Press, 1980).

Philip Rousseau, *Pachomius: The Making of Community in Fourth Century Egypt* (Berkley: University of California Press, 1999).

Robert E. Sinkewicz, *Evagrius of Pontus: The Greek Ascetic Corpus* (New York: Oxford University Press, 2003).

John Cassian, *The Conferences*, tr. B. Ramsey (New York: Paulist Press, 1997).

WORKS CONSULTED

Barry, William A. and William J. Connolly. *The Practice of Spiritual Direction*. San Francisco: Harper and Row, 1982.

Barton, Stephen, ed. *Holiness: Past and Present*. London: T and T Clark, 2003.

Bonhoeffer, Dietrich. *Letters and Papers from Prison*. Enlarged edition. Edited by E. Bethge. New York: Touchstone, 1997.

Brother Lawrence. *The Practice of the Presence of God: The Best Rule of a Holy Life. Conversations and Letters of Brother Lawrence*. London: Samuel Bagster, 1945.

Brueggemann, Walter. *Theology of the Old Testament: Testimony, Dispute, Advocacy*. Minneapolis: Fortress Press, 1997.

Cameron, Averil. "Desert mothers: Women Ascetics in Early Christian Egypt." In *Women as Teachers and Disciples in Traditional and New Religions,* edited by E. Puttick and P. B. Clarke. *Studies in Women and Religion,* vol. 32, 11-24. Lewiston: The Edwin Mellen Press, 1993.

Cavanaugh, William T. *Being Consumed: Economics and Christian Desire.* Grand Rapids: Eerdmans, 2008.

Dillard, Annie. *Holy the Firm.* New York: Harper and Row, 1977.

Johnston, William. *The Mystical Way.* London: Fount Paperbacks, 1993.

Lane, Belden C. "Desert Attentiveness, Desert Indifference: Countercultural Spirituality in the Desert Fathers and Mothers." *Cross Currents* (Summer 1994): 193-206.

Lane, George. *Christian Spirituality: An Historical Sketch.* Chicago: Loyola University Press, 1984.

Leech, Kenneth. *True Prayer: An Introduction to Christian Spirituality.* London: Sheldon Press, 1980.

Leech, Kenneth. *True God: An Exploration in Spiritual Theology.* London: Sheldon Press, 1985.

McGinn, Bernhard, ed. and tr. *Meister Eckhart: Teacher and Preacher.* New York: Paulist Press, 1986.

Merton, Thomas. *The Wisdom of the Desert Fathers of the Fourth Century.* Translated by T. Merton. New York: New Directions, 1960.

Nicholl, Donald. *Holiness.* London: Darton, Longman and Todd, 1981.

Palladius. *The Lausiac History.* Translated and annotated by R. T. Meyer. Ancient Christian Writers #34. New York and Mahwah, NJ: Paulist Press, 1964.

Sheldrake, Philip. *Images of Holiness: Explorations in Contemporary Spirituality.* London: Darton, Longman and Todd, 1987.

Sölle, Dorothee. *The Silent Cry: Mysticism and Resistance.* Minneapolis: Fortress Press, 2001.

Stewart, Columba. "The Portrayal of Women in the Sayings and Stories of the Desert." *Vox Benedictina* 2, no. 1(January 1985): 5-23

Tardiff, Mary, ed. *At Home in the World: The Letters of Thomas Merton and Rosemary Radford Ruether.* New York: Orbis Books, 1995.

Taylor, Charles. *A Secular Age.* Cambridge, MA: The Belknap Press of Harvard University Press, 2007.

Thich Nhat Hanh. *The Miracle of Mindfulness: A Manual on Meditation.* Boston: Beacon Press, 1976.

Underhill, Evelyn. *Practical Mysticism: A Little Book for Normal People.* Guilford: Eagle, 1991.

Ward, Benedicta. *Harlots of the Desert: A Study of Repentance in Early Monastic Sources.* Cistercian Studies Series, no. 106. Kalamazoo, MI: Cistercian Publications, 1987.

Von Rad, Gerhard. *Genesis.* Old Testament Library Series. London: SCM Press, 1961.

Ward, Benedicta, tr. *The Sayings of the Desert Fathers: The Alphabetical Collection.* Oxford: A. R. Mowbray, 1975, revised edition 1984.

Welker, Michael. *God the Spirit.* Translated by J. F. Hoffmeyer. Minneapolis: Fortress Press, 1994.

Williams, Rowan. *Open to Judgment: Sermons and Addresses.* Longman: Daron, Longman and Todd, 1994.

Williams, Rowan. *Where God Happens: Discovering Christ in One Another.* Boston: New Seeds, 2005.

Wüstenberg, Ralf K. *A Theology of Life: Dietrich Bonhoeffer's Religionless Christianity.* Translated by D. Stott. Grand Rapids: Eerdmans, 1998.

CHAPTER FOUR

Blessed are those who find freedom, for they will be free for others

I was not born with a hunger to be free. I was born free – free in every way that I could know. Free to run in the fields near my mother's hut, free to swim in the clear stream that ran through my village, free to roast mielies under the stars and ride the broad backs of slow-moving bulls. As long as I obeyed my father and abided by the customs of my tribe, I was not troubled by the laws of man or God. It was only when I began to learn that my boyhood freedom was an illusion, when I discovered as a young man that my freedom had already been taken from me that I began to hunger for it.

This quotation is from the autobiography of Nelson Mandela (1918–2013): *A Long Walk to Freedom*. Unlike Madiba, I think I was born with a hunger to be free. As long as I can remember I yearned for freedom: freedom from the tensions in my parental home; freedom from disciplining that did not make sense; freedom from fear of rejection, and later, freedom from the patriarchy of my family. As a little girl, I found a secret place in our garden where I could be free: free to play imaginary games; free to read just about anything I could lay my hands on; free to dream without being interrupted. I treasured this place at the bottom of the garden, snug behind creepers and bushes.

It was taken away from me at the age of eleven when, in 1947, General Smuts sent my father to Sweden to open the first South African diplomatic mission there. I was uprooted from home and school as my family went to live in Stockholm. We had no garden, the sunshine of the Cape gave way to nine months of cold darkness and, at school, everyone spoke Swedish. It was foreign and lonely. My new, not-so-secret place became my bed. After lights out, I read by torchlight under the bedclothes and I dreamt of faraway places, exotic customs and romantic heroes and heroines. Time passed and we moved to different continents. It was difficult to feel free as I struggled to cope with new languages, new schools, new homes, and later, with having to support myself. My uprooted life continued in one way or another until I got married. By then, I had a fairly clear idea of what I wanted to be "free from", but I had not begun to think of what I wanted to be "free for". This came only later when I realised that to be "free from" was only the first step to freedom.

The idea of political and social freedom is an ancient human ideal. This I think is what Madiba is referring to when he realises that his freedom has been taken away from him. The long struggle for freedom against oppressive conditions in our country has shaped South Africans in different ways. While a handful of white people still hanker after the "old days", those who were actively engaged in opposing apartheid cannot forget the joy, the sweetness, and the promise of that election day in April 1994. To be a free people in a free country, free from inequality and injustice, was finally within our grasp.

Christians to whom a just, free and equitable society is consonant with God's will for this world share this general political and social understanding of freedom. Freedom is central to the agenda of all liberation theologies that focus on actions for justice as integral to human redemption. This means the redemption of all people, societies and nations from the powers that enslave them, "and prevent them from knowing the fullness of life God intends for all humanity. Liberation is about the bestowal and renewal of life in all its dimensions," writes South African theologian John de Gruchy.

Christians, however, understand freedom as more than the

establishment of a free and just society, as vital as that is for respecting human worth and dignity. To be free is not simply the absence of interference, a freedom from, but it is, in fact, a freedom for – freedom for attaining worthy goals, freedom for goodness, freedom to cross barriers and connect with "the other", freedom to be what we were created to be , that is fully and truly human. According to theologian William Cavanaugh, "Freedom is thus fully a function of God's grace working within us. Freedom is being wrapped up in the will of God, who is the condition of human freedom."

This kind of freedom holds the possibility of the renewal of every aspect of life – personal, spiritual, social, political and, supremely important for today, environmental. The struggle to lay hold of the gift of freedom in faith, to live by it, and to pass it on is at the centre of living, moving and having our being in God. When we are free for God, we are able to be free in ourselves and this translates into the desire to pass on the gift of freedom to others. Discovering that faith is freedom is an immeasurable blessing. It is made possible by God's Spirit, the great enabler and mover, who is unceasingly at work in transforming us from bondage to freedom.

There are caveats here. In our creation myth from Genesis (2:1-14), human beings enjoy a life of oneness with God. They are given freedom to enjoy the abundance of the Garden of Eden. This is creation with God at its centre. But this myth also illustrates that we are not free to do as we like. "You may freely eat of every tree of the garden, but of the tree of the knowledge of good and evil you shall not eat [...]" (v.16, 17). There are boundaries to our freedom. Freedom is constrained because we do not live alone and our actions impinge on the freedom of others.

Freedom in the Bible has to be seen against the widespread reality of slavery that was prevalent in both Old and New Testament times. The scriptures emphasise the importance of freedom from slavery and oppression in the Exodus event. Later, the prophet Isaiah (61:1) picks up the theme of freedom, one that was echoed by Jesus in the synagogue at Nazareth (Lk 4:16-30). Isaiah says: "The spirit of the Lord is upon me [...], he has sent me to bring good news to the oppressed, to bind up the broken-hearted, to proclaim liberty to the captives, and release to the prisoners."

In the New Testament we encounter the supreme paradox. We are slaves to sin. However, by faith we are set free from sin in order to become "slaves" of God! Paul explains from his own experience: "For I do not do what I want, but I do the very thing I hate" (Rom 7:15). We are captive to sin but, he says, we are set free from the power of sin by "the Spirit of life in Christ Jesus". I understand this to mean that first we acknowledge our need to be freed from our captive selves, then the Spirit will guide us to newfound freedom as we follow the man on the borrowed donkey. Acting in obedience to God brings freedom, both my freedom and my ability to be free for others.

I cannot claim that freedom for others is exclusively an attitude of faith. Human rights, so essential for the upholding of human worth, while making no religious demands are profoundly concerned with human freedom. Many millions of caring, thinking people promote the cause of human freedom in myriad secular ways, often against daunting odds. This truth makes me ashamed for the church when it plays prescriptive power games. Women are often still excluded from exercising their gifts in some churches in various forms of ministry by asking them to "surrender" to dubious interpretations of scripture, thus denying their calling to serve God in their chosen vocations. I have even heard human rights trashed as a concept devoid of human responsibility that has no place in the church. I wonder what image of God and humanity such views express?

⁓

Do we all long to be free? I suspect most of us do, though the prospect of freedom can be frightening for some. If one has for a lifetime known only some or other kind of bondage, it could be a case of "better the devil you know than the one you don't". In the words of the poet W. H. Auden (1907–1973):

We would rather be ruined than changed.
We would rather die in our dread than
Climb the cross of the moment
And see our illusions die.

Intuitively we know that freedom involves choice, and choice can be dangerous. Things can go wrong. When we make moral choices, what we decide is shaped by our environments, our relationships and our understanding of what God requires from us. There are no guarantees that we will not come into conflict with others who share our faith commitments. We are doomed to choose and to be accountable for our choices – such is our freedom. Freedom is a sublime gift; it is also a double-edged sword. I am free to commit murder, to steal and to lie; I am also free to choose differently. In truth, the greatest freedom we human beings have is the freedom to sin. Without this freedom we would never know the redeeming love of God in Christ.

I know the longing for freedom. I also know that becoming free is not easy. It may very well take time to free ourselves from that which shackles our freedom. Sometimes this painful process is interrupted by moments of blinding, yet lasting insight; unpredictable, fleeting moments when a word, a lifted burden, a sense of fulfilment or a touch of ecstasy makes us feel whole and free. These flashes of freedom are gifts – as surprising and welcome as a mug of ice-cold river water after a long hike on a hot day –nudging us to be what we are meant to be, free for God and free for others.

I have experienced such moments in times of prayer, on retreat and when reading scripture. Can printed words on a page really make us free? Constitutions are printed words on pages that guarantee human freedom. But we know how fragile these words can be. Philosophy, theology, poetry and great works of fiction can also promote ideas of freedom. In my experience, the biblical words do something more. I have known this "something more" as an inner awakening that comes when the Spirit brings new insights into often familiar texts. Words and phrases come alive with fresh meanings that speak directly into my life. It is not something I can make happen. But when it does, it is as if new life is breathed into the printed words; they become pregnant with the promise of hope and freedom.

There are parts of the Bible that I find difficult to swallow – stories of revenge and punishment, prejudice and stigma. Particular passages that are used to justify discrimination against women exasperate me. The Bible has many examples of what I long to be "free from". What does this say about its authority in my life? I have found that as a written document it is unsurpassed in its ability to provide clues on how to understand and interpret its own texts. This attribute helps me when I resist the awkward passages. Yes, I do read the Bible through the spectacles of a woman, laced with my understanding of my faith, and as a member of a particular society and community of faith. Nevertheless, after many years of reading the scriptures, I never cease to be astonished at their ability to surprise me, to jolt my understanding, to prompt new insights, and to lift me out of fear and anxiety. Strands of freedom, hope and love are woven throughout their pages. The Bible is my prime authority, for I have learnt to trust the texts by understanding where they come from, and to acknowledge their power in my life. Whatever my spectacles may be, God's Spirit is *the* Great Interpreter of the Word nudging me, and all who seek the truth, to see, to know, to change and to rejoice. The Word is a means to know freedom in faith.

Is it possible to pin down what freedom means? Over time, theories about human freedom have occupied the minds of philosophers, theologians and writers. According to political theorist and philosopher Isaiah Berlin (1909–1997), almost every moralist in human history has praised freedom. So much so that the word has become porous and can be interpreted in almost any way. According to Berlin, there are more than two hundred understandings of freedom recorded by historians of ideas! Clearly freedom has many faces.

The need for freedom is imperative for anyone who experiences oppression. If it were not so, a term like "oppression" would have little meaning. Oppression is an extreme form of restraint on freedom that calculatingly diminishes, even denies, human worth in a variety of ways. To a lesser extent, freedom is restrained in different spheres of our lives – by other people, by physical laws, by psychological factors, by time and place, and by oppressive cultural traditions and practices. A romantic, unfettered notion that freedom means being able to do exactly as one pleases is simply a pipedream. There is no such freedom. There are always curbs on freedom. We compel children to be educated and we forbid executions. We have speed limits on our roads and regulations about constructing houses. When we make choices, there is always the possibility of conflict, because we as human beings have rights that are not always compatible with those of others. "The necessity of choosing between absolute claims is then an inescapable characteristic of the human condition," writes Berlin. Sadly, our choices often lead to suffering, oppression and exclusion. To echo philosopher Immanuel Kant's (1724–1804) famous truth: "Out of timber so crooked as that from which man is made nothing entirely straight can be built."

In his book *Faith's Freedom*, New Testament scholar Luke Johnson spells out both constraints on and opportunities for freedom. In the first instance, we are bodies and our flesh is fragile. We can only be in one place at a time. When, as a teenager, I dreamt of living in mediaeval times and meeting a chivalrous knight, or of travelling up the Amazon River in search of a lost tribe, I did so only in my imagination. Memory and imagination can momentarily transcend our bodies. But fixed in time and space, our bodies get sick, age and die. I would love to levitate or fly, but gravity grounds me. There are places I still want to visit, mountains I want to climb, rivers I want to explore, but age is now restraining me. Yet, we are not completely enslaved to our bodies. We can choose to control our desires, where we go and how we act. The truth is that our freedom is limited by our bodiliness, but we can still choose how to speak, when to listen, and how to imagine and hope.

Second, we know today, from psychology, how powerfully our psyches react to experiences of fear, anger, oppression and desire, and how these reactions influence our ability to relate to ourselves and to others. No one is free from past experiences and we ignore them at our peril. Their hold on us is powerful. People who have experienced discrimination can come to believe the images imposed on them by their oppressors. Yet, oppressors and oppressed alike have the freedom to make choices, often very difficult ones, which are significant for their freedom. We can choose to confront our inner demons and redeem our inner pain by taking responsibility for ourselves.

Third, freedom is also constrained by the societies we live in. We are all born into certain structures, countries and times. My freedom intersects with that of others. All of us are subject to the myths and rituals that are part of our lives. No one, in John Donne's well-known words, "is an island, entire of itself; every man is a continent, a part of the main". Restrictive and oppressive rules deny human freedom, as we well know in South Africa where legalised racial discrimination took away the freedoms of the majority of our people. When discriminatory and oppressive regulations dictate societal patterns of living, we lose our freedom to negotiate how we want to live our lives. Patriarchy has succeeded for millennia in robbing women of the freedom to exercise their rights and live out their dreams. Uncritically accepting social criteria of who and how I should be can make me no more than a bearer of tradition who plays various roles – mother, wife, cook, child-minder and so on. Yet experience has taught me that we do not have to be captive to societal norms and cultural constraints. Structures and rules can be resisted; culture is dynamic and change can happen. We are able to resist oppression, and to reframe and broaden our horizons by the choices we make, albeit under taxing circumstances.

Fourth, finding freedom is shaped by the way we interpret the world and look for meaning in our different realities. The freedom we find depends a great deal on what has meaning for us. Here I am not referring to some theoretical aspect of meaning, but the meaning we find in our stories. Everyone has a story to tell. Our stories are about what we feel, how we act and how we have understood a complex variety of experiences. They are fed by our relationships and traditions. At times they are stories of dissonance when fondly held beliefs are confronted by contradictions. A dear friend becomes hostile; an enemy bandages my wounds. My understanding of *ubuntu* is shattered by the indifference of our South African leaders to the plight of Zimbabweans, yet I am heartened by the generosity of those who often have little themselves towards these needy, often rejected refugees. How I understand these contradictions will depend on how I interpret the fundamental tensions between my view of the world and my experience. My search for freedom will be determined by the way in which I define myself and understand my story, by how I relate it to my faith, and by my relationships with others.

Fifth, and in addition to Johnson's list, there is the question of power. To exercise freedom I need a measure of power to control the circumstances that threaten my freedom. Yet my freedom may impinge on that of others, while it also depends on that of others. Power that wants to satisfy only my whims is a threat to the freedom of others. Exploitative, self-centred power destroys freedom. Look, for example, at the way in which we human beings have exercised our power over the earth. Instead of caring for what is good for our neighbour and ourselves in the natural world, we have sought what we perceived as essential to *our* needs and *our* comfort at the cost of putting all of life at risk. Yet, when power is used creatively as energy for freedom, it is possible to act with concern for the welfare of others and to control what is destructive.

Lastly, we human beings can claim to be absolutely free by denying the existence of God. "Modern atheism is, in many ways, an atheism for the sake of human freedom," writes Christoph Schwöbel. "Where human freedom is seen as absolute, a God who is claimed to be absolute can only appear as a threat to freedom." So be it. It is, however, ironical that ideas of human freedom and divine freedom are both similar and dissimilar. For the atheist, a person's freedom is self-constituted, with the power to regulate agency. For believers, freedom is also self-constituted giving them agency to act. Yet, for the atheist, God's existence must be denied for the sake of radical human freedom, while, for the believer, freedom emanates from the good news of God's redeeming love in Jesus Christ. Whatever the constraints on our freedom or our diverse views concerning it, I continue to believe that most people long for freedom.

At the heart of "freedom in faith" lies a paradox. Can we conceive of a God who is Creator, Reconciler and Perfecter of all things, and yet who is also a respecter of human freedom? If God commands us, does this not deprive us of our freedom? Does being obedient to God imply a loss of freedom? The answers to these questions depend on how we understand freedom. If freedom is a gift from God and central to the good news of salvation, it is to be sought, defended and enjoyed. At the same time it undoubtedly entails the responsibility to exercise freedom wisely.

The idea of freedom makes sense to me only when it is understood as a relational concept. Yes, I am free to be myself. I have agency to determine the internal norms that govern my actions, but my freedom is mediated by and depends on how I relate to others. I do not understand freedom as a mere individualistic concept. If I am free, it is because others have enabled me and empowered me to be free. By "others" I mean first of all God (and my relationship with God), and then other people (and my relationships with them). I do not understand freedom as self-fulfilment at all costs. Above all, for Christians, human freedom is vested in our relationship with God, with others and in the Body of Christ as a community of freedom. Jesus reminds us: "If you continue in my word, you are truly my disciples; and you will know the truth and the truth will set you free" (Jn 8:31-32).

To return to the two categories "freedom from" and "freedom for" and what they may mean. I understand "freedom from" to mean that I can act without interference from others, and that I am not subject to coercion or restriction. There are justifiable political, legal and moral limitations on my freedom. For example, I am not free to assault another person or to crash my car into hers or his simply because I am angry at their driving. I am not free to treat others with contempt because they are different from me, or to act in a way that usurps another's freedom of religion. Freedom depends on our ability to be agents of our own acts of will, to be subjects, not objects, to act according to reason and conscience, to follow a purpose which we choose and which is not forced upon us from outside. This we can do only if we are free. Berlin explains: "I wish to be a somebody, not nobody; a doer – deciding, not being decided for, self-directed and not acted upon by external nature or by other men as if I were a thing, or an animal, or a slave incapable of playing a human role, that is, of conceiving goals and policies of my own and realising them."

On hearing that I am attempting to write about freedom, my erudite friends tell me to read Immanuel Kant on freedom. I am afraid that I have not enough life left to begin to wrestle with Kant now; I find Berlin easier to understand. But I have tried Kant, albeit in an extremely limited fashion. I understand him (Kant) to say that we humans are endowed with practical reason and are able to exercise a law unto ourselves, a moral law. We can set ends for ourselves and we may coordinate our purposes and ends with the ends of others. This promotes community. When my desires are in harmony with those of others and when these are for the common good, true community, or what Kant calls the Kingdom of Ends, is possible. Fundamental to Kant, as I understand him, is his categorical imperative that I may never treat another as a mere object.

According to philosopher Drucilla Cornell, Kant accepts the notion of negative freedom, in the sense that we restrain our "short-term desires in the name of an overall purpose for our lives". To illustrate negative freedom, she gives the example of a young man who is a keen surfer and who is studying to be a lawyer. The conditions for surfing are perfect. The young man is faced with a choice: does he surf or does he write his exams? He weighs up his long-term desire to be a lawyer with the short-term gain of a perfect day's surfing. If he is prudent, he chooses to exercise his freedom by writing his exams. With freedom comes taking responsibility for our actions and the choices we make. Otherwise the idea of freedom becomes a mockery of our ability to act as moral agents. To exercise freedom is to make choices. This I do understand.

But what happens when the laws of nature or circumstances limit the exercising of our free will? This could occur accidentally, or because of the activities of others, or the restrictions of institutions, or through poverty or illness.

One reaction would be to withdraw into oneself and to proclaim: "No outside forces, no human malice, no attachment to things matter to me anymore." This is the reaction of those who seek to isolate themselves from the world, choosing not to be vulnerable to its onslaughts. "If I save myself from an adversary by retreating indoors and locking every entrance and exit, I may remain freer than if I had been captured by him, but am I freer than if I had defeated or captured him?" asks Berlin. Often withdrawal is the path people of faith chose. We retreat into our own faith community and insulate our territory from outside voices and external conflict. Or we are angry and resentful – reactions that can translate into depression or violent acts. There are alternatives. Choice is possible, even in the darkest moments.

This raises the knotty question of free will, a topic that has occupied a great deal of time and energy in the Christian tradition, often fruitlessly. At this stage of my life, I understand more clearly than ever before what Augustine meant when he wrote in his *Confessions*: "Give me [the grace to do as] you command, and command [me to do] what you will." With Augustine, I believe that the spark of divinity in all of us defines human reason, and that freedom is intrinsic to our ability to think, to make choices and to hope.

Freedom in faith replaces self-sufficiency, because its primary concern is how we live in relationship with one another and with God. Only God is totally free. Yet our freedom reflects something of divine freedom in our world. Human freedom is fashioned after divine freedom, but is not equal to it. Divine freedom is beyond my understanding. What I do know is that we must grasp the freedom offered to us and use it for good.

We say God is love; we do not often say that God is freedom. But love presupposes freedom, freedom to choose, to be instrumental in the flourishing of another. Love is the content of divine duty. We are free but, because we do not love as we should, God's purposes for the world are not yet accomplished. Human freedom and divine freedom are meant to work together. In the meantime, our quest for freedom is fragile and fallible. But we can at least try to do our bit, as flawed as it may be, to eliminate what hampers freedom – poverty, injustice, violence. This is the proper use of free will.

~

When I mentioned to my friend and colleague Dirkie Smit that I was thinking about Christian freedom, he suggested I read Calvin again. So I did. For many years I had steered away from Calvin. I found the kind of neo-Calvinism that dominated so much of Afrikaner Reformed theology in South Africa during the apartheid years repugnant. The militancy, austere rectitude and reactionary racist views of the neo-Calvinists I knew put me off Calvin. However, I was not unaware of the worthy social impact of Calvin's views and their contribution to reform. What I resisted was how they could degenerate into we-know-what-is-best-for-you triumphalism. I was not sure how much blame was Calvin's and how much simply the fallibility of some of his followers, but I was willing to consider Dirkie's advice.

Then, at a conference at the University of the Western Cape, he gave a paper in which he argued, somewhat provocatively, that my theology reminded him of Calvin, particularly my passion to do theology that is "simple and straightforward". Intrigued and prompted by this paper, I decided to look again at the Calvinism of my Protestant forebears.

I acknowledge that my Huguenot roots are entangled with the spectre of Calvin, and that Calvin's teachings on the need for good works and moral behaviour rubbed off on me as a child. Recently I wrote that, in the intervening years, I have travelled on theological byways that justify my being called "a ragbag theologian":

[A] strange mélange of influences and sources emerges – from Augustine to Beverly Harrison, from Calvin to Ignatius, with a couple of stops in-between, from Julian of Norwich to the Circle of Concerned African Women Theologians. I seem to be a Reformed Anglican, whose spirituality has been shaped by the Reformation and the Counter Reformation, and who draws enthusiastically from a hugely diverse collection of theologians, female and male, Lutheran, Reformed, Catholic, liberation and feminist.

When I bridle at the kind of Calvinism that dominated the nationalist Afrikaner Reformed community, I remind myself that Calvin and the Reformation influenced Anglican theology and in particular Archbishop Thomas Cranmer's (1489–1556) writing of the Book of Common Prayer (1548–1549), and that Calvin was a lay theologian intent on renewing the Catholic church, not starting a new one. In a questioning, even critical mood, I pick up my worn copy of his *Institutes*, last looked at in the early years of my theological studies.

What do I find? Clearly reasoned theology and a stunning depth of biblical scholarship. As I read Calvin's well-known essay on human freedom, my curiosity is pricked: "We must now discuss Christian freedom. No summary of gospel teaching ought to omit an explanation of this topic. It is a matter of prime necessity, and without a knowledge of it consciences dare undertake almost nothing without faltering; often hesitate and draw back; constantly waver and are afraid." Christian freedom lies at the very core of the gospel, and our consciences are vital for pursuing freedom. What is the gospel other than freedom for God? I resolve to read on. "Unless this freedom be comprehended, neither Christ nor gospel truth, nor inner peace of soul, can rightly be known." Conscience stirs the longing for freedom and monitors its proper use. The further I read, the more evident the clarity and rationality of Calvin's arguments become, but it is his liberating view of freedom that grips my interest.

Calvin argues that Christian freedom consists of three parts. The first, he says, is "that the consciences of believers, while having to seek assurance of their justification before God, should rise above and advance beyond the law, *forgetting all law-righteousness*" (my italics).

As Christians we are invited to allow our consciences to rise above the law and to grasp the freedom offered to us in Christ that enables us to resist tyranny and all that inhibits or threatens to destroy our freedom. Calvin is not saying that Christians are free from the law, but that we are free in the law and able to advance beyond it. This is a breath of fresh air for one who instinctively resists the "law". I hope one day God will not ask me: "Denise, have you fulfilled the requirements of the law?", for I know what I will have to answer. Perhaps God may just say: "My grace has saved you – know that and rejoice!"

Paul writes: "For freedom Christ has set us free. Stand firm, therefore, and do not submit again to a yoke of slavery" (Gal 5:1). All the laws and traditions, both religious and cultural, that deny a believer's freedom are no longer valid. That is why baptism in Christ removes all barriers that such laws and traditions have erected and gives us a charter for human freedom: "There is no longer Jew or Greek, there is no longer slave or free, there is no longer male or female; for all of you are one in Christ Jesus" (Gal 3:28). Women know only too well how laws, and religious and cultural traditions have banded together to deny them their freedom. Calvin may not have had women in mind when he wrote about freedom, but I find myself saying "Amen!"

Be warned – for once again we encounter paradox. I am a free individual who should act according to my God-given conscience. But I also belong to the Body of Christ. Thus my freedom and my membership in the community of faith go together. Smit explains: "This means that the Christian person is both a free individual and someone belonging to God and others at the same time, both whole and part, both self-sufficient and dependent on sociality." He continues, it is as if Calvin "anticipates modern notions of individuality as a matter of individual fulfilment in particularity and distinctiveness," for he views the "irreducible individual as 'part of the whole' embedded in and dependent on community and on forms of belonging".

The second part of Calvin's view of Christian freedom (which depends on the first) is that "consciences observe the law, not as if constrained by the necessity of the law, but that freed from the law's yoke, *willingly* obey God's will" [my italics]. Here Calvin explains that Christian freedom is the fruit of ready, cheerful obedience offered to God. Once we embrace our freedom from the severe requirements of the law, says Calvin, we will hear God calling us "with fatherly gentleness" to which we will cheerfully and eagerly respond. If freedom cannot be gladly lived, I want none of it. To become "free for others" means to be free with love and good cheer because we are filled with gratitude for what we have been given. In gratitude we become active for others, not in a sour or dutiful way, but as a loving response to the often urgent needs that surround us. We are free citizens working for justice and freedom for others. But we do so with an abiding awareness that we are but limited agents, filled with flaws and needing to examine our actions continuously. Where was this understanding of freedom in the theology of those Reformed theologians who supported Afrikaner nationalism at the expense of the majority of people in this country?

This question applies equally and even more sadly to Calvin's third part of Christian freedom. According to him, "we are bound before God by no religious obligation to outward things of themselves indifferent; but permitted sometimes to use them, sometimes to leave them, indifferently". He appears to be saying that all matters that are not matters of the gospel are of themselves "indifferent" and we are not obliged to follow them. It is unnecessary to "stir up discussion" on eating meat, on using holidays and vestments, and other "vain frivolities". When we snare our consciences with such frivolities, we enter "a long and inextricable maze, not easy to get out of". Calvin's understanding of freedom means freedom from all the unnecessary outward trappings of life. Our conscience frees us to rise above such restrictions and their stranglehold on us. The existing social order is only temporary and does not carry eternal validity.

Once again we are confronted with paradox. Yes, we may disengage from "indifferent" matters, but, as Dirkie Smit warns, this "does not disengage believers from history itself, from the wisdom of tradition and community as such, from the need to live in community with others, or in [Calvin's] own words, to belong not to oneself". This is probably what Martin Luther meant when he said: "The Christian is perfectly free lord of all, subject to none; the Christian is a perfectly dutiful servant of all, subject to all." After all is said and done, it is the mystery of God's grace that meets us in history, in our ways of being and doing that have been shaped over millennia.

This third aspect of Calvin's idea of freedom is pretty revolutionary and particularly appealing when related to gender restrictions in the church and society today. In his time the superiority of men over women was a given. One cannot say that Calvin was, in all respects, alive to gender discrimination. Yet, in historical theologian Jane Dempsey Douglas's opinion, his way of "dealing theologically with the public role of women is an unusual and intriguing one for the sixteenth century, [and] probably genuinely innovative". For instance, Calvin does argue that Paul's teaching on women being silent in church is a matter of human governance, not an eternal law that binds the conscience. Douglas comments: "Calvin appears to be very much aware that women's role in church and society is being debated, and he struggles far more than one might expect with the problems raised by the biblical texts that teach women's subordination in the church."

Calvin's contribution to the Protestant Reformation of the sixteenth century was a potent force in the subsequent political ferment in Europe's struggles for social democracy and human freedom. Douglas argues that this theology of freedom not only proved enduring, but paved the way for generations of "freedom fighters". Calvin's emphasis on the conscience of the individual and, in particular, on the individual's freedom from the constraints of culture and tradition was certainly decisive in the choices made by my Huguenot forebears. Was theirs not a journey of "freedom from" to "freedom for" as they resisted constraints on their freedom of worship and sought new lives at the Cape? How tragic that so many descendants of the Huguenots forgot their heritage of "freedom from" and opted to support racist policies, forsaking their Calvinist roots!

~

"Freedom for" is much the same as "freedom to", which means the freedom to refer everything in life to God. Above all, "freedom from" and "freedom for" should relate to fears that stalk us and prevent the abundant life offered to us. Freedom from fear is the task of a lifetime. I know that in the first letter of John (4:18) we are told: "There is no fear in love, but perfect love casts out fear; for fear has to do with punishment, and whoever fears has not reached perfection in love." This is me, for I know fear. Of all the fears I have known, none has been as consuming or as testing as my fears for my children and now, my grandchildren. Nothing is guaranteed to keep me from sleep so easily as fear for or about a child. At first it was the fear of watching over a sick child, or the icy panic of not finding a child at an assigned meeting place, or the fear of insidious influences that could have terrible consequences. Watching my nine-year-old son's back arch from a bout of encephalitis is a different kind of fear from the helpless fearfulness of watching an adult child make costly mistakes. I need to remind myself that I too did not welcome advice from adults, and that the most effective lessons I have learnt have been through making mistakes! I can think of no better way to develop trust in God than by being a parent. My love for my children has not been an antidote for fear. Prayer has. And for this I give daily thanks.

Apart from "parent fear", what do most people long to be free from? Anxiety, fear of loss of control, loneliness, suffering, political and social oppression, lack of money and security, stigma and prejudice, sexism in church and society – the list is long. In a nutshell, most of what I want to be free from are the effects of human sin – my own and that of others. Sin restricts "freedom for". But I am loath to label all fear as sinful. After all, "The fear of the Lord is the beginning of wisdom" (Prov 9:10).

What would happen to us if we lost all fear? Our planet is on the cusp of collapse; rising energy and food prices threaten world stability; corruption and political conniving make us afraid of our future; more recently the world's financial systems plunged into an abyss through greed and mismanagement, and it is not easy to sleep well in the face of rampant criminality. These are fears that arise from social and personal situations and they can be pretty unnerving. If we were to lose all fear about the effects of the wrongs in the world, we would certainly have little reason to improve matters. South Africa is a society full of fear and violence. Living with fear is hard on our bodies. No wonder depression, alcoholism, eating disorders and drug addiction are prevalent. There cannot be a woman in South Africa today who does not live in fear of rape, or a mother who does not fear for her daughters. A culture of fear can paralyse our ability to deal with the evils of poverty, hunger, despair and the kind of aggression and violence that are common on our streets and in our homes.

I have, as yet, not acquired the freedom of perfect love. I wonder whether it is possible to do so – not to fear separation from those we love, from what we value, not to fear isolation and loneliness. Jesus knew the fear of abandonment when he prayed on the cross: "My God, my God, why have you forsaken me?" Dorothee Sölle writes: "The fear of being abandoned by God is the most profound fear of separation we can feel." I can think of no greater fear. There is, however, a profound difference between fear that is necessary for survival and fear that is gnawing and destructive, slowly eroding our ability to love, to act and to trust God. Such fear doubts the truth that God is present in our world and that we are never cut off from the sustaining warmth of God's love. The redemptive activity of God's Spirit moves us to acknowledge our need to depend on and trust God in all things. Faith accepts fear; but it does not leave it untouched. Faith transforms fear.

"The terror of death is death itself," says Martin Luther. Can we be free from the fear of dying? I ask this because in recent times I have had cause to think a great deal more about death and dying than before. Most of us, at some time or other, think we will live for ever. But, as the poet Philip Larkin (1922–1985) poignantly puts it:

Most things never happen: this one will,
And realisation of it rages out

in furnace-fear when we are caught without
people or drink.
Courage is no good; it means not scaring others.
Being brave
Lets no one off the grave.

At first, death was an intermittent reality for me. It started with the loss
of my grandmother; then a young friend died in a motorcar accident;
then, much later, I lost both my parents within a couple of years. As
Sölle writes: "Every person who is close to me who dies before me,
removes a peg from my own life's tent." Now at my age, death has
become a more normal part of life as friends die. I can no longer be
surprised by the news of death. In the words of Michael Kinsley: "[it]
is a faint dirge in the background but gradually gets louder."

Quite unexpectedly, some eight years ago, I was diagnosed with
cancer. I crossed a line. Life suddenly became finite. "It is death that
is spinning the globe [...] But about the topic of my own death I am
decidedly touchy," said Annie Dillard. I no longer have the luxury of
being touchy. A routine mammogram turned into the beginning of a
waiting game. When the formerly brusque radiographer's tone sof-
tened and she said: "Would you like a cup of tea?" I knew something
was different. From the radiologist to the surgeon and from the surgeon
to further scans – waiting in doctors' rooms, filled with magazines
of beautiful, healthy, young people, pursuing more beauty and more
health, I soon learned that I had to make decisions, a freedom I had not
sought. The first was to wait a month before having surgery in order to
go on the trip of a lifetime to the Galapagos Islands, something I have
never regretted doing. Then to the operating table; green gowns bend-
ing over me and waking to hear from our family doctor that the lump
was malignant. Then a further decision: postpone radiation in order
to go on a long-planned thirty-day retreat in Wales? Finally, after six
months, I jettisoned medication because it made me feel awful. With
every decision I have had to face my fears. Am I being responsible?
What if the cancer recurs because of my wrong choices? Am I able to
face death when I love life so much, when I revel in just being alive?

What do I fear most? Most of all, the fear of separation from those I love looms larger than before. The fear of death is the fear of loss of relationships. A prolonged bout with cancer is not without its own particular fears – fears of suffering, pain and loss. There is, however, nothing exceptional about cancer and its effects. It is but one of a long list of diseases we face. Cancer is no respecter of difference. Just half an hour in the oncologist's waiting room is sobering. Babies, athletic-looking youngsters, mothers with children, the middle-aged and the elderly, all of us waiting our turn, all hoping for words of comfort, all equal as we face our mortality.

Cancer is a school for living. After every check-up, scan, blood test and mammogram (thankfully all have been negative so far), I feel exultant and grateful. I look forward to another six months in which every single day is a blessing, filled with a fierce vigour "to do", a heightened awareness of the beauty of the day, and sharp joy at just being alive. I am now beginning to understand what philosopher Charles Taylor means when he writes that contemplating death "is the privileged site from which the meaning of life can be grasped".

Recently we moved to a retirement community. I am not yet ready for "assisted living" or for finally finding myself in a frail care centre. It may be inevitable, but not yet. I am grateful too that cancer is no longer covered in stigma – a synonym for death. No longer hidden in whispers, it creates its own community with its own vocabulary. I have found a new kind of sharing that I treasure.

My experiences of the last eight years have highlighted how the most powerful determinant of health is wealth. The "haves" always fare better than the "have nots", who have far fewer options. If you are poor, you are at the mercy of our imploding health system. You queue for hours for medication and care, often to be turned away and told to come again another day. Lack of drugs, indifferent standards of care, unhygienic even toxic conditions in hospitals, and a crippling brain drain of health professionals all contribute to the present dire situation. Infant mortality, lack of maternal care, drug-resistant tuberculosis and rampant HIV and AIDS are devastating the lives of those who cannot afford private treatment, because what is offered by the state often does not meet their needs. My health care is well funded and of a high standard. How does this make me feel? Guilty, angry, grateful? All of these, and all too often, helpless as well.

Denying death distorts reality in a futile effort to control life. Then life becomes a farce. Cultural anthropologist Ernest Becker (1924–1974) in his groundbreaking work, *The Denial of Death*, points out the irony of our condition – our deepest need is to be free of the anxiety of death and annihilation. But, he continues, "it is life itself that awakens it, and so we must shrink from being fully alive". What a dreadful paradox! I suspect that the way we face our death has a great deal to do with the way we live. Woe on us if we remain slaves to permanence. The reality of death should be so firmly part of our being that it permeates our living. French novelist Gustave Flaubert (1821–1880) said: "Everything must be learnt, from talking to dying." We have the freedom to talk about our "dying". Talking about my "dying" is choosing to understand my story, processing its contradictions and incomprehensibilities, knowing that I live, I die, I am remembered and then forgotten. I find comfort in the inevitability of this process, a kind of freedom from the tyranny of wanting to be remembered "forever".

For a long time I have been intrigued by the difference between the death of the Greek philosopher Socrates (born c.469–died c.399 B.C.E.) and the death of Jesus. Socrates could have escaped his death. Jesus could have helped Pilate out of his predicament. Yet both chose death. Socrates did not accept his friend Crito's advice to leave town and Jesus told Pilate, "You have no power over me." Both these men had their own understanding of death that was the logical outcome of the way they had lived their lives. Plato tells us that Socrates said: "True philosophers make dying their profession."

As a Greek, Socrates believed that all of life was a rehearsal for death and a process of perfecting the soul for the eternal. As he understood it, death can never kill the soul, but rather liberate it to return to where it came from. Socrates' choice to die was the logical outcome of his belief in the immortality of the soul. Jesus, unlike Socrates, did not face his death with equanimity. "Now my soul is troubled. And what shall I say – 'Father, save me from this hour'?" (Jn 12:27). Yet he was able also to say: "No, it is for this reason that I have come to this hour." Jesus' life and death were not opposites, but both belonged to and were subject to divine authority. Both were in God's hands. For the Greek, death is a friend and marks the transition of going to God. For the Hebrew, death is a natural limitation to our earthly life determined by God.

The reality of death confronts us with an immediate paradox. On the one hand, death's inevitability almost makes it a non-issue – it is final. German Jesuit theologian Karl Rahner (1904–1984) reminds us that we do "not share the incessant ebb and flow of the cycles of nature, which in appearance at least repeat themselves endlessly". Death disturbs easy answers to the meaning of life and brings us up against the limits of our beliefs – there is much we simply do not know. On the other hand, the response of faith to death is one of hope. Yes, we are utterly powerless in the face of death. Yet, we confess that we "[l]ook for the resurrection of the dead and the life of the world to come". Each of us will have to come to terms with what we mean when we utter these words. I only know that I hope out of my utter powerlessness, accepting that all of life is sustained grace active in creation. Life is a gift – an unmerited gift. The gospel guarantees that my hope is not a pipedream, but a present truth. I hope that life is found in Christ and his resurrection, and that there is continuity between life as we know it and what happens when we die. I do not know what this means; I have no programme for life after death. I hope that in some utterly unknowable way I will be with Christ.

There is no defined theology of death in the Bible, and the belief in life after death is quite a late development. It is not that the Bible takes death lightly, but the main concern of the scriptures is life. Life is good; life is to be embraced. Life is the greatest gift we have from God. Life is a blessing. It is God's breath that gives life to all that lives and, if it is withdrawn, we are reduced to nothingness. The psalmist (104:29b) says: "when you take away their breath, they die and return to their dust". Death is a part of life – it is simply an aspect of our existence before God. The Hebrews saw life as an expression of their relation to God. God is the fountain of life. A long life is a ful-filled life (Gen 15:15, Judg 8:32, Job 42:17). But it is not all clear-cut. Ambiguity and paradox are not absent. God gives life, upholds life, yet God returns human beings to dust. Death is human and natural; yet death can be a threat to life or even a sign of judgment (Gen. 2:17; 3:19). Death could be the dark side of blessing. In the final analysis, God desires life and not death, and death has no inherent significance in itself. God's power extends beyond it.

Jesus says little about death. He is silent when John the Baptist is beheaded. He says nothing about the death of innocent children. I cannot think that children were not victims of accidents or disease in his day as they are in ours. He does, however, weep at the death of his friend Lazarus and he expresses compassion for a grieving widow whose son has died. When faced with his own death, he sees it as an act of obedience. Most of his teaching is about life in faith. "For those who want to save their life will lose it, and those who lose their life for my sake will save it" (Lk 9:24).

The resurrection of Jesus brings the nascent Christian commu-nity a new perspective on life. The power of death is challenged. It is final, but not final. It is also a beginning of something new: in Christ, we are a new creation. Christians claim that life after death is made possible by being one with Christ. "But God, who is rich in mercy, out of the great love with which he loved us even when we were dead through our trespasses, made us alive together with Christ – by grace you have been saved – and raised us up with him and seated us with him in the heavenly places in Christ Jesus …," says Paul (Eph 2:4-6). The belief that human beings can transcend death and enjoy eternal life with God puts a new gloss on death.

Death raises the question of the character of God. What kind of God do we have? Does God give us life for a tiny span of time and that is it? Does God, whom we believe loves us, do so only for the years allotted to us on earth? Human beings are created to be in relationship with God. Does our relationship with God come to an end when we die? When we confess our belief in life everlasting, what sort of life do we have in mind? Can it mean that we trust that God holds us in love in some way or other for eternity? I have no clear answers to these questions. Mortality is a condition of human life. I will die, but, deep down, I believe that God wishes eternal relationship rather than eternal death. I have no idea what this means, but I have faith that there is more to life than our time here.

I have signed a living will, because the futility of medically sustaining life when it is, in fact, over seems to me to be the ultimate expression of human hubris. The advances of medicine have often, paradoxically, resulted in loss of dignity for the terminally ill. Every human being has the right to die with dignity. We also have a right to expect truthfulness from our medical carers. I cannot condone medical gadgetry used to prolong life that is actually over.

I have been baffled, even angry, when good people die untimely deaths and I rail against human suffering prolonged by devastating physical and emotional pain. In the words of American poet and playwright Edna St Vincent Millay (1892–1950):

Down, down, down, into the darkness of the grave,
Gently they go, the beautiful, the tender, the kind;
Quietly they go, the intelligent, witty, the brave.
I know. But I do not approve.
And I am not resigned.

I have no neat theology that offers complete freedom from the fear of death and dying. I do know that life is on loan. When my body becomes uninhabitable, I want to remember how "the Lord your God carried you, just as one carries a child, all the way that you have travelled until you reached this place" (Deut 1:31). May I believe as I reach the end, that God is in the midst of death. I want to accept the rhythm of life – from the vulnerability of youth, to the frailty of old age that relates me to all living creatures.

Dylan Thomas (1914–1953) wrote a poem for his dying father:

Do not go gentle into that good night,
Old age should burn and rage at close of day;
Rage, rage against the dying of the light.
Though wise men at their end know dark is right,
Because their words had forked no lightning they
Do not go gentle into that good night.

Having been a doer all my life, I will not find being powerless easy. I may be tempted to rage against the dying of the light. Becoming helpless in the process of dying is difficult for us doers. But I am learning that being wholly dependent on the love of Christ is my guarantee of ultimate freedom. When all is said and done, I hope that death signals a kind of homecoming into the all-embracing arms of the Ultimate Being, in which every experience of grace, mercy and love coalesce into an eternal reality.

To believe in God means to accept that we are affirmed, desired and held in love. In Sölle's words: "There is nothing that can battle death except love [...] Speaking in Christian terms, death is always behind us, but love is before us." I hope I shall use my freedom to trust in the faithful love of the Holy One, that I shall know that relationship continues for ever, and that all of life is in God's hands, every stage of it up to its final moments and beyond. Paul's words comfort me:

Who will separate us from the love of Christ? Will hardship, or distress, or persecution, or famine, or nakedness, or peril, or sword? No, in all these things we are more than conquerors through him who loved us. For I am convinced that neither death, nor life, nor angels, nor rulers, nor things present, nor things to come, nor powers, nor height, nor depth, nor anything else in all creation, will be able to separate us from the love of God in Christ Jesus our Lord (Rom 8:35, 37-39).

Both death and the life to come are included in Paul's list. This tells us that the entire span of human life from birth to death and beyond is enclosed in the comprehensive love of God in Christ. I like the words of the prophet: "Then you shall see and be radiant; your heart shall thrill and rejoice" (Is 60:5). I will hang on to them, hoping to be surprised along the way beyond what any words can say.

"Freedom from" is not enough. "Freedom for" is the key to an unconstrained life. We have freedom to have faith in God or not. For those who choose to believe in God, mirrored for us in the person and life of our man on the borrowed donkey and mediated for us through the Spirit, freedom translates into "freedom for others". This promises us freedom from what shackles us, so that we may live in fullness with God and with others. Being "free for" is to be fully in God's hands, no matter what life throws at us. Being "in God's hands" is simply a metaphor for a trusting love affair that is central to our existence, and is expressed in our relationship with God, ourselves, with others and with the world in which we live. We are "free for" others because being in "God's hands" has enabled us to live out our freedom, both inwardly and outwardly.

What would "freedom for" look like? The first word that comes to mind is "abundance". As we free ourselves from constraints, we discover a sense of fullness, wholeness, and the desire to share our bounty. We become free for others because our personal freedom cannot remain individual. We are not truly free if we hold what we think is our freedom close to our chests. Then we are still in a controlling mode. But once we have tasted "freedom from" and are able to let go of what fetters us from living fully as human beings, we desire to share this experience with others. At the same time, others who have also found "freedom for", desire to share their newfound freedom with us. Then communities of free people take root and we partake in shared "abundance".

A second word that comes to mind is "hope". Being "free for" is to live with hope, because we know hope ourselves. Faith brings hope. Hebrews 11:1 describes the relationship between faith and hope: "Now faith is the assurance of things hoped for, the conviction of things not seen." Freedom in faith rests solidly on the belief that God has given us our freedom, that we have to accept and enjoy it, and that we dare to hope and trust that we can move beyond all that limits our freedom into a space that is filled with a lightness of being which we call "freedom". Then we can become communities of hope.

Third, to be "free for" is to be free to love my neighbour as my-self. Away with contorted, self-serving images of love! The balm of healthy love of self is the joyful acceptance that we are valued and loved by God. We see our neighbours as persons loved by God – able to love themselves and to love us. Being free for love of others is a merry-go-round of loving relationships, expressed by sharing with and caring for one another.

There are many examples of communities of people who bring hope through acts of love to others in remarkable ways, thus making "free-dom for" visible and possible. I have my favourites, like *Médicins sans Frontierès* (Doctors without Borders). This organisation, established in 1971, describes itself as an "international, independent, medical humanitarian organisation" that gives assistance regardless of race, nationality, gender or political affiliation. For years I have followed their work in different parts of Africa, from the townships surrounding Cape Town to the conflict zones of Sudan and Somalia. Of course the doctors and nurses as well as the non-medical experts that make up this organisation must at times fear for their safety. Often their work is conducted in war zones. They have, on occasion, become victims of the senseless violence in the places where they work. Sometimes they are the last to leave when the lives of aid workers are under threat. And yet, their dedication to their vision speaks of a kind of freedom against the odds, and enables them to be present for others, alleviating pain, performing field operations, providing water and sanitation, and consoling those who are frightened and needy. Their devoted acts of charity bring hope and healing in situations of dire need.

Then there is the Saartjie Baartman Centre (SBC) for Women and

Children in Cape Town – a one-stop centre for women and children who are survivors of abuse. Its work is more than timely. It is vital to counteract the abuse, rape, and other forms of physical violence against women and children that are prevalent in our country – a deeply shameful indictment of South African male attitudes. In a survey conducted in 2009 by the Medical Research Council in the Eastern Cape and KwaZulu Natal, twenty-eight per cent of men interviewed admitted to having raped someone with about half having done so more than once (*Cape Times* 19.06.09). For this study, researchers had interviewed seven hundred and thirty-nine men of all socio-economic backgrounds and ages, from both rural and urban areas. The chief researcher found that many of those interviewed did not think that they had done anything wrong! Commenting on the prevalence of the patriarchal view of sexual entitlement found by this research, Mbuyelo Botha, senior programme advisor at Sonke Gender Justice, a non-governmental organisation that also works with abused women, said: "It is also in our social institutions, such as the church or mosque, which reinforce the notion of the superiority of men."

The SBC provides shelter for women fleeing abuse: it offers short- and medium-term residential care, counselling services, legal advice and skills training. The organisation's vision is the "creation of a safe and secure society and a human rights culture where women and children are empowered to exercise their full rights". Harbouring those whose freedom has been violated and providing a space for them to recover their dignity as worthy human beings, is, in my view, being a conduit for a kind of "freedom for" that signals a new beginning in the lives of the women and children who turn up on their doorstep. Their work helps victims of violence to let go of fear and to find hope.

Lastly, and with some hesitancy, I want to mention the small church community to which I belong. We are a modest parish of some three hundred and fifty persons, mostly middle class, in whom I find notable pockets of freedom for others. Through the liberating message of the gospel, people are empowered to bring hope and support to the needy – feeding the poor at a soup kitchen, packing "love packs" for those suffering from HIV and AIDS, tirelessly raising money to fund scholarships for needy children, or to help orphanages and day-care centres – the list is long. Dedicated members of this community raise half a million rand a year to give away to these needy causes. Money does not give freedom, but committed care for others brings relief from hunger, poverty and need, and can provide a kind of "freedom for" both to those who give and those who receive. When there is faith that creation itself will "be set free from its bondage to decay and will obtain the freedom of the glory of the children of God" (Rom 8:21), we are able to care about the needs of others, and to be active in this caring. This is what "freedom for" is about. Christian freedom is being free for others. This Jesus showed us.

Jesus lived as one who was free for others. His freedom was to do the will of God, willingly, lovingly and, hopefully, cheerfully. He was a truly free human being. If I have any doubts about what it means to be free for others, I have only to look at his life. His freedom was defined by faithful obedience to God in service of others. He did not fear the social constraints of his day, nor the power of the religious and political authorities of his time. He did not fear being polluted by what He ate or by people with diseases. He touched the lepers and ate with the outcasts. He was the most accessible of persons: a woman from Samaria, a Pharisee, a tax collector, possessed people, children, the poor and marginalised – He valued them all. He was not constrained by ideologies, either religious or political. Neither was He a slave to the social conventions of his day. Because He was truly free, He heard and obeyed only the voice of God. Jesus was a human being so fully alive that He could embrace the whole world.

Jesus shifted the consciousness of his followers from a model of domination to one of service when He washed their feet. This menial, even startling undertaking was an inversion of existing social relations. Servants washed the feet of their masters. No wonder Peter reacts sharply: "You will never wash my feet!" (Jn 13:8). Jesus' act is a powerful yet simple repudiation of the dominance of master over slave. On the cross Jesus gives the final deathblow to the old ways of dominance. He chooses death in order to create new life – a life free from the old models. To be in communion with others is to be free to love others as I should love myself. To be in communion with others is to accept the freedom given to us in Christ. Then we know: "So if anyone is in Christ, there is a new creation: everything old has passed away; see, everything has become new!" (2 Cor 5:17). To be "in Christ" is to know the freedom of living abundantly as an indispensable member of the Body of Christ.

Faith in God holds the promise of a free life. I can say this because I believe that our source and our end is God in Christ through the Spirit. Freedom in faith is, in the first place, "freedom *from*" all that undermines the ultimate meaning of our lives. We are free from having to find the ultimate ground of our lives in something other than God. For the same reason "freedom *for*" – literally freedom for ourselves and for the world – is also the fruit of faith. We are free to do the works of love. We become "free for" others. Such is the blessing of freedom. Augustine and the Reformers taught that humanity is caught in a self-imposed form of slavery. We have misused and perverted our freedom. The Christian gospel promises redemption and restoration of freedom, fulfilled in relationship with God. This happens through grace. Grace is the fundamental form of God's relationship with us. Grace restores freedom – a gracious gift from God who offers us the ability to be "free for others". This is a blessing to be treasured.

NOTES

Madiba is Nelson Mandela's Xhosa clan name derived from a Thembu chief who ruled the Transkei in the eighteenth century. The use of a clan name is not only respectful, but it is more important than a surname as it refers to the ancestors from whom a person is descended. Nelson Mandela was more than the first president of a democratic South Africa. He was a man who, at great personal cost to himself, devoted his life to the cause of justice. He championed the human dignity of all persons, the reconciliation of a deeply divided society and the achievement of a constitutional democracy. His courage, great personal charm, and unwavering principles laced with compassion made him a towering world icon.

Of interest on the theme of a Christian vision for a free, just and equitable society, see a recent document entitled *Theological and Ethical Reflections on the 2012 Centenary Celebrations of the African National Congress* compiled by KairosSA. In its early days, the vision of the ANC for this country was shaped by values shared by Christians. This is no longer the case. Today many Christians are profoundly concerned about, among others, issues such as deepening poverty, the failing education system, corruption in the ranks of the powerful, and the extravagant wastage of resources by those in power. This document, which will hopefully be signed by a million people, raises these and other concerns, and cautions the government in prophetic terms.

See Ngoy Daniel Mukuda-Nyanga's *The Reconstruction of Africa: Faith and Freedom for a Conflicted Continent* (Nairobi: All Africa Conference of Churches, 1997) for a helpful guide to linking African struggles for democratic freedoms and the church's ministry of reconciliation across deep divisions.

For a reading of Reformed theology as liberating theology, see John de Gruchy's book, *Liberating Reformed Theology*. In this work, a trenchant analysis is given of Afrikaner Calvinism. He writes:

> Not all Afrikaners are Calvinists; neither is the theology of the Dutch Reformed Church to be equated with Afrikaner Calvinism. Afrikaner Calvinism is the particular ideological blend of various sources that emerged within the Dutch Reformed Church in the late 19th century, and that dominated its life during the heyday of Afrikaner nationalism and apartheid in the 20th century. While it is an aberration of Calvinism and is repudiated by many Dutch Reformed theologians today, Afrikaner Calvinism remains a potent force within right-wing Afrikanerdom, where it is still invoked to give apartheid and Afrikaner nationalism divine sanction [...] The Reformed tradition in South Africa is thus guilty of a twofold sin: it failed to prevent apartheid and it succeeded in sanctifying it. It aligned itself with an ideology of group interest. It failed to set the agenda for a society consonant with biblical norms, to align itself with the interest of the disadvantaged and therefore to hear 'the cry for life.'"

The quotation from W. H. Auden is taken from *The Age of Anxiety: A Baroque Eclogue*, ed. A. Jacobs (Princeton: Princeton University Press, 2011). See also http://www.mbird.com/2009/12/from-wh-audens-age-of-anxiety/. For the line quoted from John Donne, see his *Meditations* (XVII).

There are those who, like Berlin, see freedom in entirely negative terms as being the absence of restraint. This does not mean that such thinkers are insensitive to the way in which such freedom is to be used. They do appreciate that freedom is not unlimited and that important values govern the way in which we should use and live out our freedom. However, they simply do not associate such values with freedom or as being a part of freedom.

Ubuntu is a classical African concept, the name of which is derived from African languages in our country. Desmond Tutu in *No Future without Forgiveness* describes it as follows: "A person with Ubuntu is open and available to others, affirming of others, does not feel threatened that others are able and good, for he or she has a proper self-assurance that comes from knowing that he or she belongs in a greater whole and is diminished when others are humiliated or diminished, when others are tortured or oppressed."

Christoph Schwöbel writes: "To say that freedom is the fundamental principle of understanding what it means to be human in the modern era is almost a platitude. But like some platitudes this one seems to have hidden depths which are well worth exploring. Among the three catchwords of the French Revolution, *liberté, égalité* and *fraternité, liberté,* freedom, is the one that has proved to be the dominant and historically victorious principle."

According to Paul Guyer, *Kant on Freedom, Law and Happiness* (Cambridge: Cambridge University Press, 2000), 96, "Kant constantly reiterates that freedom or autonomy and not happiness is the fundamental ground of moral value and object of moral endeavour, 'the inner value of the world.'" Kant also says that "the innate right to freedom", which is the sole ground of all rights, "belongs to every human being by virtue of his [sic] humanity." See *Metaphysics of Morals* 6:237, quoted from Allen W. Wood's *Kant's Ethical Thought* (Cambridge: Cambridge University Press, 1999):323.

Martin Luther thought that the essence of "original sin" resembled what modern existentialists call "anxiety". Here he differed from Augustine, who held that rebellious pride was not the problem, but was rather what Søren Kierkegaard later called "fear of freedom". This understanding was picked up in modern writers such as Albert Camus and Jean Paul Sartre: human beings are insecure and threatened by fear when faced with a multiplicity of choices in a hostile universe, and resort to what theologian Paul Tillich called "meaninglessness".

First published in 1536, the *Institutes of the Christian Religion* is John Calvin's magnum opus, a work that was important for the Protestant Reformation and has remained so for Protestant theology for over five centuries. Written to "aid those who desire to be instructed in the doctrine of salvation", the *Institutes*, which follows the ordering of the Apostle's Creed, is divided into four parts. The first part examines God the Father; the second part, the Son; the third part, the Holy Spirit, and the fourth part, the Church. Throughout these four parts, it explores both "knowledge of God" and "knowledge of ourselves" with profound theological insight. The section on human freedom quoted from the *Institutes* is found in Book III, Chapter IV, sections 3.19.1-3.19.15.

The Conference on the Theology and Spirituality of Denise Ackermann (see *Ragbag Theologies* in Works consulted, Pillay, Nadar and le Bruyns) at which Dirkie Smit read his paper on Calvin took place on 5 September 2008 at the University of the Western Cape.

The verse quoted from Philip Larkin is found in his poem "Aubade". See his *Collected Poems*, ed. A. Thwaite (London: Faber and Faber, 2003), 213.

Gustave Flaubert's quotation is taken from Julian Barnes's *Nothing to be Frightened of* (New York: Alfred A. Knopf, 2008), 187. Leo Tolstoy's *The Death of Ivan Illich*, written in 1886, is a literary classic that addresses the meaning and reality of death. It captures the reluctance of human beings to accept death.

For Edna St Vincent Millay's poem "Dirge without music", see *Collected Poems* (New York: HarperCollins, 1999), 79. Dylan Thomas's "Do not go gentle into that good night" is found in *Collected Poems of Dylan Thomas* (London: Orion Books, 2000), 148.

Saartjie Baartman (born before 1790–1815) was a Khoikhoi woman slave who was sent to London in 1810 to be a freak attraction because of her large buttocks and prominent sexual organs. She became known as the "Hottentot Venus" and was subsequently taken to Paris, once again as an exhibit. When her "attraction" waned, she was abandoned and died destitute, far from her homeland. In 2002 President Nelson Mandela asked the French government to return her remains. She was eventually buried in the Eastern Cape, her place of origin.

On the topic of violence against women and children, see the *Journal of Theology for Southern Africa*, special issue, no. 114, 2002, in particular the following contributions: Isabel Phiri, "Why Does God Allow Our Husbands to Hurt Us? Overcoming Violence Against Women", 19-30; Puleng LenkaBula, "From the Womb into a Hostile World: Christian Ethics and Sexual Abuse Against Children in South Africa", 55-68; Beverley Haddad, "Gender, violence and HIV/AIDS: A Deadly Silence in the Church", 93-106.

WORKS CONSULTED

Anderson, Ray S. *Theology, Death and Dying*. Oxford: Basil Blackwell, 1986.

Auden, W. H. *The Age of Anxiety: A Baroque Eclogue*. Edited by A. Jacobs. Princeton: Princeton University Press, 2011.

Augustine. *Confessions*. Translated by H. Chadwick. Oxford: Oxford University Press, 1991.

Barnes, Julian. *Nothing to be Frightened of.* New York: Alfred A. Knopf, 2008.

Becker, Ernest. *The Denial of Death*. New York: The Free Press, 1973.

Berlin, Isaiah. *Four Essays on Liberty*. Oxford: Oxford University Press, 1984.

Berlin, Isaiah. *The Crooked Timber of Humanity: Chapters in the History of Ideas*. London: Fontana Press, 1991.

Calvin, John. *Institutes of the Christian Religion*. 1536 edition. Translated by F. L. Battles. Grand Rapids: Eerdmans, 1986.

Cavanaugh, William T. *Being Consumed: Economics and Christian Desire*. Grand Rapids: Eerdmans, 2008.

Chopp, Rebecca. *The Power to Speak: Feminism, Language, God*. New York: Crossroad, 1991.

Cornell, Drucilla. "The recognition of ubuntu." In *Ubuntu and the Law in South Africa: Indigenous Ideals in Post Apartheid Jurisprudence*. Manuscript in possession of the author for forthcoming publication.

Couture, Pamela D. *Blessed are the Poor? Women's Poverty, Family Policy and Practical Theology*. Nashville: Abingdon, 1991.

De Gruchy, John W. *Liberating Reformed Theology: A South African Contribution to an Ecumenical Debate*. Grand Rapids: Eerdmans, 1991.

Douglas, Jane Dempsey. *Women, Freedom and Calvin*. Philadelphia: The Westminster Press, 1985.

Gooch, Paul W. *Reflections on Jesus and Socrates: Word and Silence*. New Haven: Yale University Press, 1995.

Gunton, Colin E., ed. *God and Freedom: Essays in Historical and Systematic Theology*. Edinburgh: T. and T. Clark, 1995.

Gunton, Colin. "God grace and freedom." In *God and Freedom*, edited by C. Gunton, 119–133. Edinburgh: T and T Clark, 1995.

Guyer, Paul. *Kant on Freedom, Law and Happiness*. Cambridge: Cambridge University Press, 2000.

Haddad, Beverley. "Surviving the HIV and AIDS epidemic in South Africa: Women living and dying, theologising and being theologised." *Journal of Theology for Southern Africa*, no. 131 (2008): 47-57.

Ignatieff, Michael. *Scar Tissue*. New York: Penguin, 1993.

Johnson, Luke T. *Faith's Freedom: A Classic Spirituality for Contemporary Christians*. Minneapolis: Fortress Press, 1990.

Jones, Serene. *Feminist Theory and Christian Theology: Cartographies of Grace*. Minneapolis: Fortress Press, 2000.

Journal of Theology for Southern Africa, special issue, no. 114 (2002).

Larkin, Philip. *Collected Poems*. Edited by A. Thwaite. London: Faber and Faber, 2003.

Kingsley, Michael. "Mine is longer than yours." *New Yorker*, 7 April, 2008.

Makuda-Nyanga, Ngoy Daniel. *The Reconstruction of Africa: Faith and Freedom for a Conflicted Continent*. Nairobi: All Africa Conference of Churches, 1997.

Mandela, Nelson. *Long Walk to Freedom*. London: Abacus Books, 1995.

Pillay, M., S. Nadar, and C. le Bruyns, eds. *Ragbag Theologies: Essays in Honour of Denise M. Ackermann, A Feminist Theologian of Praxis*. Stellenbosch: Sun Press, 2009.

Rahner, Karl. *On the Theology of Death*. New York: Herder and Herder, 1965.

Schwöbel, Christoph. "*Imago Libertatis*: Human and divine freedom." In *God and Freedom*, edited by C Gunton, 57–81. Edinburgh: T and T Clark, 1995.

Smit, Dirkie. "Freedom in belonging? Calvin on human freedom and the Christian life." Paper given at the Interdisciplinary and International Conference on Concepts of Freedom in the Biblical Traditions and Contemporary Contexts, FFF-Zentrum, Dusseldorf, Germany, 19-22 April, 2007.

Smit, Dirkie. "Simple and straightforward? On doing theology." In *Ragbag Theologies : Essays in Honour of Denise M. Ackermann, A Feminist Theologian of Praxis*, edited by M. Pillay, S. Nadar and C. C. le Bruyns, 157–174. Stellenbosch: Sun Press, 2009.

Sölle, Dorothee. *The Strength of the Weak: Toward a Christian Feminist Identity.* Translated by R. and R. Kimber. Philadelphia: Westminster Press, 1984.

Sölle, Dorothee. *The Mystery of Death.* Translated by N. and M. Lukens-Rumscheidt. Minneapolis: Fortress Press, 2007.

St Vincent Millay, Edna. *Collected Poems.* New York: HarperCollins, 2011.

Thomas, Dylan. *Collected Poems of Dylan Thomas.* New York: New Directions Publishing Corporation, 2010.

Tutu, Desmond. *No Future without Forgiveness.* London: Rider, 1999.

Wood, Allan, W. *Kant's Ethical Thought.* Cambridge: Cambridge University Press, 1999.

CHAPTER FIVE

Blessed are those who listen with discernment, for they will hear "the sound of sheer silence"

When I was twelve years old, I compiled a list of all the places I wanted to see one day. My source was the National Geographic magazine, a publication to which I still subscribe. It was a pretty ambitious list: Machu Pichu, the Great Wall of China, the Grand Canyon, the plains of Serengeti, the Galapagos Islands, the pyramids of Egypt, the Aztec temples, glaciers in Alaska, the Darwin Straits, the Hermitage Museum, king penguins in Antarctica, Angor Wat and others I cannot remember. The excitement of travel and of seeing exotic places prompted my childish daydreaming and, I suppose, my adult determination to make my dreams a reality. I wanted to *see*, and in seeing to experience and to wonder. I am supremely a "seeing" person, with lusty eyes.

Books are even more pivotal to my being than the desire to see faraway places. Ever since I could read, I have continuously fed my passion for books, albeit indiscriminately at times. If desperate, I will read anything. I cannot go to sleep without reading. The reason reading is so central to my existence is, I suppose, a combination of a habit acquired through a lonely, displaced childhood, a love of good fiction, and an appetite for knowledge. Reading is my life. Well, perhaps, not entirely, but it *is* central to my being.

What would it be like not to be able to see or to read a book? This is no idle question. A few years ago I realised that my sight was diminishing and I was diagnosed with macular degeneration. For a while my world fell apart. I could not imagine what it would be like not to be able to read, enjoy the cinema and the theatre, or to gaze at the vivid colours of a carmine bee-eater. As far back as I can remember, I have been aware of the wonders of creation – the stamen of a tiny veld flower, or the shapes of lichens seen through a magnifying glass, the night sky over the Namibian desert or the bright reddish eye ring of our local oyster catcher. I am passionate about birds, their shapes, colours, flight patterns and habits, and watching them through my binoculars is an enduring thrill. Evagrius Ponticus tells of a certain member of what was then considered the circle of the wise who approached Anthony of Egypt and asked him: "How do you ever manage to carry on, Father, deprived as you are of the consolation of books?" He replied: "My book, sir philosopher, is the nature of created things, and it is always at hand when I wish to read the words of God." What will it be like when I am no longer able to "read the words of God" in creation?

I felt angry at God. Was this some divine trick to take away my enjoyment of books, outings and nature in order to "teach" me something I was too stubborn to learn otherwise? But reason and my understanding of my faith said this is not who God is! However, my heart could not follow my head. I raged at my eyes and at God. I consulted more specialists, hoping for a different opinion. I cancelled a sabbatical and retreated into a raw shell of despair. Anything other than blindness seemed preferable. Could I not be deaf instead?

It took a thirty-day silent retreat to purge me of my anger and absurd images of my God. I can now give thanks every morning for the gift of sight, while knowing that I am only one among many facing drastically impaired vision. I can give thanks too for ears that can still hear, while at the same time I am more conscious of those who are deprived of hearing. But I still wonder – can hearing a Bach cantata ever compensate for the loss of seeing the smile of a grandchild?

My eyesight is deteriorating, but what I see is incalculably memorable. What awaits me will not be easy, but I now feel that it might just be all right. "All right" means I will be able to bear what comes and that I may even be surprised. Perhaps, when my sight goes, I may just "see" differently and that "seeing" will be something more than what the eye can tell me. Is this whistling in the wind, a bit of brave blather? I hope not, for something has changed lately. Sounds have become more acute, more filled with meaning. I listen more intently than before. I am slowly learning that seeing can make place for a new way of listening, that hearing the inner movements of the Spirit is a different way of "seeing" and a new-found blessing.

I feel a bit like an explorer entering unknown territory, a place unlike any other I have known before, stripped of what I normally rely on, without a map, a timetable or an itinerary, as the progress of degeneration proves unpredictable. In her quirky book *Travelling Mercies*, writer Anne Lamott says:

> Keep walking, though there's no place to get to.
> Don't try to see through the distances.
> That's not for human beings.
> Move within, but don't move the way fear makes you move.

What lies ahead will require more than I dare to think of, and the darkness that confronts me is not simply the darkness of a metaphor mouthed by teachers of medieval spirituality. But I hope to "move within", for I cannot submit to the menace of meaninglessness or let fear dictate my life. Explorers often find that they discover their true identities as they trudge along. Christian philosopher Beatrice Bruteau says: "The work of prayer is to transform our identity." Will exploring new territories require more prayer? Will this new identity be that small white stone mentioned in Revelations 2:17 on which is written a new name that no one except me will know?

～

The Latin derivation of "obedience" is *ob-audire*, to listen. This is sobering. Are listening and obeying really the same? Bit by bit I am finding out that the capacity to listen discerningly, and then to heed what I hear is something from which I dare not stray. In this listening I am finding new meaning for my life in the person of Jesus. No amount of talking or thinking about God is a substitute for this kind of listening. We are made to be listeners. We listen to the gospel stories that tell of a man who lived long ago in Palestine. We listen to one another, to our traditions, and we are attentive to the gifts of the Spirit found throughout creation, in community, in experiences of love and hope, courage, power and comfort.

One of the most universal factors that identifies us as Christians is that we read the Bible. Although few of the early or medieval Christians were able to own a Bible, nevertheless the Bible was read regularly in their churches. They were listening communities. Today, whether we live in squatter camps on the edges of our townships or in comfortable homes in the suburbs, in equatorial Africa or the frozen wastes of northern Canada, and whether we worship in cathedrals, mud huts, under trees or in village churches, we all read the Bible or have it read to us. We listen to the biblical texts not merely to imbibe information or to instruct, but as an invitation to gather as communities of pilgrim people who travel with our eyes on the man on the borrowed donkey.

For a long time I have been drawn to a riveting story in the first book of Kings 19:1–18. The prophet Elijah flees to the wilderness in fear of Jezebel's threats. Miserable, afraid and alone, he wants to die. Instead he falls asleep. He is woken by an angel who, after feeding him, sends him off to Mount Horeb for forty days and forty nights. God has plans for him. He is told to stand on the mountain "for the Lord is about to pass by". What does Elijah expect will happen? I wager he thinks he will *see* something of God. But God is not in the great wind that splits mountains and rocks; neither is God in the earthquake and the fire that follow the wind. No, God is in "a sound of sheer silence". Elijah wraps his face in his cloak and stands at the entrance of the cave to receive and carry out God's wishes for the Israelites.

"A sound of sheer silence"? I cannot know what this means save to say that it is an inexplicable event full of paradox and mystery; a different reality is "heard" and obeyed. I do not want to use the word "mystery" carelessly. Benedictine Sister Jeremy Hall describes mystery as follows:

> By mystery I mean the inexhaustibly intelligible, the endlessly alluring, the depth of reality that invites us to enter again and again, to penetrate deeper and deeper, and that rewards us, not with a terminal or even a provisional solution, but with nourishment for our minds, our hearts, our spirits. God is mystery; the human person is mystery; love, whether marital or parental, the love of friendship, or divine love is mystery; beauty is mystery, we ourselves are mystery to ourselves.

I fear a world that rejects mystery altogether because we cannot accept that there are things we cannot understand. According to our scriptures, God created with one fruitful phrase, "Let there be ..." – that is all. The word "mystery" describes what I feel about Elijah hearing "a sound of sheer silence" or when I am baffled by "I slept but my heart was awake" in the Song of Solomon 5:2. Clearly there are moments in the life of faith that are inexplicable, filled with incomprehensible love and grace. They cannot be conjured up, asked for or repeated. They are beyond us. However, their effects linger for a lifetime, and when we carry these experiences over into our relationships through loving and just actions, they do not constitute simple individualistic "soul massaging", but become moments of healing and revelation.

~

We speak more easily in prayer than we listen. Prayer is a time for both speaking and listening. To begin with, I find it difficult to truly "hear" if I am not in a hearing environment. This requires quiet. My idea of hell is to be trapped in a motor car that blares hard rock on its stereo loudspeakers. I remember attending a church service in Cape Town at the invitation of a student. As I entered the church, I was overwhelmed (and amused) by a ten-piece band strumming out *Be still and know that I am God*! I am not good at tolerating noise. Equally, I struggle to be still and to hear in silence. However, I do know that silence is necessary in order truly to listen, and that wanting to "hear" means following the longing of my heart for God. Longing is my tool for seeking God in the silence.

The very word "longing" conjures up experiences of psychological and emotional hunger. We long for acceptance, for love, for companionship. We long for a kinder, more just world – no more conflict in our families, at work and across our borders. While cynicism and fatalism stifle longing and erode the possibility of longing being translated into acts that aim to bring change, the desire for something more continues to draw us.

I do not know where my longing for God comes from, other than from Godself. Can it be that God's longing for us is the source of ours for God? Is it God's grace that awakens this longing for intimacy in us because it is also God's longing? I have to believe this because otherwise I cannot, on any rational grounds, explain why I have spent most of my life pursuing my inner longing. Ever since human beings have been able to record their beliefs and experiences, they tell of a universal thirst: a search for that something "beyond", a desire for inner peace, freedom and meaning. Some may say that this reaching out to the "beyond" is simply a deep psychological need whose origins lie in early childhood and is later recast in spiritual terms. Others may dismiss it as an illusion, a huge joke played by and on a self-deceptive person. My only response is that it does not *feel* like a self-induced hoax, but more like a tool for human self-fulfilment. I cannot explain this incurable longing other than to say that it comes from deep within me. Maybe this is what Karl Barth terms "that incurable God-sickness" or what Augustine means when he says: "you have made us for yourself, and our heart is restless until it rests in you."

Israel was a small, politically insignificant group of people, yet their history became hugely significant because God's word of promise called them into being. They were a people called to respond to God in faith, to be obedient to the commandments and to worship

God; in other words, to be in relationship with God. Their history is a faltering progress fed by the longing for encounter with their God. The psalmists knew this longing. "O God, you are my God, I seek you, my soul thirsts for you: my flesh faints for you" (Ps 63:1). "As a deer longs for flowing streams, so my soul longs for you, O God" (Ps 42:1). Isaiah (26:9) cries out: "My soul yearns for you in the night, my spirit within me earnestly seeks you." But it was not their often fickle need for God, but rather God's faithful love for them that shaped Israel's history. They prayed, they hoped, they suffered and they acknowledged their powerlessness in the face of the might of their God. "In Israel's vigil the world also shares, because it epitomises a perennial human experience," says Maria Boulding, Benedictine nun and theologian.

Like the Israelites of old, coming face to face with our fragility prompts us to long for something else. The anonymous author of the *Cloud of Unknowing*, written in the latter half of the fourteenth century, knew this longing and just how fragile it is: "For now, if you wish to keep growing you must nourish in your heart the lively longing for God. Though this loving desire is certainly God's gift, it is up to you to nurture it. But mark this. God is a jealous lover. He is at work in your spirit and will tolerate no meddlers. The only other one he needs is you."

On the opening evening of a conference in Heidelberg, Germany, to celebrate the hundredth anniversary of the birth of renowned biblical scholar Gerhard von Rad (1901–1971), philosopher Hans-Georg Gadamer (then aged a hundred and one) stood up and said of Von Rad: "There was a silence in him that came out of a deep listening." Everyone who knew Von Rad attested to the truth of this statement. Being told one is a good listener is a compliment. Listening nurtures relationships. The willingness to really hear another can bridge differences. Yet, the idea that we can "listen" to God is often considered way out, spooky or even aberrant. But is this not what the "sound of sheer silence" is about?

We are made to listen. When Jews recite the *Shema Yisrael*, they begin with the call from Deuteronomy to listen to God: "Hear, O

Israel: the Lord is our God, the Lord alone … " (Deut 6:4-9. See also Deut 11:13-21; Num 15:37-41). Proverbs 8:34 reads: "Happy is the one who listens to me." Israel also knows that God hears because their God is one who listens to the people – their cries of distress, their longings, their needs. When a dispute arises over Moses' authority, "the Lord hear[s] it", comes down in a pillar of cloud and says "Hear my words", and settles the dispute between Miriam, Aaron and Moses (Num 12:1-9). When Hezekiah becomes sick to the point of death, "the word of the Lord" comes to Isaiah. "I have heard your prayer," says God (2 Kings 20:1-7).

As Christians we take the Word as our source. We read, study and reflect on the scriptures that frequently tell us to "hear the word of the Lord". We believe that Jesus is God's Word made human and his relationship with God is one of speaking and listening. Our reading and meditating on biblical texts is a particular kind of listening. We are prompted by our desire to "hear" the One with whom we long to be in relationship. Dwelling on the words, turning them over and chewing on them, listening inwardly for the prompting of the Spirit are acts of loving attention.

Nurturing my longing happens when I take time off, away from the busyness of daily chores. It happens in the silence of listening. What do I hear when I try to listen? Often there is nothing, except my own breathing and internal noise. Occasionally, very occasionally, "hearing" happens. Listening inwardly implies unlearning, letting go of what I think I know. I am an unfinished self: I know who I am, yet there is a "me", one that I do not really know. There have been moments when, while listening, I have detected that "sound of sheer silence", beyond "the great wind" of my own rattling thoughts, beyond "the earthquake" of my own desires, and below "the fire" of faith seeking an experience. My world is turned upside down. An unexpected, unsolicited and unwarranted something happens. A new awareness, a different insight forms in my consciousness and changes my reality.

This kind of listening necessitates a deliberate act of unlearning. It is not simply a case of sitting quietly and waiting, though being patient is essential. We cannot make Spirit-prompted insight happen. It is freely given, not manipulated. We think we know who we are and what we should experience. We have to abandon such thoughts, to dump all our presuppositions about ourselves and God. We should be prepared only to be surprised. We may have to enter a place devoid of comfort. We may well confront our meanness, conceit and unbelief. We will be stripped. "It is a full pleasure," says Julian of Norwich, "to our courteous Lord that a helpless soul comes to Him simply, plainly, homely." It may be difficult to see ourselves as "homely". I think Julian means that we homely creatures are simply ourselves, nothing more. Our worth, our dignity, our pettiness, our self-doubt and our holiness all make up our homeliness. We come as we are; we may even meet an "I" we never knew existed.

We listen partially and fitfully, and often do not want to hear. We fear that the word we hear will demand obedience that will fetter our freedom. Experience has taught me that listening for that sweet voice in silence is not a tyrannical call to some level of unattainable obedience. It is solely the call of incomparable love. In Thomas Merton's words: "My life is a listening, His is a speaking. My salvation is to hear and respond. For this, my life must be silent. Hence my silence is my salvation."

Listening implies waiting, and an openness to surprise. The root of prayer and of our whole life is an unconditional "Yes" to God even when we do not understand what is going on. The Spirit opens us to the kind of listening that hears and receives the Word of love. Our personal listening is our prayer. This may sound like a highly individualistic and self-centred activity. It should not, for this is only half the story. Prayerful listening makes no distinction between the public and the personal. We "listen" in order to act. Elijah heard that silent voice and obeyed by returning from the wilderness to anoint Hazael and Jehu kings over their territories in obedience to God's instructions. Our deeds are the touchstone of our listening. Saying "Yes" to God is made manifest in tangible actions for justice, peace and freedom.

What I do alone in silence has everything to do with how I

relate to others. We listen as members of a community of listeners. There is no private listening without public consequences. A community inhabits a common world that is mediated by meaning and motivated by values. However, a community is not a self-contained unit. Communities interface with one another within complex, pluralistic, multilayered structures. The church is not and cannot be a community untouched by the world around it, though there are strange manifestations of Christian community that wish to be so. Christians listen together to the Word and hopefully become more aware of the multilayered reality that makes community. The preparation for listening to God is listening to others. We join with people of faith throughout the ages, unknown believers of every age and place whose lives have been shaped and fed by the same Word. "The human condition is itself a privileged place for listening," says Boulding. Our listening is a privilege, for it is in the service of communal relationships.

Discerning listening requires silence. Effective silence needs solitude. The silence to which I am referring has its own being and its own reality. Syrian theologian Isaac of Nineveh (died c.700) said: "If you love truth, be a lover of silence … More than all things love silence; it brings you fruit that the tongue cannot describe. In the beginning we have to force ourselves to be silent. But then there is born something that draws us to silence. May God give you the experience of this 'something' that is born of silence." Being willing to be silent is an act of trust. Words are no longer necessary. We can let go of our preoccupation with "thinking about" and rest in a place of simple trust that in the "not knowing" there is Presence. Then words can return. "Words give way to silence and silence in turn gives birth to words. These words are that much deeper, coming as they do from the void," writes theologian Celia Kourie.

In today's world, silence and solitude seem luxuries, accessible only to some. Who can take time off to be silent in solitude, without jettisoning responsibilities, taking precious leave, losing income, or perhaps even endangering one's job? Going on a silent retreat is a privileged activity. What mother coping with the inevitable exhaustion of tending young children has the time or energy to go away on retreat? But there *are* ways of stripping silence and solitude of their trappings of privilege. The conflicts will remain: the ringing telephone; the daily demands of family and work, and the lack of time. However, in the small hours of the morning before the world awakes, there is time to listen, wait, and be welcoming to what may come. Silence and solitude are possible at home provided one has a place that is quiet, a Bible and half an hour for oneself. After the Gestapo had shut down the community at Finkenwalde, Bonhoeffer encouraged seminarians to continue the practice of daily meditation. He shared his conviction that "[...] daily, quiet attention to the word of God [...] even if it is only for a few minutes" becomes "the focal point of everything which brings inward and outward order into [one's] life".

English psychiatrist Anthony Storr's book, *Solitude: A Return to Self*, suggests that the capacity to be alone is an aspect of inner security built up in our early years. A clinging child is an insecure child who has no confidence that when mother leaves she will return. A child who has the capacity to be alone, first in the presence of the mother and then in her absence, is a child who can be in touch with and express her or his own inner feelings. Meaningful solitude can never be imposed. It simply has to be found. So why do we shy away from solitude? Probably for a number of reasons. We may fear being lonely or even bored. Boredom is the enemy of listening. If we crave action and cannot wait expectantly in silence, we will be disappointed. And, when we go into a place of silence, we discover that the real noise is within ourselves – and this we shy away from. Solitude is not loneliness. Loneliness is an ache. Solitude is refreshment. Solitude is creative silence. We all need times of solitude and we all need to risk just being quiet by ourselves. English Anglo-Catholic writer Evelyn Underhill (1875–1941) writes that in silence we are able to "contemplate our Christian treasure from inside".

I emphasise relationship, and rightly so. Relationship lies at the heart of existence. The capacity to be alone is not inimical to relationship, but rather a valuable resource to wean us momentarily from reliance on external stimuli and enable us to focus on changes in our inner attitudes. Such activity must surely be beneficial for our relationships – with God, ourselves, with others, and with our world. When we are able to be alone with ourselves, we are able to relate to others. "Nothing is more like God than silence," says Meister Eckhart. To be alone is to explore increased awareness and self-discovery. This I learnt from Desmond Tutu. Throughout very difficult and repressive times in the 1980s, when states of emergency swept over our country, the Arch (as he is affectionately known) faithfully took time off from his public activity against apartheid to pray and to mediate. On the one hand, he marched in the streets, lobbying, preaching, teaching and writing in the cause of justice. On the other, he prayed and he listened to God. He taught me that prayer and praxis are inseparable.

Completely "green" or uninitiated, with no real understanding of what I was letting myself in for, I went on my first retreat at a local convent many years ago. Those ten days were a baptism, not of fire, but rather of a painfully drawn-out confrontation with my own inner noise. I struggled to grow quiet and I continue to do so. I am not a natural.

Looking back on many different experiences of retreats (single days, eight to ten days at a variety of retreat centres here and abroad, a time at Shantivanam in Tamil Nadu, India, and a thirty-day retreat at a Jesuit centre in Wales), I know that I need to find solitude at least once a year by going on a retreat. The inner cacophony has barely diminished; I have known boredom and restlessness; I have resented indigestible food; I have been tempted to cheat and read a good book. One may ask why I persist with retreats. I can best answer this question by describing a fairly recent experience of a thirty-day retreat. But first, what *is* a retreat, and where does the idea of going away alone to pray come from?

Time-out is not an exclusively Christian practice. It is found in most world religions. Although I am familiar only with retreats in my tradition, I am aware of useful tips for quietening down, such as listening to one's own breathing and the practice of mindfulness as described by the Buddhist monk Thich Nhat Hanh. For Christians, the purpose of a retreat is to listen discerningly to the inner movements of the Spirit, coupled with a willingness to reappraise one's life and embrace the unexpected. A retreat is a time away from one's normal routine and everyday environment to a quiet place dedicated to prayer. For some, the very word "retreat" is problematic. We do not need to retreat from life, but rather to engage with it, they say. Others object to the idea of a retreat for it elevates those who are privileged to go on retreat above those who are unable to do so. No, a retreat is not an escapist activity. Yes, it is a privilege, and also a necessity. Going on retreat is not about having some sort of esoteric knowledge or experience away from the daily struggles of existence. I go on retreat to explore the following question: how can I live my faith, in my context today with myself and with others, in a way that is pleasing to God and involves all of me – my longing, my mind, my heart, and my allegiance?

Modern-day retreats have their origins in the ordering of monastic life. However, our scriptures often tell of solitary encounters with God. Moses was tending his sheep when he came to Horeb, the mountain of God, where his dramatic, if somewhat unnerving, encounter with God took place and changed the course of Israel's history (Ex 3). Elijah withdrew to the Wadi Cherith and stayed alone, fed by the ravens until he received instructions from God to go to Zarephath (1 Kings 17:1-9). Jeremiah, that stubborn and often despairing prophet, cried out: "Is there no balm in Gilead?" and then uttered his longing: "O that I had in the desert a traveller's lodging place, that I might leave my people and go away from them!" (Jer 9:2). This is his plea for solitude to come to terms with frustration at the intransigence of his people.

Jesus' need for times of withdrawal and quiet is our template for retreats. He began his ministry with forty days in the wilderness, dealing with hunger and being tempted to forsake his calling. This "wilderness" describes a place apart and forsaken, a place of testing and reflection that shaped Jesus' life. Again and again we are told that Jesus prayed alone. His need to pray was essential to his ministry of service. Jesus' life was as busy as anyone's today with considerably less privacy than most. Followed by crowds seeking miracles, hounded by disputes, surrounded by the poor and needy, he had no room of his own for early morning prayer. Yet he needed quiet to pray and was driven to seek solitude, often at night (Mt 14:23, Lk 6:12, Mk 1:35). He appears to have taught the apostles to do likewise. "Come away to a deserted place all by yourselves and rest awhile" (Mk 6:31). The numinous experience of the transfiguration took place away from the crowds "up a high mountain" (Mt 17:1-9). And then, at his most wrenching moments in Gethsemane, Jesus prayed in agony to submit to God's will by withdrawing "about a stone's throw" from his followers (Lk 22:41). Listening and responding to God's call on his life, he needed to retreat to places where he could be alone in prayer.

It is not easy to endure the inevitable emptiness that comes when we are still and alone. I hear birds, traffic, a car door slamming, and the cacophony of my own thoughts – anything but that mysterious whisper on the other side of silence. But I have learnt that waiting in silence is an act of love. I get no neat answers to problems or maps for life falling into my lap from on high. Whatever understanding occurs comes piecemeal, in fragments of insight, as layers of self-imposed clutter are peeled away. Waiting expectantly in silence and prayer is, in reality, one activity. Prayer happens in the silences. As Merton says: "Prayer then means yearning for the simple presence of God, for a personal understanding of his word, for knowledge of his will, and for the capacity to hear and obey him."

It is true that insight can occur dramatically, in a sort of road-to-Damascus way. On a visit to Syracuse I saw the place where according to popular legend, Archimedes rushed naked from the bathhouse exclaiming "Eureka!" (I have found it!). He had been thinking about a problem set him by King Hieron when, suddenly and unexpectedly, he found the answer. His insight was that of creative genius. What I have known is something different. It is an awareness that drops silently and unprompted into my consciousness and causes a radical shift in my perception of myself, others and God. I have no words to describe it other than to say that it is given, but not asked for; unexpected and not planned. The shift that takes place remains, and is always a movement towards greater wholeness in myself, and a sweet sense of the closeness of God.

If all this sounds easy, it is not. Taking time off for silent prayer is only the start. Obstacles, distractions and doubts then surface, seeking to torpedo my efforts at silent waiting. Obstacles are a sticky, persistent barrier to prayer. For instance, I know only too well that when my longing to "experience" God's love becomes the purpose of my prayer, it is an obstacle. "Feeling good" then becomes the goal of prayer instead of prayer being "ultimately the loving response – somehow made explicit – which accepts God's will to love", as Karl Rahner puts it. God takes the initiative; we wait with openness to whatever God has in store for us, accepting that whatever it may be, it will be an expression of God's love for us.

Another, and perhaps the greatest obstacle to prayer, is our refusal to acknowledge our spiritual poverty. If we cannot do this, we cannot pray. Everything, all I have and am, is from God. Every day, I need to be converted and begin again. My poverty is knowing that, of myself, I am without merit or achievements, yet I am loved unconditionally. Facing my poverty jolts me to depend utterly on God, but this does not happen easily. Anxiety and fear do not vanish overnight. However, I remind myself that there is nothing worth hanging on to, and that it is simply sensible to leave all to God. "There is nothing special in ourselves to love. We go out of ourselves, therefore, and rest in him who alone is our help," says Merton. He continues: "To really know our nothingness we must also love our nothingness. And we cannot love unless we can see that it is good. And we cannot see that it is good unless we accept it." Our greatest consolation is the truth that "we do not know how to pray as we ought". Ultimately it is God through the Holy Spirit who prays in and through us (Rom 8:26-27).

The experience of our own nothingness is not turning away in disgust from our mistakes and illusions, trying to separate ourselves from them. This kind of turning away from self is nothing more than false humility which, in reality, is saying, "I am worthless", whereas, in fact, we mean "I wish I were not what I am." This gets us nowhere and is a real obstacle to prayer. It signals dissatisfaction, discontent and unwillingness to come to terms with who we are. The acceptance of our spiritual poverty is the beginning of honest prayer.

Distractions are different to obstacles and I can claim to be an expert on them. My mind is wired for distraction. It jumps, ducks and dives, and dredges up irrelevancies. Untameable, it resists inner quietness. Driven by unattractive desires to control, it struggles to let go and just be. Fortunately, I know now that if one has never known distractions, one does not know how to pray. How can I be so sure? I pray because I hunger for God – a longing that is at a much more profound level of my being than all the superficial wanderings that surface in distractions. Yes, the distractions persecute me at times and so force me to pray more intently. In this sense, they are better instructors for prayer than all the clear and beautiful concepts my mind can muster. Distractions cannot be shaken off and it is useless trying to get rid of them. They are unavoidable in the life of prayer. I have learnt that it is silly to get into a knot about being distracted. It is better to accept distractions and let them take their share of one's prayer time, and, if one is able, to laugh at their persistence. Then it is possible to move on to direct attention to God, knowing that prayer is a gift, and that distractions will surface again. Fortunately, the disciples asked Jesus to teach them to pray (Lk 11:1-4). He did, and the Lord's Prayer is ours every time we need to pray.

The challenge of doubt surfaces when I am trying to pray. I have learnt that as faith deepens, so does doubt. "You cannot be a person of faith unless you know how to doubt. You cannot believe in God unless you are capable of questioning the authority of prejudice, even though that prejudice may seem religious," says Merton. Faith and doubt develop together. Doubt is no enemy of faith. The deeper one's awareness, the greater the level of distrust of conventional wisdoms and the more the questions arise. Since I have understood that questioning my beliefs is essential to growing in faith, I have welcomed doubt.

If this sounds contradictory, paradoxical, even alarming, remember that many of those who led saintly lives were plagued by darkness and doubt. Mother Teresa (1910–1997), who tended the poor in Calcutta from 1959 until her death, knew the darkness of feeling abandoned by God. Writing to a spiritual confidant, she wearily remarks on an absent Christ. "Jesus has a very special love for you," she assures him. "[But] as for me, the silence and the emptiness is so great that I look and do not see, listen and do not hear, the tongue moves [in prayer] but does not speak [...] I want you to pray for me [...]." Even before her sojourn in India, in conversation with an Archbishop, she says, "Where is my faith – even deep down right in there, there is nothing but emptiness and darkness [...] I have no faith – I dare not utter the words and thoughts that crowd in my heart and make me suffer untold agony."

I do not want to analyse her words or her frame of mind. Mother Teresa is not unique in her radical doubt. Her honesty about her darkness and doubt, while still calling on God in prayer, reminds me of Job. Such are the contradictions and paradoxes of the life of faith. Yet despite her doubt, Mother Teresa was still able to say:

The fruit of silence is prayer,
The fruit of prayer is faith,
The fruit of faith is love,
The fruit of love is service;
The fruit of service is love.

Doubts are to be spoken to God, unambiguously, hiding nothing, without any attempt to disguise or resort to pleasant, pious talk. Doubts force us to speak the truth in prayer. Doubt often takes on the guise of resistance – that familiar human reaction that leads us rather to make do with the devil we know than risk change.

Obstacles, distractions and doubts will surely surface when we take time off. However, there is much more to being on retreat than dealing with these problems. Retreats are, in essence, about prayerful encounter with the One who loves us and seeks to make a home in us (Jn 14:23). I have tried different ways of being on a silent retreat. What works best for me is a directed retreat in which I receive daily guidance from a spiritual director in a quiet place away from the busyness of my life. There I meditate on passages from scripture, learn to quieten my restless mind, and end by making notes in my journal. This is how I learn to listen responsively to the Bible. Karl Barth says that "[…] the Bible was not about the cultivation of a religious existence enriched by tradition, but solely about listening to God's voice." This reflective prayer is called *meditatio* or meditation in the Christian tradition.

There is a further way of relating to God in prayer. In recent times, monastic communities have brought the ancient Christian practice of *contemplatio* (contemplative prayer) to the fore. For the first fifteen hundred years of the Christian era this prayer was common and positively viewed. The monasteries taught *lectio divina*. Reading of the scriptures is *lectio.* The active part of *lectio* is *meditatio*, discursive meditation, followed by affective prayer called *oratio*. A third dimension of prayer is called *contemplatio* – a simple resting in the presence of God. These phases may all take place in the same prayer period, interwoven with one another. By the sixteenth century, meditation and contemplation were viewed as two separate forms of prayer, each with its own aim and method. Gradually the tradition of contemplation diminished. Trappist monk Thomas Keating reminds us: "The genius and contemplative experience of Ignatius of Loyola led him to channel the contemplative tradition, which was in danger of being lost, into a form appropriate to the new age." Ignatius's *Spiritual Exercises* combine the powers of memory, intellect, will and contemplation, including the use of imagination in prayer. The aim of the *Exercises* is contemplation in action.

Keating, whose work *Open Mind, Open Heart* is very helpful for understanding the dimensions of contemplative prayer, writes that this kind of prayer is not so much absence of thoughts as detachment from them. In the words of Evagrius: "Prayer is the laying aside of thoughts." Gregory the Great described it as knowledge of God that is impregnated with love. Contemplative prayer is based on the conviction that the Spirit is with us as we pray. This requires a certain detachment and the ability to wait with patience and expectation.

There are, however, no recipes for retreats. Some combine physical work, *lectio divina* and meditation. I cannot manage six prayer sessions every twenty-four hours. Being a chronically bad sleeper, I do not pray in the middle of the night. I am pretty sure that God prefers me to rest. I find the use of my God-given imagination helpful when I meditate, for it allows me to get into the biblical stories as a participant. After all, it was Albert Einstein (1875–1955) who said: "Imagination is more important than knowledge." I have found that using my imagination is particularly fruitful when I encounter Jesus in the gospels. Struggling with difficult truths compels me to imagine a better way, and a healing alternative, for my life. Imagining can translate into the kind of action that makes what we hope for become reality. I have also known times of waiting upon God devoid of words or thoughts.

Prayer is an activity of the heart, not solely of the mind. This statement is not a plea to reject reason or to decry the mind. Neither is it a reaction against discursive prayer. I must speak to God and cannot abandon reason. Reason constrains me to accept my subjectivity as I try to understand. Reason, hopefully, makes me accept ethical responsibility for what I do. Reason shapes all theological reflection. Saying that prayer is an activity of the heart does not exclude the mind. Heart and mind join in prayer. What I am getting at is a move from reasoned prayer to an awareness of the movements of our hearts, *because prayer is an act of love.* We pray because we are in love with God. Being in love means we long to hear and respond to the voice of the Beloved. The anonymous author of *The Cloud of Unknowing* knew this: "By love He may be gotten and holden, but by thought or understanding, never."

Anthony de Mello (1931–1987), a Jesuit teacher of prayer, says: "The head is not a very good place for prayer. It is not a bad place for starting your prayer, but if your prayer stays there too long and does not move into your heart, it will gradually dry up and prove tiresome and frustrating." Reason cannot access the mystery of God. I am not advocating that we jettison the ability to think and be rational. But to rely solely on the mind is a barrier to being open to the Spirit moving in us, often in imperceptible ways. Prayer is heart stuff that opens windows we did not know existed. Harry Williams knew the awesomeness of prayer: "In prayer we enter the realm of reality and see things as they really are, from God's point of view."

I am slow to launch into wordy prayer. I am learning not to be afraid of wordless waiting on God. In *Report to Greco*, philosopher and novelist Nikos Kazantzakis (1883–1957) writes: "When I pronounce a word, for instance, Lord, this word shatters my heart. I am terror-stricken and do not know if I shall be able to make the leap to the following words: Have pity on me." We need not bludgeon God with words. I cannot imagine that God is intrigued by what I have to say. God is, I believe, more interested in what I feel, where my heart is and in my ability to trust and to love.

Reading the journals I have kept on retreats, I can see that I have been helped to live my faith in more concrete ways. My longing, my mind, my heart and my allegiance continue to be ruffled, but I cannot be without this ruffling. It is intrinsic to the life of faith. As I said, I am not a natural. I will need all the time I have left to continue finding out what it means to live a more fulfilled life.

A thirty-day silent retreat at St Beuno's, a Jesuit retreat centre in northern Wales, changed my life profoundly. I had heard of St Beuno's many years before from my spiritual director and friend Francis Cull. His time there had left its stamp on his spirituality. When he spoke of his experience, I thought: "Good for him, but beyond me."

In 2006, shortly after surgery for cancer and still reeling with anger about my eyes, I took off for Wales, knowing that I needed time out. I soon found out that a thirty-day retreat actually takes thirty-six days. The first three days we spent being introduced to what lay ahead, and the last three were for a gentle re-entry into the bustle of life. Silence meant silence, except for forty-five minutes each day with one's spiritual director. Mine was a funny, feisty, very wise Irish nun whose deft directing of me was a blessing in every possible sense. Every afternoon at five o'clock there was a Eucharist in the chapel.

As the thirty days stretched ahead of me, I wondered how the days would be filled. But once I got into the rhythm of St Beuno's, the days passed quickly and were surprisingly structured. There was time every day for a good two-hour walk across fields and over stiles, up and down hills, often in soft rain or howling wind. I talked to a lot of cows and smiled at ruddy-faced farmers. I can barely draw a stick person, yet I discovered that I enjoyed dabbling in water colours in the art room for an hour a day. And then, of course, there were hours for prayer in my comfortable room. We ate all meals in silence, but despite this the twenty of us on the thirty-day retreat were astonishingly aware of each other throughout our time together. Some of us have kept in touch with one another, a fact I find both surprising and satisfying.

As a Jesuit retreat centre, St Bueno's follows the *Spiritual Exercises* of Ignatius of Loyola. Inigo, later known as Ignatius, was born of a wealthy family in Loyola, in the Basque region of Spain, in 1491. (A year later Christopher Columbus "discovered" America.) Ignatius started life as a soldier and lived it up in the traditional sense of this phrase. In 1521 he was badly wounded in battle: one of his legs was broken and the other injured. The broken leg was set crooked, broken again and reset with excruciating pain. During his long convalescence, he asked for stories of chivalry, the staple diet for knights of his time, but when none was available, he read the lives of the saints instead. As he read, he found two warring impulses within himself: the first was to indulge in all the delights life could offer, and the second was to go on a pilgrimage to Jerusalem. Reflecting on being tugged in opposite directions, he found that contemplating the pilgrimage was uplifting, even joyous, whereas a return to his previous ways left him feeling arid and unfulfilled.

This experience he described as a "transformation of the soul" and it was crucial to his discovery of the gift of discernment. It laid the foundation for two central concepts of the *Spiritual Exercises*: "consolation" and "desolation", described by Ignatius as discerning "the moods and motions of the soul". Ignatius then undertook his pilgrimage to Jerusalem and, on his way, stayed at Manresa, near Barcelona. I visited the cloister there, still a place of pilgrimage, set high above a plain on a craggy mountain. Here Ignatius had rested on his journey and began drafting the *Spiritual Exercises*. He continued refining them over the years. Their purpose was to obtain spiritual freedom, quaintly described as the ability "to conquer oneself and regulate one's life without determining oneself through any tendency that is disordered". Eventually, during a stay in Paris, Ignatius, together with a group of friends, formed the Society of Jesus, known as the Jesuits. The *Exercises* were first published in 1548 as a manual for a retreat over thirty days. "By the term spiritual exercises every method of contemplation, of vocal and mental prayer and other spiritual activities [is meant] [...]," Ignatius explained.

Right at the outset of the retreat we were introduced to Ignatius's well-known prayer.

> Take, Lord, and receive all my liberty, my memory, my understanding, and my entire will, all that I have and call my own. You have given it all to me. To you, Lord, I return it. Everything is yours; do with it what you will. Give me only your love and your grace, for this is sufficient for me.

I wrote in my journal: "Can I ever pray this prayer? I doubt it. Will I ever find inner freedom from all attachments and selfish desires that thwart my relationship with God? It scares me." I was prepared to abide by the rules, not to cheat, and to wait with openness. I knew I longed to encounter God, and I also knew, instinctively more than rationally, that doing the *Spiritual Exercises* would not be a ride in the park. I was angry, wrestling with a God whom I secretly resented for not sparing me from failing eyesight in order that I might "learn" something. As I said, I knew full well that such an image of God was totally at odds with my theology and with my life of faith. However, this knowledge did nothing to stop my inner self from being gnawed by fear and anger.

Every person's experience of a thirty-day retreat is unique. I do not intend recounting more about mine, except to say that when it was over, I knew, without reservation, that God wants only what is best for me, for all of humanity and for all of creation. I believe that the pulse of God's creative power is at the centre of all things, inexorably moving all towards completion. I cannot explain why earthquakes, tsunamis, wars, genocides, famines, rape, violence, sickness or whatever type of suffering happens. In other words, I have no answers for the theodicy problem – why does God allow suffering if God is loving and all-powerful? All I know is that I have to do what I can within the ambit of my life to relieve suffering. I left St Bueno's with the assurance that "[...] the Lord your God carried you [me], just as one carries a child, all the way that you have travelled until you reached this place" (Deut1:31). This is more than enough for me. The blessing of having heard that "sound of sheer silence" at that place in Wales eight years ago moved me to a different way of being. And surprisingly, when I left I was, and am still, able to pray Ignatius's prayer with my whole being.

Socrates spoke of his inner *daimon* that warned him against taking a certain course of action. From childhood he had heard something akin to a voice that guided his actions. That voice, for instance, barred him from entering public life. What Socrates describes can be called the voice of discernment. Ignatius's struggles were at times intense and overwhelming. With courage and honesty he faced his scruples, engaging with and reflecting on what was happening to him. This enabled him to write the rules for discernment, which are part of the *Spiritual Exercises* – a great gift to people of faith through the ages. Both Socrates and Ignatius discovered how vital discernment is for life, albeit in different ways. Listening in silence is all very well. What is vital is that we listen with discernment.

There are no guarantees, no matter how intently we try to listen. Rowan Williams tells a story about the Anglican monastic theologian Herbert Kelly in relation to discernment. When asked by one of his novices, "How do we know what the will of God is?" Kelly replied: "We don't. That is the joke." Exactly! We never know precisely what the will of God is; however, we attempt to discern what we can in prayerful listening. Often we face having to choose between several courses of action. What will more fully resonate with the life and teaching of the man on the borrowed donkey? What sort of action opens up more possibilities for God to work? These are not questions that immediately yield answers. But they are the stuff of, the raw material for discerning reflection.

Discernment means being attentive to our inner promptings and assessing them. The wisdom of the desert taught that discernment is "right judgment in all things". This means distinguishing the movements that strengthen, encourage, console and inspire us from those movements that make us restless, or tepid in prayer, or that foster fear, tension, aridity and envy. In Ignatius's language this means discerning between consolations and desolations. Practising discernment is essential to the spiritual life.

Discernment lies at the heart of the *Spiritual Exercises*. Listening without discernment and acting on such listening can either be a self-indulgent pastime or a dangerous exercise. Without discerning these inner movements, we are not able to sift what is life-giving from what is not. It can be a perilous practice as it involves self-criticism, questioning and risk, and often requires us to redirect our lives. Discernment is about acquiring self-knowledge. As the Chinese Taoist philosopher Lao Tzu (sixth to fifth centuries B.C.E.) sagely remarked: "He who knows others is clever; he who knows himself has discernment." Listening discerningly is a process of distinguishing what is consonant with God's desire for us (consolation) and what is not (desolation), and then doing something about it. Such listening takes place guided by the Spirit and finds expression in our relationships with others and ourselves.

Awareness of God's gracious self-giving, coupled with our commitment to openness and change, makes for discernment. Growth in discernment is a lifetime's work. As time passes, our awareness of the inner movements becomes more pervasive and more frequent. It is as if we listen to that voice of sheer silence and actually begin to hear the quiet whisperings of God. We experience something of that inner certainty of finding God in all things, from the most mundane to the most exceptional. My experience of the *Spiritual Exercises* has been profound. Having tasted God's self-giving love, I am changed. I am still too full of my old ways. I admit this readily, but deep down I am not the same person I was before going to Wales.

I have written much here on prayerful listening as an exercise of loving. This does not negate the centrality of listening to others. We are relational beings who are made to love one another. Listening to another with an open mind and a caring heart expresses loving concern and nurtures relationship. Being listened to with empathy can also be affirming and healing. We need to be heard. Paradoxically, silence and solitude are essential for our prayer life, yet we are not created for a solitary journey. As Dietrich Bonhoeffer said: "The first service one owes to others in fellowship consists of listening to them. Just as love of God begins with listening to his Word, so the beginning of love for the brethren [sic] is learning to listen to them."

To end where I started: these days I am having to forgo the pleasure of holding a book in my hands for most of my reading. For now, I can see better when reading on my iPad. I am grateful for modern technology and for friends who have promised to come and read to me when I can no longer see. I want them to read Merton, Julian, the poetry of Emily Dickinson and W. H. Auden, the latest fiction and a good thriller now and again – the list grows daily. I will listen on my iPad to comedy and criticism, to Bach and Mozart, Ella Fitzgerald and Lucky Dube. As time passes, and I practise listening inwardly, I hope I will understand more about my world and myself, and be at peace with what I find. I want to be caught up in the paradox of listening for the "sound of sheer silence", laugh with delight, and be able to let go of my desire to walk on the Great Wall of China or to see the red disas in bloom this January along the aqueduct on Table Mountain. I will rely on the eye of my heart and its storehouse of treasures. And I will trust "that all will be well, and all manner of things will be well", because God's love is present and real for the entire creation.

NOTES

Macular degeneration (or AMD) belongs to a group of diseases characterised by the breakdown of the macula, that part of the eye that is responsible for central vision. The tissue of the macula thins and deposits pigment on the macula that eventually obscures vision. AMD is age related and particularly prevalent in white females.

Geoff Quinlan pointed out to me that like the Latin root for obedience, the Greek *akouo* means to hear, and *hupakouo* can mean to listen, but also to obey.

"The sound of sheer silence" is an oxymoron (Hebrew *qōl dĕmāmāh dakkāh*). Literally it refers to a voice or often a sound, and to silence, which is thin or fine like an edge. Thus a sound (voice) of fine (thin) silence.

Gerhard von Rad was a German Lutheran pastor and Old Testament scholar. His scholarship prepared the way for the blossoming of Old Testament studies in Germany and elsewhere. From 1949 until his death he was a professor of Old Testament studies at the Ruprecht-Carls University of Heidelberg. Hans-Georg Gadamer (1900–2002) was a German philosopher whose magnum opus, *Truth and Method*, sought to explore the nature of human understanding. I am indebted to friend and theologian Michael Welker for this story.

I am grateful to Francine Cardman for the following reference: Sister Anna Maria Reynolds, C. P., "'Courtesy' and 'Homeliness' in the Revelations of Julian of Norwich", see http://www.umilta.net/homeliness.html.

Observant Jews say the *Shema Yisrael* every morning and every evening and this repetition is a *mitzvah* (a religious commandment). Its primary theme is the Oneness of God and its second verse (Deut 6:5) is "You shall love the Lord your God with all your heart, with all your soul [...]" This prayer is contained in the *tefillim* – the small box containing scriptures that is worn on the forehead and the arm.

Scripture has many references to God communicating with people. For further reflection see: Abraham, Gen 15; Moses, Ex 19 and 20; Joshua, Jos 5; Samuel, 1 Sam 3; Nathan, 2 Sam 7; Isaiah, Is 6, and Jeremiah, Jer 1. Also see Joseph, Mt 1 and 2; Zachariah, Lk 1; Mary, Lk 1; John, Lk 3:22; Philip, Acts 8, 29-40; Peter, Acts 10, 13-16; Paul, Acts 19:21, 1 Cor 12.

For the quotation from Isaac of Nineveh, see Jennifer Wild, *The Westminster Collection of Christian Meditations* (Louisville: Westminster John Knox Press, 2000).

Finkenwalde was an "illegal" theological seminary established by Dietrich Bonhoeffer in Stettin (Szczecin in Poland today) in 1935 on the banks of the Oder River. Here Bonhoeffer sought a new kind of monasticism in training pastors for the Confessing Church. The Gestapo closed the seminary in 1939. His experiences in Finkenwalde contributed to his well-known work *Costly Grace* and are described in *Life Together.*

I cannot resist seventh-century monk John Climacus's somewhat fulsome comment:

> Talkativeness is the throne of vainglory on which it loves to preen itself and show off. Talkativeness is a sign of ignorance, a doorway to slander, a leader of jesting, a servant of lies, the ruin of compunction, a summoner of despondency, a messenger of sleep, a dissipation of recollection, the end of vigilance, the cooling of zeal, the darkening of prayer. Intelligent silence is the mother of prayer, freedom from bondage, custodian of zeal, a guard on our thoughts, a watch on our enemies, a prison of mourning, a friend of tears, a sure recollection

of death, a painter of punishment, a concern with judgment, servant of anguish, foe of license, a companion of stillness, the opponent of dogmatism, a growth of knowledge, a hand to shape contemplation, hidden progress, the secret journey upward. For the man who recognises his sins has taken control of his tongue, while the chatterer has yet to discover himself as he should.

Evelyn Underhill's (1875–1941) writings on Christian mysticism grew out of her experience of religious conversion in 1907 when her spiritual struggles led her to study Christian mysticism. She is noted for her insistence that mysticism is not something esoteric, but essentially practical. See her *Practical Mysticism* (Guilford: Eagle, 1991).

Shantivanam Ashram is a Christian retreat centre dedicated to the Holy Trinity. It is located in Tamil Nadu near the Kavery River. Henri le Saux, a French Benedictine monk (known in India as Abishiktananda) and Jules Monachin founded it and built its first structures with their own hands in 1950. They were later joined by Bede Griffiths (1906–1993), also a Benedictine monk who was born in England, went to India in 1955 and arrived at the ashram in 1968 where he stayed until his death. Here liturgies are conducted in English, Tamil and Sanskrit, and those who live at the ashram work among the rural poor. Bede Griffiths contributed greatly to Indian Christian thought, and Shantivanam became the centre of contemplative life, enculturation and inter-religious dialogue.

Archimedes (born c.287–died c.212 B.C.E.) was one of the leading Greek scientists of antiquity. He is credited with inventing the compound pulley and the hydraulic screw for raising water from a lower to a higher level. A physicist, an engineer and an inventor, he revolutionised integral calculus two thousand years before Leibniz and Newton. The Archimedes Principle states that any body partially or completely submerged in a fluid is buoyed up by a force equal to the weight of the fluid displaced by the body.

Mother Teresa was born in Macedonia in 1910 of Albanian descent. At the age of twelve she felt a call to serve God, and at eighteen joined the Sisters of Loretta, an Irish community of nuns with missions in India. She went to India in 1931 and first taught at a girls' school in Calcutta. From 1948 for the next forty years or more, she worked among the poor in the slums of this city. There, in 1950, she was given permission to start her own order, the Missionaries of Charity. In 1979 she won the Nobel Peace Prize for her humanitarian work. She died in 1997 and was subsequently beatified by Pope John Paul II.

Lectio divina (Latin for "divine reading") is an ancient Christian practice treasured by the Benedictines and others living the contemplative life. It is a slow, contemplative praying of the scriptures, so that the word can bring union with God. Together with daily manual work and liturgy, *lectio divina* is meant to give rhythm to daily life and cultivate the ability to listen deeply to what Benedict called "the ear of our hearts". *Lectio divina* formed part of the monastic rules of Pachomius, Benedict, Augustine and Basil, and continued throughout the Middle Ages up to present times.

The reference to Karl Barth is taken from Martin Rumscheidt's article, "The formation of Bonhoeffer's theology" in John de Gruchy, ed., *The Cambridge Companion to Dietrich Bonhoeffer* (Cambridge: Cambridge University Press, 1999) 50–70, quoting from Barth's *The Epistle to the Romans*.

The Jesuits are the largest male order in the Roman Catholic Church with around twenty thousand members worldwide. They played an important role in the Catholic Reformation under the leadership of Ignatius of Loyola. The Constitutions of the Society of Jesus state, among others, that members are to go wherever ordered to do so to "save souls"; they are not to wear a special habit, and are to take vows of poverty, chastity and obedience. The Jesuits have a chequered history, but today play a vital role in education and in continuing the spiritual tradition of Ignatius of Loyola. They are at the disposal of the Pope, a relationship that has not been without tensions. Jesuits are required to do a thirty-day retreat twice in a lifetime if possible. The *Spiritual Exercises* are their foundational training, and they, in turn, have opened its genius to all who care to participate. The present Pope Francis is a Jesuit.

Daimon is what the Greeks called the inner voice that they believed was an intelligent being that guided people. Socrates spoke with easy familiarity about his *daimon (daemonion)*, an inner mystical voice, and recorded that when it did not favour a question that had been asked, it remained absolutely silent. Socrates could not make his *daimon* speak. See Plato, *Apologies, Crito and Phaedo of Socrates*, tr. H. Cary (Charleston: BiblioBazaar, 2007). *Diakrisis*, a Greek word for distinguishing, discerning or judging, occurs in the New Testament, see, for example, 1 Cor 12:10.

The red disa (*Disa uniflora*) is an orchid, also known as the "Pride of Table Mountain". It flowers on the margins of mountain streams and in wet rock clefts.

WORKS CONSULTED

Barry, William A. *Finding God in All Things*. Notre Dame: Ave Maria Press, 1991.

Barry, William A. and William J. Connolly. *The Practice of Spiritual Direction*. San Francisco: Harper and Row, 1982.

Bonhoeffer, Dietrich. *Life Together*. London: SCM Press, 1970.

Boulding, Maria. *The Coming of God*. London: Fount Paperbacks, 1986.

Bruteau, Beatrice. "Prayer and identity." *Contemplative Review* (Fall, 1983), 2.

Caraman, Philip. *Ignatius of Loyola*. London: Fount Paperbacks, 1994.

Clare, Mother Mary. *Encountering the Depths*. Edited by R. Townsend. London: Darton, Longman and Todd, 1981.

Conroy, Maureen. *The Discerning Heart: Discovering a Personal God*. Chicago: Loyola Press, 1993.

De Gruchy, John ed., *The Cambridge Companion to Dietrich Bonhoeffer*. Cambridge: Cambridge University Press, 1999.

De Mello, Anthony. *Sadhana a Way to God; Christian Exercises in Eastern Form*. New York: Image Books, 1984.

De Villiers, P. G. R., C. E. T. Kourie and C. J. S. Lombard, eds. *The Spirit that Empowers: Perspectives on Spirituality*. Acta Theologica Supplementum. Bloemfontein: University of the Free State Press, 2008.

Fleming, David L. *Draw Me into Your Friendship: The Spiritual Exercises*. St Louis: The Institute of Jesuit Sources, 1996.

Hall, Sister Jeremy. *Silence, Solitude, Simplicity: A Hermit's Love Affair with a Noisy, Crowded and Complicated World*. Collegeville, MN: Liturgical Press, 2007.

Johnston, William. *The Mystical Way*. London: Fount Paperbacks, 1993.

Johnston, William, ed. *The Cloud of Unknowing and the Book of Privy Counseling*. New York: Doubleday, 1973.

Jones, Alan. *Journey into Christ*. New York: Seabury Press, 1977.

Kazantzakis, Nikos. *Report to Greco*. New York: Bantam Books, 1965.

Keating, Thomas. *Open Mind, Open Heart: The Contemplative Dimension of the Gospel*: Rockport, MA: Element, 1991.

Kolodiejchuk, Brian. *Mother Teresa, Come be My Light: The Private Writings of the "Saint of Calcutta"*. New York: Doubleday, 2007.

Lamott, Anne. *Traveling Mercies: Some Thoughts on Faith*. New York: Anchor Books, 1999.

Merton, Thomas. *Thoughts in Solitude*. New York: Farrar, Straus and Giroux, 1988.

Merton, Thomas. *New Seeds of Contemplation*. London: Burns and Oates, 2002.

Merton, Thomas. *The Inner Experience: Notes on Contemplation*. Edited and introduced by W. H. Shannon. London: SPCK, 2003.

Nolan, Albert. *Jesus Today: A Spirituality of Radical Freedom*. Cape Town: Double Storey Books, 2006.

Plato. *Apology, Crito and Phaedo of Socrates*, tr. H. Cary. Charleston: BiblioBazaar, 2007.

Storr, Anthony. *Solitude: A Return to Self*. New York: Ballantine Books, 1988.

Schweizer, Eduard. *Good News According to Mark*. London: SPCK, 1987.

Underhill, Evelyn. *Mysticism*. London: Methuen, 1960.

Underhill, Evelyn. *Life as Prayer*. Edited by L. Menzies. Harrisburg: Moorehouse Publishing, 1946.

Underhill, Evelyn. *Practical Mysticism*. Guilford: Eagle, 1991.

Wild, Jennifer. *The Westminster Collection of Christian Meditations*. Louisville: Westminster John Knox Press, 2000.

CHAPTER SIX

Blessed are those who are grateful, for they will delight in the ordinary

I was blessed with a mother-in-law who had a grateful heart. She could find reasons for being grateful, even in adversity. Her ability to be thankful for even the smallest gifts shaped her well-being and her happiness. She believed in the ultimate goodness of people, despite the fact that a lifetime dedicated to working for Child Welfare exposed her to some of humanity's worst aberrations. Her ability to be grateful came from the core of her being. She was not conventionally religious. Yet, in her last years, when widowed and struggling to walk, she would say: "I am grateful to God for so much." I have often wondered what she meant. For me, Alpha Ackermann was a woman blessed with a grateful heart that opened her to the bounty of God's grace in this world. She helped me to understand that gratitude is key to human well-being. Being grateful is to find and appreciate grace in the ordinary and the every day. This is truly a blessing.

I grew up being told I had to be grateful. As my home was often fraught with tensions, disruptions and restrictions, I struggled to find grounds for gratitude. But there was cause for gratitude. Although my parents were frugal, I did not want for material things. We lived comfortably, far removed from "the starving children in Europe" of whom I was constantly reminded following World War II when I balked at eating cabbage. Yet there were times when gratitude felt like something forced on me – something dishonest and at odds with my experience. While I resisted being told to be grateful, I can also remember the warmth of gratitude for unobtrusive acts of kindness and generosity. I do not think I resented being taught to say "thank you" for gifts and outings. However, it was only later that I began to learn something of the true nature of gratitude and how it relates to the ordinary everyday moments of life.

I have much to be grateful for: fifty-six years of a good marriage, three children and five dear grandchildren, shelter, food, good friends, walking on the mountain, swimming in the bracing south Atlantic, enjoying the birds and flowers of the *fynbos*, celebrating family occasions and a generous amount of travel. And there is even more. As I write these words, memories of loving moments, images of unforgotten sights and the joy of having prayers answered for those I love flood my consciousness. I know the delight of frequent flashes of thankfulness for very ordinary, often insignificant, objects or happenings. To be ungrateful would be downright mean-spirited. Sometimes I wonder whether I am simply lucky or particularly blessed. What about the woman at my door who is HIV positive with five children to care for, depressed and poor; or those filled with hopeless anger at the annual inundation of their shacks on the Cape Flats; or people in tumbledown plastic shanties on the wind-swept wastes of Darfur; or the traumatised women and children in Somalia, Congo, and Syria; or the mother on the front page of the newspaper whose three-year-old daughter was raped and murdered? What does gratitude mean for these people? Does the magnitude of human suffering erode our ability to be grateful? Can only the fortunate know thankfulness?

I know that among the "fortunate" gratitude is by no means as-sured. Some people seem constitutionally unable to feel gratitude. The assumption that one is entitled to good fortune because one has earned it hardly engenders gratitude. Gratitude does not sit well with self-interested entitlement. Self-interest is an insidious, ever-present skunk in our souls. The stench of self-interest (often claimed as a necessary ingredient for survival) frequently overwhelms doing good towards others. The marvel is that I know people who can still be grateful in the midst of appalling circumstances. One wonders what makes the difference. Do some have an inner disposition for gratitude that enables them to appreciate the smallest and most ordinary of occurrences? I do not know, but it is an attitude at which to wonder.

Writing about gratitude is like entering a hornet's nest. I will be stung as I try to avoid pious platitudes or the blithe certainty of a Pollyanna. Yet, I believe that thankfulness cannot only be about what we have, or about favoured circumstances or even about who we are. True gratitude comes from accepting the truth that God loves us. Knowing this shifts thanksgiving from what I have and who I am to what is freely given to every single human being. It is an experience of God's unending and enduring care in both the good and the bad times, in the great moments and those that are very ordinary. I know this is difficult to accept. Suffering can erode faith in God's loving care. Nevertheless, just the effort of focusing on the small and very ordinary happenings of the day for which we can be grateful helps. I am abidingly grateful for having learnt this.

Is gratitude a virtue? A virtue is a moral quality that is considered good and desirable. Gratitude is probably the most underestimated and neglected of human emotions. Nevertheless experiencing gratitude is essential for living well. Can we cultivate gratitude because we consider it a virtuous quality? The Greek word *arête*, generally translated as "virtue" (or sometimes as "excellence"), has since ancient times been the subject of much debate. For centuries moral and practical philosophers have had something to say about the character of virtue while not always agreeing on the origin of virtue or who is virtuous. Generally speaking, many agree that virtues are dispositions or qualities of character, rather than skills or capacities.

Aristotle (born c.384–died c.322 B.C.E.) is very clear that virtues are not inherited faculties or human passions but "states of character". He concludes: "Virtue, then, is a state of character concerned with choice ..." Thus virtue is the way a person chooses to act. When a person is virtuous her or his actions are considered good. We choose what is good because we have given the matter thought. Philosopher Anthony Kenny, in discussing Aristotle's ethics, writes: "Virtuous action must be based on virtuous purpose. Purpose is reasoned desire so that if the purpose is to be good, both the reasoning and the desire must be good." Aristotle describes "the good" as "that for whose sake everything else is done". He did not think that people could be persuaded to be good by rational argument. A person becomes good by training and by adopting good habits and making good choices. To develop a virtue, a child must grow up in a community in which virtues are taught and expressed. We learn from early on that, for the sake of our relationships, we must try to do what is good. But Aristotle warns that "virtue is (also) in our own power, and so too is vice". We can choose to act for good or not. We have the power to be either "virtuous or vicious". Is gratitude a virtue? I think so. It is a matter of choice.

At the heart of my attempt to write about blessings lies the perennial question: what makes life worth living? Living gratefully is a virtue by which a person will be appreciative, content and hopeful. Gratitude is a virtue that, when experienced, is inclined to elicit appreciation and thanks. Gratitude engenders goodwill and the disposition to act in ways that flow from goodwill. Feeling grateful or thankful is much the same. Both involve someone other than oneself. Experiencing acts of kindness and generosity, receiving gifts, or simply getting something for nothing all evoke a sense of gratitude and make one feel valued. However, being morally virtuous is not an end in itself. Virtue for a Christian is not its own reward. *God is our reward.*

Gratitude does not occur in a vacuum. To be grateful is primarily, but not exclusively, to be grateful to someone – to another person or to the Holy One. Sunlight on a luminous raindrop, the perfect markings of an impala, and the plumage of a sand grouse can all evoke a surge of gratitude for the God-given bounty of life. The delight of a grandchild, courtesy of a driver, help of a neighbour or generosity of a friend can elicit an experience of instant gratitude. Being grateful is not exactly the same as being glad. To say "I am grateful that it did not rain today", probably means "I am glad that […]." True gratitude has an interpersonal element and should go hand in hand with a sense of appreciation. If I were to telephone my mother on her birthday to wish her well merely because it is the right thing to do, I am aping gratitude instead of being grateful for all that she has done for me.

However, not all apparently thankful attitudes are virtuous, for instance, if one thanks someone for a favour but feels no real appreciation towards the giver. Such a perfunctory "thank you" is no more than a socially acceptable response to an act of kindness. Thankfulness that is motivated by self-interest – a show of gratitude to improve one's standing with another – will not contribute towards authentic human relations. True gratitude is laced with appreciation. It feels good and is not necessarily a flashy emotion. It tends to run quietly and deeply.

A useful way of testing one's own experience of gratitude is to ask how one feels when receiving a gift? Indebted? Embarrassed? Unworthy? Obligated to give in return? Moved to gratitude? The exchanging of gifts can go wrong. It can place a person in an inferior position vis-à-vis the giver and leave that person with a sense of obligation. A sense of obligation takes away the element of delight in giving – particularly when we are giving something of ourselves – or of being able to receive gladly. It is not always simple to receive with thankfulness. If, on receiving a gift, one feels obliged to give something in return, the freedom of being able to receive gratefully is impaired. French philosopher Paul Ricoeur (1913–2005) says: "Gratitude lightens the weight of obligation to give in return and reorients this toward a generosity equal to the one that led to the first gift." Expecting reciprocity of any kind weakens the freedom of giving. We should be able to give and to accept with no strings attached.

Aristotle bridled at this kind of attitude. He did not include gratitude among his virtues. He thought gratitude incompatible with magnanimity and undermining of the status of his "great-souled man"! He wrote: "And he is the sort of man to confer benefits, but he is ashamed of receiving them; for the one is the mark of a superior, the other of an inferior." In Aristotle's view, a self-sufficient person who is magnanimous finds it demeaning to be indebted or grateful to others. Christians, however, are indebted to our Creator (and to one another) as we acknowledge and delight in God's great generosity that infuses this ailing world with grace. I can understand why Augustine chooses not to use the term "gratitude". He prefers *gratia* because for him it is always a matter of divine grace.

Ingratitude is not only unattractive, it is also hurtful, discreditable and a common human vice. Immanuel Kant felt that ingratitude was one of the three vices that are the "essence of vileness and wickedness". Scots philosopher David Hume (1711–1776) wrote that "[o] f all the crimes that human creatures are capable of committing the most horrid and unnatural is ingratitude ..." Shakespeare, in *Twelfth Night* (Act 3, scene 4), did not mince words:

> I hate ingratitude more in man
> Than lying, vainness, babbling, drunkenness,
> Or any taint of vice whose strong corruption
> Inhabits our frail blood.

Why these strong sentiments? Clearly the ramifications of ingratitude are understood as dire for human well-being. I know how I feel when I encounter thanklessness. It leaves a sour taste and can spoil a relationship. Yet, I know that when I expect to be thanked, I am often acting out of self-interest. I am also shamed by those who have the least and who act without self-interest by sharing the little they have.

A flash-back: I remember the priest's table in his very modest home, north of Inhambane on the coast of Mozambique. Six months previously, after a protracted civil war, a peace accord had been signed between the contesting forces of Frelimo and Renamo for control of the country. I accompanied Francis Cull on the invitation of Bishop Denis Sengulani to help church members rebuild their fractured communities. Twelve were expected for a lunch consisting of rice, black sugarless tea, cassava leaves and cassava roots. As we sat down more people joined us. The dishes were passed around. We all ate a bit less so that all twenty-seven of us could be fed. What there was was shared and gratefully received.

A world without gratitude is a nightmarish prospect, bereft of care for others or the delight of giving and receiving. I can barely imagine the quality of relationships in such a world! A grateful community is one whose members can flourish. We are not born with the instinct to be grateful, but we can choose to be grateful by cultivating a sense of gratitude. Continuing to choose to act out of gratitude, rather than to be ungrateful, will foster better human relationships and contribute to the common good.

What does gratitude have to do with faith in God? "Everything" is the short answer. Gratitude is like the proverbial stone cast in a pond that causes ripples to spread out in ever-widening circles. We know those ripples from the moment we are aware of God's grace. As our awareness of God's mercy, love and care for us deepens, gratitude surges out, touching the far edges of our lives. There can be no genuine faith without gratitude. Knowing the gratitude that comes from having tasted God's bounty is a blessing that can never be erased or forgotten. My interest in this topic is a response to the experiences of God's grace and mercy I have known in my life and in the lives of others. But it is also more. Learning to be thankful for both the small acts of kindness as well as the daunting magnitude of God's grace has changed my life. I do not feel a victim of circumstance. Joy in ordinary, everyday things is fed by my sense of gratitude. In poet Mary Oliver's words, I am continually "a bride to amazement" as the "ordinary" becomes a delight!

It was ingratitude that got us into trouble in the first place. According to our creation tale, Adam never thanks God for Eve, but blames God for having made a woman that leads him into sin. When God asks Adam: "Have you eaten from the tree of which I commanded you not to eat?", he responds with what Professor of Jewish Education Solomon Schimmel calls "*chutzpah* and ingratitude": "The woman whom you gave to be with me, she gave me from the fruit of the tree, and I ate" (Gen 3:11-12). It is too late for gratitude.

In their defiant quest to know as the Creator knows, neither Adam nor Eve shows any humility or gratitude. They cannot accept their vulnerability. Self-sufficiency was their (and often our) motto.

Ingratitude is a theme that runs throughout the Old Testament. The Israelites, after being freed from slavery in Egypt and fed in the wilderness, rail against God and against Moses: "Why have you brought us up out of Egypt to die in the wilderness. For there is no food and no water, and we detest this miserable food" (Num 21:5). Grumbling, murmuring and fault-finding were common sins (see Ex 17:1-7; Ps 95:8-11). King Solomon, blessed with great wealth and "very great wisdom, discernment, and breadth of understanding" (1 Kings 4:29), forgets what God had done for him. At the end of his life, he takes hundreds of wives from outside of Israel, forsakes God and follows Astarte, the goddess of the Sidonians. He does what is "evil in the sight of the Lord" (1 Kings 11:1-8). Thanklessness is a constant theme throughout the tales of the kings of Israel. It leads to apostasy and much suffering for the people.

However, the Old Testament is not all about ingratitude. The Israelites offered a basket of the first fruits of the harvest to God at the altar, accompanied by a long prayer acknowledging God's saving acts (Deut 26:1-16). There are also numerous psalms and prayers of thanksgiving. "I will bless the Lord at all times; his praise shall continually be in my mouth. My soul makes its boast in the Lord; let the humble hear and be glad [...]. O taste and see that the Lord is good; happy are those who take refuge in him" sings the psalmist (Ps 34:1-2, 8). Or, "O give thanks to the Lord, for he is good; his steadfast love endures forever" (Ps 107:1).

In the New Testament, when the Pharisee prays to God saying "God, I thank you that I am not like other people", his thanks are simply an arrogant sentiment masked as gratitude (Lk 18:11). There is no humility, no effort to look into himself. This is in total contrast to the tax collector who beats his breast saying "God, be merciful to me, a sinner" (Lk 18:13). Jesus encounters ingratitude when he meets ten lepers between Samaria and Galilee (Lk 17:11-19) They call out: "Jesus, Master, have mercy on us!" Jesus tells them to go and show themselves to the priests. "And as they went, they were made clean." However, the story does not end there. Only one, a Samaritan, turns back "praising God with a loud voice", and throws himself at Jesus' feet, thanking him. Then Jesus asks: "Were not ten made clean?" Jesus' reaction to the lack of gratitude of the nine is a mixture of surprise and dismay. Such acts of miraculous grace are surely a cause for thanksgiving. In our story of the man on the borrowed donkey, Judas Iscariot does not appreciate what Jesus offers him. Instead he betrays his friend for money – an act of gross ingratitude and greed.

By contrast, Jesus' life is one of gratitude. Again and again he blesses and thanks the Beloved. From the joy of being blessed comes gratitude. No wonder he could give his life so freely and no wonder his actions astonished the world. He was from God and he is with God – his power derives from his relationship with God. It is not a controlling, self-interested power, achieved by wealth or position, but a power that is life-giving and one which can transform the world. Philosopher and theologian Søren Kierkegaard (1813–1855) suggests that gratitude in our relationship with God and others leads to that self-awareness which constitutes our being. Our ability to experience thankfulness shapes our identity. It is key to human well-being.

Why is the Holy One worthy of gratitude? Endless mercy and constant faithfulness and love despite our foibles are more than sufficient cause for gratitude. The twentieth century Protestant theologian Karl Barth describes being faithful as "a steady and lasting perseverance in thought, word, attitude, and act. It is endurance and persistence in a union, commitment, and obligation laid upon man with both kindness and strictness." More precisely he adds: "Gratitude, or, more correctly, thanksgiving, does in fact give us precise and exhaustive information about what is commanded of man in his relationship to the gracious God and therefore about what is decisively and comprehensively commanded of him." For Barth, thanksgiving is not an optional extra. It is central to our relationship with God.

Thomas Merton writes: "All sin is a punishment for the primal sin of not knowing God. That is to say all sin is a punishment for ingratitude [...]. Our knowledge of God is perfected by gratitude;

we are thankful and rejoice in the experience of the truth that He is love." He continues by pointing out that to be thankful is to recognise the love of God in everything we are given. All we have is from God – life, breath, growth, beauty, truth, love and relationship. Dare we be ungrateful?

Gratitude and grace are deeply linked in the life of faith. God is gracious and we respond with gratitude. The roots of thanksgiving are found in knowing the loving grace and mercy of God. God is the ultimate giver – the One who pours out favours to which we respond. In fact, gratitude is a distinguishing mark of having faith in a loving God. It is "a kind of moral barometer as well as a moral motivator," says Schimmel. I know that I can assess the quality of my relationship with God by the welling up of gratitude within me. When I lag or sink into that lukewarm place, I remind myself of the immensity of God's grace – how it is totally unmerited and freely given. This helps me to set aside the moral turpitude that often assails me and I can thank anew.

Feelings of gratitude to God also motivate good behaviour towards others. God's grace and mercy are poured out on all human beings, whether we acknowledge this reality and live by it or not. We are all in the same boat – treasured recipients of blessings, called to live with gratitude. The unmerited quality of God's blessing should make us more humble and a thousand-fold more thankful, as well as more tolerant of our own and others' lapses in gratitude. To give thanks and to have a grateful heart means that we recognise that all that we receive from God is divine favour, and free at that.

How do we express gratitude to God for the unmerited grace we receive? Barth has no doubt as to what we should do – we should pray. Barth believes that not praying is an act of rebellion against God. It is an act of unbelief. I agree that if I do not believe in God there seems little point in praying. However, prayer is more than an act of obedience to a god who wishes us both to speak and listen.

To have faith in the Source of all Life is to desire to know God more closely, to reach out to the Beloved. Prayer is not a rule to be obeyed, but the fulfilment of a loving longing. We pray because we cannot be mute before the One we love; prayer is an act of love in response to God who floods this world with grace.

Thus the relationship between gratitude and prayer is inseparable. It is impossible for a person of faith not to thank God. By giving thanks we recognise that the favour we receive has no strings attached, so our response is spontaneous and comes from the heart. In case prayer sounds like a hard maintenance job or a monotonous list of requests and thank you's, we can remind ourselves, as French Trappist priest André Louf does:

> In order to pray more and better we must often do less, let go of more things, give up numerous good intentions, and be content to yield to the inner pressure of the Spirit the moment [the Spirit] bubbles up in us and tries to win us over and take us in tow. Ultimately all our attempts at prayer and all our methods must come to a dead end and wither away in order that the Spirit of Jesus may facilitate and validate his own prayer in our heart.

Experience has taught me that gratitude is a plant that needs daily watering. Hundreds of years ago Ignatius of Loyola understood this and gave us the *Examen* for reviewing the day. I know of no better way of cultivating a grateful heart than the daily use of this tool to examine my consciousness. There is nothing complicated about the *Examen*. It is an exercise in prayerful attention to the past day. Gratitude lies at its heart and it simply requires a couple of minutes to review the day to find cause for gratitude. Essentially this is the practice of finding God's presence in all things, and discerning moments when one did not respond to God's love. The *Examen* concludes by giving tomorrow and what it might entail to God.

This profoundly simple exercise is the essence of being in relationship. It keeps us talking and listening to God at the end of each day. Ignatius exhorted busy people "[to] practice God's presence in all things, in their conversation, their walks, in all that they see, taste, hear, understand, in all their actions, since his Divine Majesty is truly in all things by his presence, power and essence [...]." So we delight in the presence of God and are grateful for enduring grace.

We can measure our ability to be grateful by being always conscious that what we have is not ours by entitlement. This requires awareness – that dawning realisation that we are totally dependent on God and our lives are in God's hands. At our most vulnerable, when words desert us and hope is fragile, we can remind ourselves that God's "grace is sufficient for you, for power is made perfect in weakness" (2 Cor 12:9).

I am convinced that gratitude is a delight and a blessing that lights up the most ordinary events of every day. Living out of gratitude is transformative. Being thankful helps us to be more contented, more accepting and more hopeful about life. Conversely, we can block our ability to experience gratitude by sinking into perpetual dissatisfaction, regret, resentment and envy. These reactions are unpleasant. They are insidious and require self-scrutiny to lay them to rest. How do we register these feelings and how can we recognise these spoilers of gratitude?

To begin with, gratitude is the opposite of *perpetual dissatisfaction*. In her book *Radical Gratitude*, Mary Jo Leddy, founder of Romero House, a refugee centre in Toronto, devotes a chapter to spelling out its effects in her part of the world. Overwhelming consumerism, the culture of money and pervasive messages of advertising that entice people to need more and more are as familiar to South Africans today as they are to North Americans. The culture of money, Leddy explains, has its own set of values, its own spirit, symbols and codes of communication. It consumes us and material realities become all-important. Leddy comments: "Economics is a useful tool, but it is neither a wise master nor a just god."

Being perpetually dissatisfied with what we have makes us captive to craving for more. There is never enough. Once this message lodges in us, it transmutes to other levels of our being. As Leddy says:

I don't have enough
Becomes **I am not enough**
Becomes **I am not good enough.**

This process breeds inner dissatisfaction, a sense of powerlessness, inadequacy, even guilt. We can no longer see the good in ourselves or in others. We judge others, we want them to be different or we envy them. We take the world and all that is in it for granted. What there is is never regarded as good enough. Finally, we are persistently dissatisfied with our Creator who does not do enough for us.

I cut my theological teeth on liberation theology with its insistence that God has "a preferential option for the poor". I have never understood this to mean that God loves poor people more than those who are materially more comfortable. I do not want to qualify God's love or restrict God's all-embracing mercy and compassion for all humanity, but I do know that in the gospel stories it is overwhelmingly the poor and the marginalised who follow Jesus. He has harsh words for those with power and money, and he sees himself as anointed "to bring good news to the poor" (Lk 4:18). He has a special concern for those who are afflicted and destitute. Now, I have not been poor. The community I come from is largely self-sufficient, materialistic, dissatisfied and too often ungrateful for what it has. I find the perpetual dissatisfaction of those who are materially comfortable not only odious, but also squalid.

Second, gratitude is the opposite of *regret*, which is often a source of much unhappiness. I know how deadly "if only ..." can be: if only I had not chosen that path; if only my attitude to my child had been different; if only I had taken more trouble to repair this or that relationship; if only I had not rushed into making that decision – the list can be endless. Dwelling on the past, on issues we can do nothing about and harbouring regrets is futile. Once regrets dominate our lives, bitterness and resentment can creep into our consciousness.

It is far better to take note of the good and be grateful for it than to focus on the bad in a particular action.

Third, much that has already been said also applies to *resentment*. Resentment towards another is also the reverse of gratitude. It thrives on a perceived lack of regard, justice or fairness. We feel hard done by and this we resent. Resentment is not necessarily vicious in the sense that it resorts to violent deeds; it is a deeply harboured sentiment. Just a disdainful look is enough to make us feel resented and so we ourselves become resentful. Being on the receiving end of resentment is unpleasant. Resentment involves wanting to get even. In contrast, a thankful person has no need to get even. When we are grateful we are more inclined to do a favour for another than we are when we feel resentful or resented. Resentment sullies relationships, while gratitude can lift feelings of vengeance and promote forgiveness. It is better to see the goodness in another's actions. Furthermore, thankfulness and humility go hand in hand, hence growing more grateful is demanding, as most of us lack true humility. It simply requires more than we are prepared to take on – less of "self". It is not easy to accept indebtedness to another. Neither is it undemanding to practise gratitude in humble service as Jesus did when he washed the disciples' feet.

Can we be thankful and harbour no feelings of resentment when we experience injustice, the violation of our dignity or a mean and ugly act? Probably not. But what are we to do? It is difficult to find two more disparate people than the Dalai Lama and German philosopher Friedrich Nietzsche. In very different ways, they both arrived at the conclusion that resentment and regret are not worth harbouring. According to Nietzsche "But if you have an enemy, do not requite him evil with good, for that would put him to shame. Rather prove that he did you some good." In other words, we should avoid feeling hard done by, but rather make some good out of what has happened to us.

The Dalai Lama has often said that he is grateful to the Chinese for their occupation of his country, for it has given him the opportunity to practise love for his enemies. He has never condoned what the Chinese have done, neither has he refrained from speaking out against it. Nevertheless, true to one of the central tenets of Buddhism of practising gratitude to one's enemies, he is able to say:

> Even our enemies give us the best training in patience. When we reflect on these holy instructions, in a way we should feel grateful to the Chinese. If we were living in the same old system, I very much doubt that the Dalai Lama could have become so closely acquainted with world reality. I used to live in a very sheltered environment [...]. I had to sit on a high throne assuming the attitude of being the Dalai Lama [...]. It is quite possible that I could have become narrow-minded, but because of the Chinese threats and humiliations, I have become a real person. So what happened in Tibet can be seen as a blessing in disguise.

These attitudes may strike us as strange and beyond our capacity to emulate, but they are arresting. The Dalai Lama's attitude towards the Chinese occupation of Tibet shows that he accepts, without condoning, this modern-day act of colonisation. Persecution, exile and hardship are forced on him against his will. Yet he is able to find reasons for gratitude in this tragic history.

Is this approach akin to the Christian idea of the providence of God? I find the idea of God's providence difficult to accept when it gives rise to a kind of "holy" fatalism or inertia in the face of human suffering and injustice. Nevertheless some of the great spiritual teachers in our tradition have argued for self-abandonment to divine providence – nothing happens outside the will of God, therefore we abandon ourselves to God's will. French Jesuit Jean-Pierre de Caussade (1675–1751) writes about abandonment to divine providence. To understand divine providence we have to empty the soul "of all trust in its own action", he says, for such confidence is spurious and leads us to exclude divine action from our lives. "What happens to us each moment by God's design is for us the holiest, best and most divine thing. The whole essence of the spiritual life consists in recognising the designs of God for us at the present moment."

While I believe that God wants only the best for us, this understanding of God's providence can make light of terrible events and the suffering they produce. The idea of divine providence is not easy to grasp in a world that is overwhelmed with sin and suffering. I certainly cannot accept that God wills anguish, hardship and wretchedness. Neither can I feel grateful for them. When faced with the horrors of life, I am struck dumb. There is no answer to the ever-present question of human suffering and God. "Gratitude does not dispel the mystery of suffering and evil in the world and may even deepen it," writes Leddy.

I confess: the whole question of human suffering defeats me. I cannot pretend to understand rationally what it means to believe in a God who wills what is best for us in the face of interminable suffering. I know that largely we bring suffering upon ourselves. I do not blame God for human wretchedness. However, I also know that the innocent suffer, like the three-year-old girl who was raped. I resist this; I feel searing anger and at times a deep stream of doubt floods my consciousness. I have no answers. Do I feel resentment towards God when bad things happen? Yes, I have. But these moments, together with my inability to rationally justify having faith in God in the face of human suffering, have not cancelled out my experiences of a loving, caring God, or my faith in that innocent man on the borrowed donkey who suffered torture and death. I somehow know that it is wrong only to be grateful when things go well or when it suits me. The centre of my faith remains Jesus. So, even when things go wrong, Christians still remain grateful for the inescapable reality of Jesus – for his life and work.

I am now able to see that my whole life – the good, the bad and the indifferent – has ultimately shaped me for something better than I was when I set out to make sense of it long ago. Of course, bad things happened along the way – and still do. However, many of the incidents that initially seemed wrong and insurmountable, like rejections, brokenness, wrong turnings and missed opportunities, have not been entirely futile, and I must admit that these experiences have taught me lessons for which I am grateful. Ultimately, however, no matter how wrong-headed we are, there is forgiveness in Christ and we remain recipients of God's benevolence. So although we may not be grateful for suffering and sin, we can give thanks for being forgiven and grasp the opportunity to start afresh. I cannot call myself a Christian if I eschew gratitude.

Lastly there is *envy*, in essence the opposite of gratitude. Years ago, I read Austrian psychoanalyst Melanie Klein's thoughtful study on the relationship between envy and gratitude. Klein was convinced that envy "is the most potent factor in undermining feelings of love and gratitude at their root [...]." She distinguishes between envy and jealousy. Envy is the "[...] the angry feeling [towards] another person [who] possesses and enjoys something desirable – the envious impulse [is] to take it away or to spoil it". Jealousy and envy, despite appearing similar, are not quite the same emotion. Envy is essentially hostile and destructive. Jealousy can also be destructive, but it usually stems from the fear or suspicion that one may be replaced in another's affections, thus it involves an element of emotional attachment. Envy is simply destructive hostility and is often unconnected to any idea of relationship. Gratitude, according to Klein, is closely bound up with generosity. It experiences the world as a friendly place and enhances one's capacity for enjoyment. To be grateful is to be satisfied with what one has.

Klein helped me to understand that envy stems from dissatisfaction with oneself. This leads to self-alienation and self-hatred. Envy cannot accept with grace that someone else may have qualities that one does not have oneself. Envy wants to destroy what it cannot have. Envy cannot tolerate being indebted. Envy spoils one's capacity for enjoyment. Envy is definitely an "after-me-you-come-first" sort of emotion. Envy is disastrous for human relationships – it breeds hostility towards those who are perceived to be successful. The recent attacks in South Africa on refugees and immigrants, who are perceived as more successful than local traders, may also have been prompted by envy. Envy is the reverse of gratitude. While one can understand and overcome resentment and regret, envy has no redeeming features. Only true gratitude can dispel envy.

The story of Saul and David's relationship is a biblical case study on envy. Saul, "a handsome young man", becomes the first king of Israel. His rule is fraught with dissension and eventually God says to Samuel: "How long will you grieve over Saul? I have rejected him from being king over Israel" (1 Sam 16:1). Instead God chooses David, a "ruddy" young shepherd with "beautiful eyes" (1 Sam 16:12). We are then told that the "spirit of the Lord departed from Saul and an evil spirit from the Lord tormented him" (1 Sam 16:14). I am not sure what this means, but I can see that the stage is set – a spirit of envy grips Saul that ultimately drives him to murderous acts. Saul, a man blessed by God with so much promise, is destroyed by his envy of David. In his play *David*, D. H. Lawrence has Saul say of himself: "I am a man given over to trouble and tossed between two winds." Yet at his burial, David laments over Saul in a poem of great beauty and irony, a generous homage free of rancour.

I have often wondered whether the hostility of the religious and political authorities towards Jesus was not also motivated by envy. The power of his teaching, the vividness of the parables and the lessons they contained, his ability to see through their connivances to catch him out, the miracle healings and the devotion of his followers could all have evoked envy in the hearts of those who were threatened by his very presence. Nowhere do I read that there was any gratitude expressed by the religious authorities of his day when Jesus restored sight to the blind and enabled the lame to walk.

The very word "Eucharist" means thanksgiving, and takes us to the heart of worship as an act of thanksgiving towards God. I like responding to the request at the beginning of the Eucharistic prayer to "[…] give thanks to the Lord our God", with the words: "It is right to give God thanks and praise." The prayer continues: "It is right and indeed our duty and joy […] always and everywhere to give thanks through Jesus Christ your only Son Our Lord." The Eucharist is the great feast of thanksgiving. The fact that Jesus took bread and gave thanks and then said: "Do this in remembrance of me [...]" grounds the Eucharist as the central act of thankful remembrance of all that Christ has done for us. It is also more than thanksgiving and remembrance: it is a gift to us. Martin Luther (1483–1546) knew this, for he believed that in the sacrament it is God who is the giver. The reformer John Calvin also saw the Eucharist as a gift. He wrote: "The Supper itself is a gift of God, which should [be] received with thanksgiving." Thanksgiving is central to the Eucharist – the gift is Christ himself. He is both the source of the gift and the gift itself. The action of the Holy Spirit creates the bond between the worshipper and the true gift received in faith.

My experience of the Eucharist is that of an Anglican. The preaching of the word and the taking of bread and wine are, in fact, one whole central act of worship. It is difficult for me to imagine separating the ministry of the word from Communion. The themes of praise, thanksgiving, sacrifice and remembrance follow in related steps in the Eucharistic prayer until the final breaking of bread takes place. The prayer begins with the exuberance of praise as we say together: "Holy, holy, holy Lord, God of power and might, heaven and earth are full of your glory, Hosanna in the highest!" Thanks and praise continue to be intermingled as we call to mind the great acts of our salvation in Christ, summed up in the broken bread and the cup of wine. The ground is prepared for our proclaiming of the great mystery of faith:

Christ has died
Christ is risen
Christ will come again.

Partaking in the Eucharist without humility is unthinkable, so we say: "We do not presume to come to this your table, merciful Lord trusting in our own righteousness ..." We trust only in God's righteousness and limitless mercy. After eating the bread and drinking the wine, we pray: "[W]e offer ourselves to you as a living sacrifice in Jesus Christ our Lord. Send us out into the world in the power of the Holy Spirit to live and work to your praise and glory." Like most people, I draw back at the thought of sacrifice. Frankly, it scares me. I need to remind myself that sacrifice is not primarily about suffering. It is about being holy, being our whole selves. The truth is that we are all very much beginners at the job of true sacrifice, but we dare not evade it.

The Eucharist is more than thanksgiving. Without getting into a debate about whether Christ is truly present in the elements or not, what is incontravertible is that Jesus did four things: he took, he blessed, he broke and he gave. When Francis Cull first made me aware of the importance of these four actions, my celebration of the Eucharist changed. Previously it had been a rite that I could assent to intellectually, but which had little impact on my life of faith. Like Michael Welker, quoting Immanuel Kant, the Eucharist had for me all too frequently been "a dismal enterprise". This changed once I grasped that Jesus' four actions were powerful metaphors for my life of faith. It was as if I woke up. The bread and the wine took on practical significance for my life as follows:

Jesus first *takes* the bread and the wine and offers it for blessing. Bread is taken in a world in which bread is not justly distributed and people starve daily for lack of. Wine is taken in a world where wine is abused and drunkenness and alcoholism are common. The ingredients of the Eucharist are earthy – "the work of human hands," not manna sent from on high. So I am reminded that everything is tainted, yet everything can be redeemed. We present ourselves at the table as part of the polluted world, and we are accepted, warts and all, with all our hang-ups, defences and conceits. In Kenneth Leech's paraphrase: "Blessed are you Lord God of all creation. Through your goodness we have this person to offer, which the womb of woman has given and human hands have influenced, shaped and damaged. It will become the Body of Christ." Indeed cause for thankfulness!

Jesus then *blesses* the bread and the wine. We are taken and then blessed. To be blessed means to be made happy, to be showered with divine mercy, to start afresh as a new creation and the recipient of grace. This is possible only through the transforming power of the Holy Spirit who brings about change. This promise of transforming power sums up the whole of the Christian life and prayer. The Eucharistic prayer is at the centre of all Christian prayer and of all our common life together. Come, be blessed, eat and drink, and remember that mine is the power that can transform the world!

After blessing it, Jesus *breaks* the bread. I am beginning to understand more fully, as the years pass, how much I need to have the bunkum I have absorbed over a lifetime rooted out in order to be the person I am intended to be. As Leech says, the breaking is as much a breaking down as it is a breaking through. The breaking of the one bread is the symbol of Christ's body scattered throughout the world, yet still one. In the words of the *Didache,* that early manual of Christian teaching: "As this broken bread was scattered upon the mountains, and being gathered together and made one, so may thy church be gathered together into thy kingdom from the end of the earth." So the breaking is both an act of division and of unification. It binds me to all people eating the bread throughout the world. For this communion of people I am intensely grateful.

Finally, Jesus *gives* the bread and we share anew in Christ's life. This is the climax of the Eucharist. We share in the life of Christ. In Leech's words: "We receive the Body of Christ which we already are: so we eat what we are, and become what we are." We are reminded, blessed and renewed by the simple action of eating bread and sipping wine. How can we not be thankful? In Jesus' actions we see the pattern for our spirituality: offering, blessing, breaking and sharing.

We share the bread and wine in an unsharing, wasteful world. When I see a person picking through my garbage, when waste poisons the earth and pollution hangs heavy in the air, I am compelled to ask: what does the Eucharist mean in my context today? Can I still hold on to my personal feelings of gratitude in the face of injustice, inequality and environmental degradation?

I remind myself that inequality and self-centredness do not have the last word; that the Eucharist is a very social, if not subversive, act. Luke 22:14-28 tells us that immediately after Jesus took the cup and the bread, his disciples squabbled about who was to be regarded as the greatest among them. Jesus reminds them that service is the core of discipleship: "For who is greater, the one who is at the table or the one who serves?" When John (13:1-20) relates the events of the same day, he starts with the story of Jesus washing the disciples' feet. Jesus tells us that we should do as he has done by washing one another's feet. The bread and the wine are symbols of sharing our resources in the service of others. The Eucharist has profound social implications. We cannot eat the bread or drink the wine if we are reluctant to be part of God's transforming acts in the world. We are fed in order that we can do likewise. Otherwise there is little point in our rituals. Only when our rituals are intrinsically part of our actions for justice in a world of overwhelming need can the Eucharist be a sacrament of equality in an unequal world. The Eucharist is a weekly reminder that all who partake of the feast can please the Giver of the gift by giving to others.

Christianity has a great diversity of traditions and there are differences within our traditions as to how we interpret our faith. Anglicans can, for instance, be evangelicals or Anglo Catholics, or anything in-between – all within one large communion. Undoubtedly this produces stresses and strains, but it is also an opportunity for accommodation and acceptance. Christianity has found a home in widely different cultures, societies and countries. At the Shantivanam Ashram in Tamil Naidu, I was anointed with a red mark (a *tilaka*) on my forehead, then served the Eucharist on a brass plate decorated with flowers, accompanied by Indian music. In Inhambane in Mozambique the Eucharist was served under a wild fig tree on a plate of banana leaves. In Mamelodi outside Pretoria, we danced the peace to the music of marimbas before singing our way through the Eucharist. In New York, a solemn silence allowed us to ponder the mysteries of communion. Different cultures, different practices, different understandings, yet we all say: "We who are many are one body for we all partake of the one bread."

If gratitude is truly a blessing, can it be acquired? Can I *become* grateful? I think so – but it needs awareness and some practice. The virtue of gratitude can be cultivated. God knows our need to live out of thankfulness and shows us the way through being a God of bounty. Being perennially dissatisfied with the present and nostalgic for better times is a dead end. We need to learn to love the age we live in. It is the best age for each of us, the age in which God has placed us. We cannot live well longing for another time. We certainly cannot pray with thanksgiving unless we believe that it is by grace that we exist this day. "God has chosen our age for us … We have no right to prefer another one," Jean Leclerq warns us. We can only taste the blessing of God's bounty when we are grateful for being alive in the here and now.

Kathleen Norris writes:

> True gratitude is magnificat; that is, it magnifies. It refuses to remain strictly private but, like poetry itself, employs the personal to convey something more universal, stories that others may well claim as their own. Gratitude in this sense reverberates through one's relationships with others and the world. As *Magnificat*, gratitude is praise in the light of the past and it uses past experience to bolster the ability to enter into an unknown future with trust and hope. As *Magnificat*, gratitude is not a "thank you" for a new sense of ease or comfort. If nothing else, Mary's song in the first chapter of Luke reveals that *Magnificat* has its own reward. And yet such wanton thanksgiving seems to provide Mary with strength for accepting the gift of the incarnation and for taking off for territories unknown.

Gratitude is our *magnificat*, enhanced when ordinary, everyday happenings spark a moment of delight. A stranger's smile, a new tendril on a vine, the smell of freshly brewed coffee, sliding between clean sheets after a long, hot day – these are ordinary events all magnified by a flash of gratitude. The "ordinary" is momentarily lit up by a shaft of thankfulness, and then the day moves on. However, we can "bank" the moment of the delight and allow it to grow as we keep our antennae alert to receive what the day has to offer us.

Being grateful may just become easier as time passes. At my age, time races on. Just the gift of life is enough. Enough means acceptance of my weaknesses and strengths. Saying "thank you" is easier than it has ever been. Central to growing old with gratitude is looking back with a mixture of acceptance and surprise, and, at the same time, never losing the ability to wonder at the events of today. All of life is a gift and we are recipients of life's gifts. This is what I learnt from Alpha Ackermann. Yes, I am grateful, and yes, I am not consistently or sufficiently grateful. I know the fruits of thankfulness. I also know the havoc that dissatisfaction, regret, resentment and envy can wreak. Gratitude is indeed "a labour undertaken by the soul" and we *can* learn to be more thankful – and thus happy. The place to start is with the small, often insignificant and very ordinary everyday moments, meetings and sights. Delight in the ordinary and be blessed by gratitude.

NOTES

Fynbos is the Afrikaans word for "fine bush" and refers to the slender leaves of the flora of the Western Cape. *Fynbos,* the shrub and heath-like vegetation of this area, makes up the world's sixth floral kingdom and is both the smallest in area and the richest in species.

Two books have contributed significantly to this chapter. The first is a collected volume of essays entitled *The Psychology of Gratitude* (see Emmons and McCullough). It begins with the philosophical, theological and historical foundations of gratitude and then covers current research from the field of psychology on this topic. The second is Mary Jo Leddy's work, *Radical Gratitude*. Quotes from Immanuel Kant's *The Metaphysical Principles of Virtue*: Part II of *The Metaphysics of Morals* and David Hume's *A Treatise of Human Nature* are taken from *The Psychology of Gratitude*. It is interesting to note that Kant very clearly postulates that there is only one unqualifiedly good thing in the world and that is good will; see Alan Wood, *Kant's Ethical Thought*.

The word "gratitude" is derived from the Latin *gratia*, meaning "favour", and *gratus*, meaning "pleasing".

For a discussion on virtue in the thinking of Socrates and Aristotle, see Anthony Kenny's *Ancient Philosophy* (see Works consulted). The Stoic Lucius Annaeus Seneca (born c.4 B.C.E.–died 65 C.E.), who wrote a series of *Moral Discourses*, argued that understanding the intention of both giver and receiver of benefits is of utmost importance in understanding gratitude. Good consequences that are devoid of good intentions do not create a debt of gratitude. Then the intention is to bind the receiver to the giver.

The history and origins of leprosy is complex and unclear; see John R. Trautman M.D., "A brief history of Hansen's disease", on http://www.ncbi.nlm.nih.gov/pmc/articles/PMC1911721/pdf/bullnyacadmed00073-0005.pdf. Leprosy, known as Hansen's disease, is a serious skin disease that develops over a long period of time and until 1968 was believed to be uncontrollable and incurable. According to the *Oxford Companion to the Bible*, the disease known as leprosy in the New Testament is different from the disease known as leprosy today. It is clear that what is referred to as leprosy in the Bible covers a wide range of skin disorders. What is also clear is that so-called lepers in the Bible were treated as ritually unclean and thus shunned.

The quotations from André Louf and Jean Leclerq are taken from Hannah Ward and Jennifer Wild, *The Monastic Way* (see Works consulted).

A charming and most readable book on the *Examen* is *Sleeping with Bread: Holding what Gives you Life* by Dennis Linn, Sheila Fabricant Linn and Matthew Linn (Mahwah: Paulist Press, 1995).

As part of her analysis of processes of alienation in North American culture, Leddy says that average Americans watch television for twenty-six hours a week. By the end of their lives they will have watched thirteen years of continuous programming. Advertising takes up twenty-seven per cent of prime television time. Thus the average American watches three solid years of advertising alone in the course of a lifetime – a sobering thought for the average South African.

The discussion of gratitude towards your enemies and the quotation of the Dalai Lama come from Patrick Fitzgerald's article "Gratitude and justice".

For the theodicy question, namely the question of human suffering in the face of a loving and all-powerful God (inevitably raised in discussions on the providence of God), see chapter 4 on lament in Denise M. Ackermann, *After the Locusts: Letters from a Landscape of Faith* (Grand Rapids: Eerdmans, 2003).

Various names are used today to describe the Eucharist: the Lord's Supper, Holy Communion, holy mysteries, synaxis, mass, liturgy. According to the Windsor Report (1971) of the Anglican-Roman Catholic International Commission and the later Eucharistic Doctrine Elucidation (1979), the term "Eucharist" is found in the *Didache* and in the writing of Justin Martyr, a Christian apologist of the second century. I have drawn on the texts of Michael Welker and Kenneth Leech for the section in this chapter on the Eucharist.

I am indebted to Lewis Hyde (*The Gift: Imagination and the Erotic Life of Poetry* (New York: Vintage, 1983) who describes gratitude as a "labor undertaken by the soul".

WORKS CONSULTED

Ackermann, Denise, M. *After the Locusts: Letters from a Landscape of Faith.* Grand Rapids: Eerdmans, 2003.

Anglican Prayer Book 1989. Church of the Province of Southern Africa. London: Collins Liturgical Publications, 1993.

Aristotle. *Nicomachean Ethics.* Translated by D. Ross. Revised by J. L. Ackrill and J. O. Urmson. Oxford: Oxford University Press, 1998.

Barth, Karl. *The Christian Life, Church Dogmatics IV/4, Lecture Fragments.* Translated by G. W. Bromiley. Grand Rapids: Eerdmans, 1981.

De Caussade, Jean-Pierre. *Self Abandonment to Divine Providence.* Translated by A. Thorold. Edited by J. Joyce. Springfield, IL: Templegate, 1962.

Emmons, Robert A. and Michael E. McCullough, eds. *The Psychology of Gratitude.* Oxford: Oxford University Press, 2004.

Fitzgerald, Patrick. "Gratitude and Justice." *Ethics* 109 (October 1998): 119-153.

Fleming, David L., ed. *The Christian Ministry of Spiritual Direction.* St. Louis: Revue for Religious, 1988.

Foot, Philippa. *Natural Goodness.* Oxford: Clarendon Press, 2001.

Gerrish, B.A. *Grace and Gratitude: The Eucharistic Theology of John Calvin.* Minneapolis: Fortress Press, 1993.

Honderich, Ted, ed. *The Oxford Companion to Philosophy.* Oxford: Oxford University Press, 1995.

Hyde, Lewis. *The Gift: Imagination and the Erotic Life of Poetry.* New York: Vintage, 1983.

Kenny, Anthony. *Ancient Philosophy: A New History of Western Philosophy, Vol. 1.* Oxford: Clarendon Press, 2004.

Klein, Melanie. *Envy and Gratitude: A Study of Unconscious Sources.* London: Tavistock Publications, 1962.

Leddy, Mary Jo. *Radical Gratitude.* Maryknoll: Orbis Books, 2003.

Leech, Kenneth. *True Prayer: An Introduction to Christian Spirituality.* London: Sheldon Press, 1980.

Linn, Dennis, Sheila Fabricant Linn and Matthew Linn. *Sleeping with Bread: Holding what Gives you Life.* Mahwah: Paulist Press, 1995.

Nietzsche, Friederich. *The Portable Nietzsche*. Translated by W. Kaufmann. New York: Viking, 1968.

Norris, Kathleen. "Gratitude at Last." *Christian Century* (June 3-10, 1998): 582.

Ricoeur, Paul. *The Course of Recognition*. Translated by D. Pellauer. Cambridge, MA: Harvard University Press, 2005.

Schimmel, Solomon. "Gratitude in Judaism." In *The Psychology of Gratitude*, edited by Robert A. Emmons and Michael E. McCullough. Oxford: Oxford University Press, 2004.

Trautman, John R. M.D., "A brief history of Hansen's disease". [online] http://www.ncbi.nlm.nih.gov/pmc/articles/PMC1911721/pdf/bullnyacadmed00073-0005.pdf.

Ward, Hannah and Jennifer Wild. *The Monastic Way: Ancient Wisdom for Contemporary Living: A Book of Daily Readings*. Grand Rapids: Eerdmans, 2006.

Welker, Michael. *What Happens in Holy Communion?* Translated by J. F. Hoffmeyer. Grand Rapids: Eerdmans, 2000.

Wood, Alan. *Kant's Ethical Thought*. Cambridge: Cambridge University Press, 1999.

CHAPTER SEVEN

Blessed are those who know when enough is enough, for they will be able to share with freedom

I am a "have" living in a world of great need. I have had a job, a roof over my head, the opportunity to travel in ample measure, and the security of medical insurance and a pension. There are clothes, more than I need, in my cupboard; there is food in my pantry, a car in my garage, and there are more books in my house than I can read in a lifetime. Only once have I sampled hunger – an experience almost too trivial to mention. I was at university in the fifties. The head of my residence regularly won the annual prize for managing on the most frugal budget. Needless to say, the food was bad and excessively skimpy. We were a post-war generation who did not have money to spend, and my parents lived far away in another country so that food from home was not an option. Those three and half years of living in a residence have left vivid memories of a gnawing feeling in my empty stomach! I can still see that half slice of old bread covered with a piece of stiff French polony that was our Sunday evening meal. In my second year, I led a march to the rector's house, carrying my plate of meat on which I had discovered a worm. I was threatened with expulsion if I did not return to my residence immediately. I capitulated. The thought of having to leave university and go home was not on my agenda. Underqualified at the age of nineteen with a bachelor's degree in history and English, I went to work as a very indifferent typist. The challenge of living on a meagre salary was easily brushed aside with the insouciance of youth and the security of being white in an apartheid country. I belonged to the privileged and have always known that the next meal will be there.

Why these personal snippets? Because I am immediately thrust into "the belly of a paradox". I can attempt this piece only by facing myself. This blessing has been the most painful and the most difficult to write about because it stands as an accusation against my life of privilege. I know that it is necessary to work out when enough is enough if one wishes to follow the man on the borrowed donkey. The further I examine what constitutes "enough" in my life, the more I feel that I can never measure up to what is asked of me. My life is one of enormous contradictions. I am a Christian, a follower of the man who had nowhere to lay his head, whose possessions were paltry, and who lived among the "have-nots" of his time. Everyday I ask myself: "When is enough enough?" I wish I could say I know the answer to this vexing question. Being a "have" skews my assumptions and confronts me with guilt and dismay. The "enough" question will simply not let me go.

I write in a land of great need. There are so many stories of poverty in the South African context that it seems shabby to single out one. However, this story tells of the impact of poverty on a single-parent household – a pattern that is repeated more than a thousand-fold throughout our country. It is the testimony of a young woman in her thirties from Mpumalanga, given at the Poverty Hearings. I do not know her name so I will call her Dorcas.

> At home we are nine children and my mother. We all sleep in one shack. The children sleep outside in summer, as the shack is too small to fit all of us. When it rains, all nine of us must find a way to fit inside to sleep. I have HIV and TB. I had medication for six months but now I do not have it. All nine of us are supported by a pension from my mother. My eight year old was chased away from school because he did not have shoes. He was wearing my shoes (grey worn-out takkies [canvas shoes]) and the teacher took them from him and chased him

away. We have no food. My mother is from Klerksdorp – we have no relatives here – even you can be my relative. My help comes from neighbours.

Dorcas's plight haunts me. Can I be her relative? Will she survive? Dorothy Day, founder of the Catholic Worker Movement and social activist for justice for the poor, encapsulated the dilemma of the "haves": "How can we say to these people [the poor], 'Rejoice and be exceedingly glad, for great is your reward in heaven', when we are living comfortably in a warm house, sitting down to a good table, decently clothed?" I wonder whether I will live to see a different life for the hundreds of thousands of Dorcases in our country or an end to the dozens of young men waiting at traffic intersections for someone to stop and offer them a job for the day. When will street children disappear from our streets because they are housed in places of refuge? When will children in poor areas have proper school buildings, dedicated teachers and educational resources? Will this happen in my lifetime? Is my lament nothing more than the whinge of a privileged old woman who fails to understand the complexities of addressing past injustices and present problems of governance?

I return to Dorcas's plight, and the questions come fast and furiously. While greed and rampant consumerism have brought about the world's present economic woes, how do those of us who attempt to follow Jesus deal with the truth that we too are consumers in a world of great need? Can Christians bring alternative practices and values to the marketplace? What criteria determine whether a transaction is just and in accordance with God's will? I believe that we are all called to be agents for the coming reign of God that we pray for daily. But we are continuously tripped up by greed, the need to acquire and possess, and desires that are self-centred. We suffer from a frequent lack of awareness of how consumerism infiltrates our consciousness, and even our different faith communities. How can we know the blessing of sharing God's bounty ungrudgingly so that there will be enough for everyone?

That I am no economist will become abundantly clear as I struggle to understand my theme. However, I reject the notion that economics and theology live in two different worlds and have nothing to say to one another. Neither economics nor theology has a privileged status; they simply approach human activity in different ways. Economic exchange is one of the activities people undertake, but it is not the only activity. The term "economy" comes from the Greek word for "housekeeping". We share a common household and our well-being depends on our actions, our ethical principles, our civic virtues, and on just and caring housekeeping.

Former Archbishop Rowan Williams writes that theology can contribute two things to the discussion of an ethical economic future. First, it challenges the idea "that there is a mysterious uniqueness about economic life" that is outside the scope of our choices and ability to understand. Second, Christian theology can offer a critical account of how things should be and provide a basis for "talking about character and thus about virtue." So I am rushing in, but without fear that this is territory on which only angels may tread. Angels, I hope, welcome and share an interest in economic justice! We are all members of the household of God, in which no one is dispensable or of less value. What affects one, affects all. When the parts flourish, the whole flourishes. Dorcas's life and mine are bound together. The common narrative in our lives is that we are both made in the image of God. We share this image; it defines our common humanity.

I remember that Dom Helder Câmara (1909–1999), the Brazilian Archbishop who was known for his concern for the poor, once remarked: "When I help the poor I am called a saint, but when I ask why they are poor, I am called a communist." I am neither of these, but I know that the question of "enough" will not let me go, and will require more than compassion for the needy or palliative, short-term responses from me. I confess to feeling daunted. However, sidestepping this issue is not an acceptable alternative. My effort to understand the predicament of "enough" will raise more questions than provide answers. I am truly stuck in that paradoxical belly.

As I struggle to navigate through unknown territory, filled with contradiction and paradox, I want to consider the following themes: first

I want to look at my own context, then at the impact of globalisation on our world and what I understand of the free market. Next I attempt a short piece on capitalism, followed by the impact of consumerism on the environment and the church. Finally, I ask if scripture gives us guidance for the "enough" question, and conclude that sharing is necessary, but not always straightforward. The chapter ends with what partaking of the Eucharist can mean for followers of Jesus.

Living in South Africa is an experience of deep contrasts. We do not need that incomprehensible measurement called the Gini Coefficient to tell us that there is a huge disparity between the rich and the poor in our country. I cannot possibly imagine what "enough" means for those who have not enjoyed my privileges. Economic inequality is a daily reality: grinding poverty and unemployment; indifferent health care for the poor (many of whom like Dorcas suffer the onslaught of diseases such HIV and AIDS and drug-resistant tuberculosis); a deteriorating educational system; the lack of transport which results in the elderly having to walk miles and stand in queues for hours, sometimes days, for their meagre pensions. Beggars at traffic lights are a common sight. Women market their bodies on street corners of a nearby suburb where the walled gardens contain large homes with their own swimming pools. Informal settlements around our cities grow daily as people flock from the countryside to try to eke out a living in the urban areas. The urgently needed redistribution of land seems to have stalled, further exacerbating the unhappy processes of urbanisation. About fifteen million people of the population of approximately fifty million live on social grants, making South Africa proportionately the biggest spender on social grants in the world. Yet, only about six million pay individual income tax, accounting for just less than thirty per cent of the total tax income!

I know that pervasive poverty and the unequal distribution of resources is not only a South African problem. It is a worldwide blight. Approximately one-fifth of the world's population live in absolute poverty, with hunger, disease, squalid living conditions, insecurity and fear as a constant. Mostly these conditions occur in poor or "developing" countries. Children born in these countries are thirteen times more likely to die before the age of five than those born in the wealthier parts of the world.

Jolted and dispirited by this picture, I am also angry and bewildered. Throughout the struggle for freedom in our country, I supported the ideals of the African National Congress (ANC). Now I am confronted almost daily with the terrible waste of diminishing resources, together with mounting corruption and greed in this organisation's ranks. I search in vain for the morality that made this organisation respected throughout the world. I am bewildered that our new leaders can celebrate their last electoral victory and the hundred-year birthday of the ANC with vintage French champagne and Cuban cigars and, with arrogant insensitivity, drive around in luxury cars sporting all manner of unnecessary gadgets while pleading the cause of the poor. I am angry when national lottery money is given to fund organisational festivities, while charities that support abandoned children, feed the hungry and house the destitute are allowed to implode for lack of funding. I am deeply troubled by the lack of shame at these excesses and the blithe indifference to what will happen when the poor rise up and say: "Enough!" In a recent public address, Dr Mamphela Ramphele, academic and leader of one of our new political parties, Agang, tellingly remarked that "corruption is a tax on the poor". And so it is. The "new haves" are not excluded from the need to examine what "enough" means.

I have a further concern. The feminisation of poverty is a pernicious problem in our country. Of our approximately twenty-five million women, nearly sixty per cent live in rural areas. These women have little access to resources, are often poorly educated, suffer from chronic illnesses, and are frequently the sole providers for their children. Girls help mothers carry their responsibilities and this takes them out of school, perpetuating the cycle of poverty and lack of skills development. According to a South African Department of Health survey, just over thirty per cent of women between the ages of fifteen and forty-nine who visited health clinics in 2010 were HIV positive. When these infected women succumb to AIDS-related diseases, the number of child-headed households increases. They have no income other than a social grant. I think of Nandipha Ndungane, a teenager who is head of a family of six living in an Eastern Cape informal settlement and trying to survive on a pitiful social grant. "My grocery list is simple – samp [Indian corn] and sour milk," she says. What is the future for this family decimated by AIDS? According to Statistics South Africa, some forty-seven per cent of South Africans live on less than the "lower-bound" poverty line. This means that a huge segment of our people, mostly women, do not have three hundred and twenty-two rand (about thirty dollars) a month for essential food and other items.

As the worldwide demand for certain raw materials slows down, the South African mining sector has come under pressure and has retrenched workers. The shrinking market and perceived low wages have made local labour strikes the order of the day. The manufacturing sector has also suffered. In the Western Cape, clothing factories, which largely employ women, have closed because they cannot compete with cheap Chinese imports. This highlights a further contradiction: our governing alliance is ostensibly concerned about the plight of unemployed workers and promises to create a million jobs in the next five years, but its pandering to the Chinese prevents it from putting a brake on cheap Chinese imported goods. Every time I buy an item of clothing, I have to be careful not to give a Chinese worker a job at the expense of our own people.

Our situation has been exacerbated by the world economic meltdown, an event that was not of our making. The result of unmitigated economic failure let loose on the world has made Karl Marx's words truly prophetic: "Modern bourgeois society, [...] a society that has conjured up such gigantic means of production and of exchange, is like the sorcerer who is no longer able to control the power of the nether world whom he has called up by his spells." However, the appalling scandal of the present economic implosion is that *children are dying* and it is calculated that *over a billion people went hungry in 2010, the majority of whom live in Africa.*

I am no economist. In fact, I find "economic speak" largely incomprehensible. But, in my untutored attempts to understand the way things are, I can see that living in a globalised world is a further challenge. "Globalisation" is a common buzzword or term used these days to describe the economic interdependence of countries. This is not anything new. The great empires of Assyria, Babylon, Persia and especially Rome in their day became global networks of trade, military and political power. The Phoenicians, the Arabs and the Chinese have a long history of international trading. More recently, the colonial powers of Britain and France, for example, took advantage of the economic resources of distant countries, enabling the colonial power to thrive economically, but leaving the colonised territories exploited and largely underdeveloped. Today, the economic and military power of the United States has created a modern-day "empire" of globalised power with China fast following suit.

Nor is globalisation new in our part of the world. For a very long time people have migrated across national boundaries and there has been religious and cultural interaction between peoples, countries and regions. As the world shrinks, many aspects of our lives are affected: our cultural identities, the ways in which we conduct our politics, our exchanges of ideas and knowledge, and our social interactions. It is a process fostered by the explosion of electronic media and communications. Globalisation is here to stay. "In this globalised world, no single country can live or work on its own. We are all tied together in a common destiny," Nelson Mandela said in Cape Town in 1999. So, while our poverty can, in part, be attributed to the inequalities spawned by apartheid, present ineffectual policies and inefficient governance, what happens in the northern hemisphere and the countries of Asia also affects our economy. We too are part of the globalised economic reality, as we found out when the economies of many northern countries imploded in 2008.

Is globalisation a two-edged sword bringing benefits to some and misery to others? I am not competent to analyse this question adequately. I can see that there are advantages in the flow of people and capital across borders. I benefit hugely from the increased mobility offered by globalised transport, communications and computer technology. I make use of international goods and services. I watched the triumph of the Tunisian and Egyptian people over tyranny on my television and felt a sense of solidarity with them. Their world momentarily became part of mine.

At the same time, I also see how the economic system under which we have lived for so long is now disreputable, linked as it is to corporate greed. I watch the increasing power of transnational corporations with distaste and a great deal of trepidation. These corporations engage in business that includes sales, distribution, extraction and manufacturing in more than one country at a time. They are also responsible for a great deal of the capital flow across borders and account for roughly two-thirds of the world's trade in goods and services. They have global power and their decisions are driven solely by profit. They are aided by large international banking institutions, which have played a major role in recent disreputable economic practices.

The transnational corporations are largely based in Europe, North America and Japan. Statistics overwhelm me, but when I read that the largest three hundred control at least one quarter of the world's productive assets (worth some five trillion dollars), I feel vaguely sick. When I am then told that the sales of some of these corporations exceed the gross domestic product of reputable countries in Europe, I feel resistance rising in me. We do not vote for these transnational corporations, yet they control our lives with a disproportionate amount of power. When the Shell corporation wants to prospect for gas by fracking in pristine areas of our Karoo, my resistance turns to anger, fanned by the knowledge that their sales equal the gross domestic product of Iran and that their regard for the environment is zero. Ever since their rape of the Niger Delta, I have tried never to stop at a Shell filling station. On his release from prison, Nelson Mandela said: "Together we live in a global neighbourhood and it is not to the long-term benefit of any if there are islands of wealth in a sea of poverty. We need a globalisation of responsibility as well." "Responsibility" is a word missing from the vocabularies of too many of these transnationals!

Having said all this, I drive a Japanese car; I use a computer made in the United States; my watch comes from Switzerland; I have electrical appliances that are made in Europe; I take medicine that is developed and manufactured abroad; I am sure that I have bought items of clothing produced by sweatshops in India or China, and my book shelves are packed with books printed in an array of different countries. I am a participant in the globalised world; my life is riddled with contradictions, and my rather pitiful resistance to Shell mocks me at every turn in my home. We may not have power over the financial institutions of the world, but we too are cogs in the wheels of "want more, buy more". We are all tainted by greed that leads to over-consumption. Can we even begin to know when enough is enough?

I wonder about some of the shibboleths we live with, such as that of the "free market", a mantra I have heard repeated for as long as I can remember. When exactly is a market free? Is it the "free market" that has dumped us into the worst economic crisis since the 1930s? Can a market truly be free in the sense that everyone involved in the market is free to trade, buy and sell in a manner that is fair to all?

For me that entity called "the market", which seems to hold such sway over our lives, is simply a description of commercial activity where goods and services are bought and sold – from soap to financial services, to stocks and bonds, to commodities like precious metals and agricultural produce. We have lived with markets for millennia, but today's market has a life of its own that I do not understand. It is clear, however, that "the market" has created modern society and contributes hugely to the shaping of our identities.

In South Africa, "the market" can mean different things to different sections of our population. In fact, we live with at least two in parallel. The first is the market of capitalism with all its potential and its dangers. The second belongs to what is called the informal economy, exemplified by open-air markets found throughout the African continent. Here the basic necessities of life are sold: anything from used tyres, scrap metal, cheap clothing and plastic wares to hunks of meat, sizzling boerewors and spicy chicken on open fires, and mounds of vegetables. These markets teem with life, bartering activities, and a mixture of smells and sights. They play a vital role in providing sustenance and employment for the poor. They cater for those who are economically disadvantaged, who do not trade in stocks and shares, and whose basic needs centre on economic survival. The *spaza* shops that are scattered throughout the townships and rural areas in our country are another manifestation of this informal market.

So when is a market free? This is a question for the worldwide capitalist market system inhabited by traders in securities, bankers, international trade organisations and multinational companies. We can guess the answer. Who has the power in this "free market"? If twenty per cent of the world's population consumes sixteen times as much as the poorest twenty per cent, the power to purchase in the market seems to lie with the "haves". Clearly, not everybody has the same freedom or access to the same benefits of trading. As self-interest is this market's dominant motive, it can be open to socially destructive possibilities.

Let us, for example, consider the power of advertising. Advertising favours those who seek to sell their goods with disproportionate power over those who seek to buy goods. Advertising aims to seduce people to want more and therefore to buy more. It bombards the public with images calculated to evoke hopes and desires that are often not entirely honest. I view all advertising with the utmost suspicion and am fortunate that it has a reverse effect on me. The more I am bombarded, the more resistant I become to whatever product is being thrust at me. At the same time I am aware of its power over the minds of my grandchildren – and by extension, all children. Images of the "good life" projected on television are calculated to arouse both dissatisfaction with one's present lot and a desire for the illustrated goods to ensure a glamorous, exciting and privileged existence. No wonder it is such a lucrative industry!

In our system, companies employ people and provide them with a living. The market in which they operate has no concept of the common good and to expect this is naïve. Market-driven economies are there for profit. Can one realistically expect business to accept corporate responsibility for the effects of its trading, while at the same time it is trying to make maximum profits? I remind myself that to rail against the market as though it were an individual with a conscience is to forget that markets are, in fact, of our own making. They are tools, systems and institutions devised by us in our pursuit of growth, money and the good life.

So what does all this mean for Dorcas? I wager that she longs for a bigger house, schooling for her children, and enough money to feed and clothe them. She wants to be well, and needs medication and health care for her condition so that she can work and be free from the worry of providing for her family. Is this a lot to ask? Although I cannot make the connections, I also wager that Dorcas's lot and the circumstances I have described above are somehow linked. Her world, my world, and the world of transnationals do not exist in separate universes. The "enough" question of the "haves" is bound up with Dorcas's and her children's lives.

I call myself a social democrat and my early formative years spent in Sweden gave me a taste of how a social democracy can work. Since 2008 it is clear that the modern capitalist-oriented market has much to answer for. Alternatives are debated and radical solutions sought while bankers, who were bailed out with taxpayers' money, are awarded huge bonuses as I write. I know on which side of this debate I find myself, but I want to try to be fair – so here goes.

It is fashionable today to decry capitalism in South Africa, ironically, especially by politicians who with unfettered greed are benefitting from it hugely. However, one may ask whether all capitalism has been detrimental to human well-being. According to economist Deirdre McCloskey, whose views are not entirely unsympathetic to those of us who seek a different economic ethic, to define capitalism as a vice incarnate does not take cognisance of the development of the middle classes and the stability that they have brought to many societies. She seeks to defend the virtues of bourgeois capitalism. McCloskey points out that countries that were poor in the 1950s, such as Japan, South Korea and Thailand, have become well-to-do under capitalism. Countries that in the 1950s were relatively well-off but still had people living in slums, ill-nourished and ill-clad, such as Britain, Italy and the United States, became richer in terms of housing, clothing and food. Many of the poor moved to the middle classes. Clean water, inoculations and better food purchased with higher incomes raised the average life expectancy in the world from roughly twenty-six years in 1820 to sixty-six years in 2000!

Anti-capitalist rhetoric from societies like North Korea, Myanmar and Zimbabwe is clearly based on the refusal to embrace democracy. Nationalising large businesses, closing down any attempts by small people to buy and sell, while not providing developmental pro-grammes that nurture skills is simply bad politics. The results have been tragic: famine and abject poverty for most of their citizens, not to mention the excesses of tyrannical rule. "Countries where stealing rather than dealing [according to] rules, become poor and remain so," writes McCloskey. It does not matter what kind of stealing it is, she continues. It can be the stealing of failed socialist states, or private or government stealing or bureaucratic stealing and even stealing at the point of a sword. "By doing evil we do badly. And we do well by doing good," she says. This is undoubtedly the woeful reality of a number of countries on our continent.

McCloskey flatly repudiates the present model of capitalism. She argues that when business people "[…] believe that capitalism and profit are good for business but have nothing to do with ethics, that the poor should shut up and settle for what they get, and that we certainly do not need a preacherly ethic of sin and service for com-mercial society; we are in trouble". She adds: "They think Jesus got it all wrong in the Sermon on the Mount."

Any arguments that are based on material achievement only, says

McCloskey, are unconvincing for "what has man profited if he shall gain the whole world and lose his own soul?" Her interest lies in what she understands as bourgeois virtues. A virtue is having good intentions towards people and actively seeking their good. It was Immanuel Kant who proclaimed: "So act that you use humanity, whether in your own person or in the person of another, always at the same time as an end, never merely as a means." McCloskey describes seven virtues that are needed for human beings to flourish: hope, faith, love, justice, courage, temperance and prudence. These virtues are certainly not incompatible with those of the Christian faith.

McCloskey's views are interesting, well presented, and in some cases difficult to refute. However, I am left with one insurmountable problem – acquisitiveness, greed, and the desire for more are deeply part of our humanity. I know this in myself. I cannot separate capitalism from greed. I also know that it is perfectly understandable that those at the bottom of the economic pile desire to join those above them. They want more, and why should they not? The desire for upward mobility is a powerful motivating force that is often exploited by the marketplace of "things". The poorer one is the more one dreams of having money, and the greater the temptation to spend one's scarce resources on buying lottery tickets, or gambling at one of the casinos that are proliferating (in my view polluting) our landscape, or to be duped into having a credit card one cannot afford. Capitalism, as we presently know it, is based on the desire for more – and more. Unless capitalism can coexist with economic justice, and unless the "haves" can fetter their desire for more and more, I cannot see stable and contented societies being achieved.

Consumerism is a worldwide phenomenon. Whether one lives in Africa, North America or the Far East, the consumerist culture is a dominant social force. I note with some sadness that students at some of our universities are now referred to as "clients" – they are consumers of services, rather than human minds acquiring knowledge and learning to think critically. Consumerism is the dominant ideology of our day. In order to live we consume – some much more than others – resources in the form of food, energy and manufactured goods. "Consumption" is not necessarily a bad word – the fact that we consume helps us to develop and enlarge our capabilities. However, when our patterns of consumption determine our behaviour, shape our identities and give meaning to our lives, and when greed is assuaged by ever-greater consumption, we have succumbed to consumerism. This means that we are overly preoccupied with acquiring consumer goods and that our longings and desires are focused on their attainment. Sadly, this is so whether we have the means to satisfy our desires or not.

Being a consumer can consume us. When we vest our self-imagine in what we have, and covet what others have, we become caught in a spiral of desire, insatiable and wasteful at the same time. We are trapped in a death-dealing web of more, more, more. Having becomes the dominant theme in our lives instead of being. We lose sight of the truth that all we have is not only transitory, but it is undeserved and to be held lightly.

Wanting more can lead to ever-increasing debt. "Neither a borrower nor a lender be," says Polonius to his son Laertes in Shakespeare's *Hamlet*. Yet today we find it almost impossible not to make debt, and debt has become deeply embedded in our culture. It was not always the case. Canadian novelist and poet Margaret Atwood hits the nail on the head: "debt goes in and out of fashion, and today's admired free-spending gentleman is tomorrow's despised deadbeat." For over sixty-five years my mother kept meticulous account of what she spent. She had lived through the Great Depression of the 1930s and could never be other than frugal. My family ran no accounts at shops and if we could not pay cash for something, we did without it. If debts were made, they were paid back in the shortest possible time – probably a throwback to a Calvinist ethic of frugality – a tradition in which my father was raised. There was definitely a connection between debt and sin.

Atwood observes that "in Aramaic, the Semitic language spoken by Jesus, the word for 'debt' and the word for 'sin' are the same". Yet, it was during the Reformation that the ban on usury – charging interest on loans – was lifted for Christians. It makes one think! Our God-given ability to imagine and to be creative can be stifled because our imagination is simply captured by "things". I frequently hear parents bemoaning their children's desire for more and I read with repugnance of those whose toddlers' parties cost up to half a million rands! These "diseases of our time" are, in fact, symptoms of a creeping sickness in our society. In the words of Richard Foster:

> [...] the lust for affluence in contemporary society is psychotic. It is psychotic because it has completely lost touch with reality. We crave things we neither need nor enjoy. We buy things we do not want to impress people we do not like [...]. Covetousness we call ambition. Hoarding we call prudence. Greed we call industry.

This book is dedicated to my five grandchildren, each one of them full of promise with much to offer. I want them to inherit a world in which their lives will not be caught up in the desire to consume more and in which human beings will not be measured by what they have. I long for their lives to be touched by the wonder of creation. I want them to see rhinoceroses in the bush, to marvel at a Cape vulture in flight, and to drink water from a tap. But I have profound concerns for the future of the natural world. If we continue to consume at the present rate and allow unconstrained greed to rape the environment, the future of our grandchildren will be marred by the loss of species, the eradication of forests, and the pollution of the seas and ground water. We are making debt on their behalf. I do not need statistical support for the simple truth that the planet is in crisis. It is a given. The question is: how can the tide of consumerism and its destructive effects be stemmed and what can a Christian perspective offer to grappling with when is enough enough? Karl Marx famously predicted: "All that is solid melts into air." He was thinking about global capitalism, but his words are sadly true for our natural world as well.

To begin with, the depth of our dilemma needs to be understood with clarity, away from the obfuscation of politicians and those with vested interests in "business as usual". This generation is faced with two particular problems that are interlinked. First, we almost totally depend on cheap energy, specifically oil and coal; these resources will be exhausted sooner rather than later. Every year they diminish, yet it is generally assumed that continuous growth is the ultimate goal, that this growth will benefit everyone and that it can be contained within the limits of the planet. This cannot be possible. Our present model of "consume more" cannot work. Charles Landry, who has written on how to make a "creative city", says: "Barring manna from heaven it is safe to say that civilization will not survive in its present form. This is not to make an ideological point. There is just not enough planet to maintain culture as we now know it." A "consume more" culture is doomed, yet we keep building, developing and making more, while not investing enough in alternative energy sources such as solar and wind power. Today New York city uses as much electricity as the entire African continent. This cannot go on.

Second, the world's climate *is* changing. The processes of photosynthesis needed to transform carbon dioxide into oxygen have been disrupted over the last two hundred years by our colossal discharge of carbon dioxide and other gases into the atmosphere. The planet is getting hotter, deserts are growing, polar ice and glaciers are melting, all sooner than we anticipated. On a recent trip to the Antarctic I saw how age-old glaciers are shrinking, and the disintegrated Larsen ice shelf dots the Weddell Sea. The results of these changes are unpredictable, but nature will not act according to our rules. The earth is in "bio-deficit", writes theologian Timothy Gorringe. What excesses of climate change will my grandchildren face?

Economists speak of natural capital: water, fish stocks, tropical forests, wetlands, the atmosphere – ecosystems generally. Assessments of the world's ecosystems confirm that many have already collapsed. Water and food are becoming more limited by the day. South Africa is, or rather was, rich in natural capital. Our seas once teemed with fish, but sadly this is no more so. Our wetlands are falling prey to unchecked so-called "development". Bird and plant species are diminishing with startling rapidity as their habitats are destroyed and trade in wild life (insects, reptiles, birds, apes, pangolins and so on), rhino horn and elephant tusks continues unabated. Yet, in our country I hear a variety of objections to environmental concerns: it is a luxury that those who "have" can indulge in. The powerful élites of the north, having already ruined their environments, are now advising us to spare ours, and while poverty is our main environmental problem those dispensing advice are the major polluters of the world and the main consumers of the earth's resources. It is ironical that these polluters and consumers have the temerity to counsel those who live with less.

I know that the main contaminators of the planet are the rich industrialised countries. I know that, as "haves", my family and I consume more of the earth's resources than the poor people a couple of kilometres from our homes. I use more energy, water, oil products and food than most of the people living in my country, while at the same time I am an amateur "greenie" who attempts to recycle, cut down on electricity, and rail against any despoiling of our environment. I do not believe that unlimited "growth" is possible if we are to survive as a species. That type of progress is based on unequal rewards for work, the unending accumulation of goods and services, the continuing underdevelopment of groups of nations and the rape of the environment. This is not the kind of world I want for my grandchildren. Where is our common sense that Karl Barth identified as his favourite gift from the Holy Spirit?

We need, moreover, to understand that ecology has everything to do with relations. Everything is bound together in an infinite web of all-inclusive, interacting relations. We are as much in relation with creation as we are with others and ourselves. Our welfare and the welfare of nature are inseparable. When our environment implodes, we will perish. Yet our views are so human-centred and utilitarian. We have lost our balance. What is not useful for our immediate needs can be discarded. A pertinent example of this loss of balance is the spectacle of people in my city drinking bottled water when our tap water is perfectly healthy. The simple and natural act of drinking a glass of water has become a choice between a dazzling array of bottled "spring" waters (most of which I suspect come from our taps anyway), which also adds to the problem of disposing of plastic. It is tragic that we are not fully in a caring relationship with the earth's resources as our shared destiny.

While heartstrings (including mine) may be tugged by the picture of a polar bear stranded on a piece of shrinking ice, it is the farmer in the developing world trying to cope with diminishing rainfall and its effects on crops that should also be cause for concern. It is most likely that this farmer supports an extended family and could be a woman trying to eke out a basic means of survival in a rapidly changing environment. Unless we develop the idea of environmental justice as a way of bridging the opposing interests that threaten the future of human existence on earth, my grandchildren and their children will have a very unpredictable, even precarious future.

Because we are relational creatures, we should desire what is beneficial for our neighbour, for all people and for our planet, not just for ourselves. Sadly, we are all complicit in using the earth's resources faster than they can be replenished. Forests do not grow overnight, nor can the atmosphere be purified at the click of a finger. One may wonder whether we are living in denial or claiming our freedom to make rational choices for the future of our world. I believe that we have agency to act in such a way that the earth's sustainability can be preserved. Every living thing shares our one *oikos*, one interrelated household. This requires respect for a "being with", for the integrity of creation, and a letting go of human grandiosity, greed and selfishness.

I have no doubt that God is present in the natural world. Teilhard de Chardin said: "The world is God's body. God draws it ever upwards." Thus we respect and cherish it not only for the sake of our continued existence, but also for God's sake. The psalmist sings the cosmic song: "The heavens are telling the glory of God; and the firmament proclaims his handiwork" (Ps 19:1). Can we sing this song? Do we see God's hand in nymph cicadas emerging in their millions from the floor of the forests in the eastern United States every seventeen years only for a couple of days, or in the mating dance of a blue-footed boobie, the migration of millions of wildebeest and zebra over the plains of Serengeti, the lumbering power of a rhinoceros, or the call of the fish eagle? Every tree, every weed, every creature that breathes is infused with the energy of God. We dare not be unmoved by the power present in creation.

Swedish diplomat and Nobel Prize winner Dag Hammarskjöld (1905–1961) in his only work, *Markings*, said:

> God does not die on the day we cease to believe in a personal deity, but we die on the day when our lives cease to be illuminated by the steady radiance, received daily, of a wonder, the source of which is beyond all reason.

Daily wonder at the riches of creation is not a bad place to start reminding ourselves that what we do to our environment we are actually doing to ourselves and to the Creator.

We cannot live as if creation is something separate from ourselves, or divorce ourselves from the marvels that surround us. We need "both bread and beauty," writes Leonardo Boff. When we cease to wonder at beauty we are no longer truly human. In his weekly column in a local newspaper, *Die Burger* (18.06.11), Dirkie Smit repeats a riveting story of how we can become impervious to beauty. One cold winter morning, on a Washington metro station, a young man takes up his violin and plays a series of demanding pieces by Bach for forty-three minutes. Over a thousand people scurry by, a few pause and then walk on, while a three-year-old boy tries to get his mother to stop and listen. The violinist young man is Joshua Bell. His instrument is a 1713 Stradivarius worth millions of dollars and he is one of the most talented young violinists in the world today. Are we, like those passers-by, unable to take a few minutes out of the day to wonder at beauty?

Human life cannot flourish without the beauty of the natural world. I know how I feel when I get out on to a mountain, or walk in the Kirstenbosch Botanical Gardens or along a sandy beach at sunset.

I know the awe of looking at the inhabitant of a minute shell, or the feathers of a guinea fowl, or tiny crystals in grains of sand through a magnifying glass. I have a hoard of memories of hikes in different parts of our country, memories of vistas, mountain pools, forests, dunes and bushveld. So much beauty for eyes that hunger to see! While I lament the degradation of the natural beauty that surrounds us, I remind myself of what William Morris said: "Have nothing in your house that you do not know to be useful, or believe to be beautiful." The call is to live with justice, simplicity and beauty because we treasure the riches of the earth. This I want for my grandchildren.

~

It is fashionable today, particularly in some Christian circles, to speak contemptuously about consumerism without acknowledging the undeniable truth that not only are we all consumers but that religion itself is not immune to consumerism. Religion is very marketable. From religious trinkets and paraphernalia to albums of Gregorian chants and spiritual songs, there is money to be made in religion. Today, there is a marketplace for different spiritualities and our cafeteria-like mentalities cause us to flit from one offer of nirvana to another. The insatiable desire for "stuff" – be it religious "stuff"or for spiritual experience clothed in terms like "growth", "becoming" and "self-realisation" – traps us into an ideology of self rather than being seekers after relationship with God.

In a thoughtful book called *Consuming Religion*, Vincent Miller explores how consumer culture changes our relationship with our religious beliefs, narratives and symbols. He defines consumerism as "[…] the high levels of consumption in advanced capitalist societies and the great significance and importance that it is given in these societies". Consumer societies are those "[…] in which consumption plays an important role in establishing social identity and solidarity. These tend to be marked by a high level of consumerism […]."

Miller points out that both Christian desire and consumer desire know endless, insatiable longing. Human beings are made to desire.

We long for closeness with the Author of our faith. We long for closeness with those we love. We also long for things, and for the comforts
that we think can buffer us against life's blows. All these longings
become entangled. Miller warns that Christian culture is in danger of
being distorted and exploited by consumer culture. The vexing problem is that the shape and texture of the desires cultivated in consumer
societies are similar to Christian forms of desire. Thomas Merton said:
"We are made in the image of what we desire" – a sobering thought!
To be human is to desire. As consumer desire increases, the search for
gratification becomes unending. Desiring becomes pleasurable in itself. We rationalise our greed. In his book entitled *Greed*, James Childs
writes that greed "is a perennial human vice, a genuine character for
all seasons". He continues: "Greed is not all ostentation and spending
or the lust for great wealth. It is also manifest in the hoarding compul-
sion that turns people into misers."

What has Gucci in common with Jerusalem? The answer is – what
we think will make for fulfilment. Consumer culture says Miller,
"is neither about attachment nor about enjoyment". It is ultimately
about "seeking". We may have hundreds of compact discs in our
collection, more than we can listen to, but we are intent on finding
"just the right one". Pleasure is found in accumulating. In a similar
way, seeking also prompts Christian desire. "Desire for God is the
ultimate form of desire in Christianity, but it is tied to a host of other
important desires, including the desire for the kingdom of God, the
coming of God's justice on earth both for ourselves and for others
[…]. We should and, in the end, can only enjoy God," Miller points
out. He continues (perhaps prompted by Augustine) that: "However
unwisely we may choose what to set our hearts on, we will eventually
be spurred on to seek more, since we are made for fellowship with
the divine and only that will satisfy the profundity of our desire."

So when is enough enough? How do we "haves" deal with the
paradox of having more than we need while being followers of
Christ? What is enough for creating human well-being? How do
we negotiate between quality of life and quantity of goods? How
can we live as people who know that the earth is the Lord's and

all that is in it? "When is enough enough?" is a question that has to be grappled with by those of us who profess faith. It can all too easily induce guilt, paralyse us, or simply enable us to put it aside because facing it is too demanding. The life of faith is a process of transformation. We need to be transformed again and again. No one has arrived. We are continually being moved by God's Spirit away from the innate need for power, control, possessions and the stuff of self, towards a life of greater charity, justice and compassion. If only we could let go, for if we are not willing to move out of our comfort zones, we cannot be transformed.

Vulnerability cannot be avoided. We remind ourselves that, as Richard Rohr says, Christianity is the only religion that dares to call God a *lamb*. We have to let go of that false self that thinks it knows who we are, and what we need – it is a fiction interested only in self-maintenance. The true self is an abundant self, filled with a steadiness of purpose and a sense of contentment. Being trapped by the desire for more and more is as unhealthy and inappropriate as being trapped by guilt. We forget that, as Julian of Norwich reminds us, God looks on us with pity and not with blame. Wrestling with the "enough" question requires discernment and self-awareness, qualities that can awaken to our deepest self.

What does my heart desire? Am I able to say to God: "My desire is for you and you only"? We cannot be forced to desire to be good against our own will. But mercifully God's grace works for our own good – after all Jesus changed Paul's life against his will. Surrounded by the struggle to live in the paradox of hunger and over-consumption, we are offered abundant life (Jn 10:10) in the One who said of himself "I am the bread of life. Whoever comes to me will never be hungry" (Jn 6:35). Here we are shown that our insatiable desires are absorbed by the abundance of God's grace. "Those who eat my flesh and drink my blood have eternal life," says Jesus in John 6:54. The food that endures is for eternal life.

When turning to the scriptures for answers on the dilemmas of being a "have", contradiction and paradox surface once again. On the one hand, the scriptures are littered with injunctions against greed and possessions. The ancient writers were deeply aware of the needs of the poor and the importance of giving alms, and in the Old Testament greed is often coupled with oppression of the poor. To those in need, "[g]ive liberally and be ungrudging when you do so, for on this account the Lord your God will bless you in your work and in all that you undertake" (Deut 15:10). Giving is praised: "They have distributed freely, they have given to the poor; their righteousness endures forever" sings the psalmist (Ps 112:9). But those who are consumed by the need to possess are warned: "Such is the end of all who are greedy for gain; it takes away the life of its possessors" (Prov 1:19). The prophet Isaiah does not mince words about corrupt prophets and rulers: "The dogs have a mighty appetite; they never have enough. The shepherds also have no understanding; they have all turned to their own way, to their own gain, one and all" (Is 56:11). Care of the poor brings honour to God: "Those who oppress the poor insult their Maker, but those who are kind to the needy honour him" (Prov 14:31).

On the other hand, as Luke Johnson points out, "[...] in that part of the Wisdom tradition in which the deuteronomic principle of blessing and curse is rigidly maintained, wealth is seen as a straightforward sign of God's blessing." Once again paradox confronts us. God favoured Jehoshaphat and established his kingdom "[...] and he had great riches and honour" (2 Chron 17:5). "Happy are those who fear the Lord, who greatly delight in his commandments [...] the generation of the upright will be blessed. Wealth and riches are in their houses" (Ps 112:1-3). In Wisdom's right hand is a long life "[...] and in her left hand are riches and honour" (Prov 3:16). Job is an example of a rich man who can still claim to be righteous.

As part of the Roman Empire the New Testament writers knew all about the divide between the wealthy and the poor. In their time the landowners, administrators, military and merchants comprised about ten per cent of the people. The rest were poor peasants. There was virtually no middle class. Galileans were taxed three times over:

they paid a tithe to the temple, a tribute to the Roman emperor and more tax to the Jewish king through whom Rome ruled by proxy. The backbone of their economy was agriculture, while some folk were fishermen and artisans. These taxes were skimmed off their crops, flocks and the work of their hands. Jesus' parables basically address two classes – the rich landowners and the poor peasant labourers. Not surprisingly, the poor had to work very hard just to stay afloat. Revolt and rebellion lurked below the surface, ready to explode.

Jesus has a great deal to say about greed and priorities. He warns: "Take care! Be on your guard against all kinds of greed; for one's life does not consist in the abundance of possessions"(Lk 12:15). The Sermon on the Mount is a treasure trove of advice and warning. "Do not store up for yourselves treasures on earth, where moth and rust consume and where thieves break in and steal; but store up for yourselves treasures in heaven, where neither moth nor rust consumes and where thieves do not break in and steal. For where your treasure is, there your heart will be also" (Mt 6:19-21). And again, "You cannot serve God and wealth [...]. But strive first for the kingdom of God and his righteousness, and all these things will be given to you as well" (Mt 6:24, 33). Jesus calls his disciples to leave everything and follow him (Lk 5:11). The rich young man has to sell everything to have treasure in heaven and follow Jesus (Lk 18:22). Paul cautions the Colossians (3:5) against "greed (which is idolatry)". Idolatry is the ultimate expression of unfaithfulness to God and is severely punished throughout the Old Testament. Timothy (1 Tim 6:17-18) also weighs in with a warning and some advice: "As for those who in the present age are rich, command them not to be haughty, or to set their hope on the uncertainty of riches, but rather on God who richly provides us with everything for our enjoyment."

However, "having" is not rejected out of hand. The wealth of Zaccheus, the tax collector, was not a barrier to his hosting Jesus in his home. He subsequently promises to give half his possessions to the poor and to repay those whom he has defrauded, to which Jesus says: "Today salvation has come to this house [...]"(Lk 19:9). After Jesus says that it is easier for a camel to go through the eye of a needle than for someone who is rich to enter the kingdom of God, the disciples ask: "Then who can be saved?" Jesus replies: "For mortals it is impossible, but not for God; for God all things are possible" (Mk 10:27). When Paul needs to collect money for the church in Jerusalem, he encourages the converts in Macedonia to give generously, saying "[...] it is a question of a fair balance between your present abundance and their need [...]" (2 Cor 8:13-14).

Seeking guidance from the scriptures on the question of "having" is not straightforward. Can the Bible therefore be a moral and ethical guide in this complex and unnerving dilemma? To seek guidance from the scriptures requires accepting that they contain a variety of ethical models as the contexts in which they were written reflect the practices of different times. Some teachings have more lasting moral authority as general ideals for all, while others refer more specifically to time and culturally bound practices. A defined code of behaviour for the Christian use of possessions is often tangled up with the times in which people lived and wrote, with different understandings of the law and personal circumstances. Reading the scriptures requires discernment.

Actions and intentions cannot be separated, and the way in which we acquire, use and disperse material possessions expresses our attitudes and responses to those around us, to ourselves, and most of all to God. Having possessions is not wicked per se. However, making possessions into a god is; ignoring the plight of the poor and the needy is, and believing that having is more important than being is wicked. In fact, anything that prevents us from responding to the call of God is unrighteous. Most noxious and most subtle of all is "owning" spiritual possessions – being aggrandised by our visions and ideas such as our self-imposed asceticism as opposed to the "orgies" of others; our virtue in the face of the vice of others that makes us feel more worthy than the other. This is a poisonous form of "having", and a particular temptation to those of faith. Attempts to live a morally and ethically responsible life are at best fragile, require courage, and must be open to being revised when found wanting.

The age-old virtue of detachment is helpful in wrestling with the "enough" question. Attachment is, of course, part of life. We fall in love and become attached. Zen-like detachment is not the Christian way. However, when we realise that loving has become no more than meeting our own needs, that we have become dependent and self-seeking, it is time to pull back and become detached so that we can re-assess what and how we love. Our lives are a dance between attachment and detachment.

In the first letter to Timothy (6:7), Paul strikes a sober note on the question of detachment: "we brought nothing into the world, so that we can take nothing out of it". Food and clothing are sufficient, he says, and continues to point out (v.9) that desiring to be rich is harmful and can lead to ruin. "For the love of money is the root of all kinds of evil …," he warns (v.10). Worst of all, there is the danger that we will wander away from the faith. Detachment from "having" becomes imperative. We need to turn away from the culture of having and towards the truth of the first beatitude: "Blessed are the poor in spirit for theirs is the kingdom of God." Is detachment something we can achieve through our own efforts or is it a gift from God? It is both. We move to detachment through our own efforts aided by God's grace. It will require prudence, temperance, fortitude and also faith that it is God's desire for us. Our desire for more things is then transformed.

Paul calls on his followers: "Do not be conformed to this world, but be transformed by the renewing of your minds, so that you may discern what is the will of God – what is good and acceptable and perfect" (Rom 12:2). I know that a renewal of the mind cannot take place through an act of will. Willingness to be open, discerning, obedient and trusting is essential. Ultimately, however, renewal comes about as a free gift from God through the Holy Spirit. This is the same Spirit who was at work in Jesus and this makes him the model for our faith.

Undeniably Jesus was poor and had no possessions; he and his followers were supported by the generosity of others. Minute by minute, hour by hour, he lived in obedience to God. Johnson points out that when he wanted to preach, he was called to heal; when he wanted to rest, he was called to teach; when he wanted to teach, he was called to feed, and when he wanted to live, he was called to die. Jesus was not conformed to this world; instead he transformed it, and this he did by totally divesting himself of "self" and committing himself completely to minute-by-minute obedience, in loving trust of God. Unless we live in the truth that we are naked before God and that all that we are and have comes from God alone, our use of material or spiritual possessions can become forms of greed, acquisitiveness and idolatry. There is no proof against moral failure. I resort to the truth that everything on earth belongs to God, that all I have is temporary, to be held in trust, to be accounted for, and to be used wisely. Denise cannot become Dorcas. Nevertheless Denise can choose not to take her eyes off the man on the borrowed donkey. His life and his teaching are her guides.

The longing to rest in God is certainly not accepted as an ideal by all. However, those who know this holy restlessness, this insatiable desire for ever-greater closeness to the Source of our being, are aware that consumer culture cannot assuage this longing. Holy restlessness differs from the desire for more things because it longs for God to reign on earth so that peace, freedom, love and justice will be brought about. To pray "May your kingdom come" is a profoundly practical prayer. "When is enough enough?" is a seriously practical question. What is "enough" for me and how do I share out of my "enough"?

There are a plethora of objections from the "haves" to the idea of sharing more: I have worked hard for what I have. Surely I am entitled to spend it on myself? How can I know that what I give is responsibly used where needed and will not line the pockets of some crook? I already give – to the church, the soup kitchen down the road, the beggars at my door – that's enough. Giving only breeds dependency. Surely what I have to share cannot really make a difference to the lives of millions upon millions who are in need?

With regard to the last point, it is true that the vastness of world-wide poverty and need is overwhelming, but this objection is a cop-out. "If you think you are too small to make a difference," says the Dalai Lama, "you have never been in bed with a mosquito!"

Is giving a simple matter? Not quite. I find that I am pretty sceptical about certain kinds of aid. I know that much of it is politically heavily motivated. I also know that money generously given to fight apartheid and, more recently, to combat HIV and AIDS has too often failed to reach those in need because both of these worthy causes have, at times, succumbed to being self-sustaining industries. I read that more than two trillion dollars have been transferred from rich countries to poor countries over the past fifty years, with Africa being the biggest recipient, yet poverty and need persist on our continent. I hear arguments that seek to explain why this is so ad nauseum: corruption and poor governance; the hangover from colonialism; the severity of conditions placed on aid by donor countries, and so on. Undoubtedly these are contributing factors. However, let us consider the case of the local person who manufactures mosquito nets and employs ten people in her or his factory. Along comes a noisy celebrity who, to great acclaim, has collected money to donate a hundred thousand free nets. The local manufacturer is promptly put out of business, and workers and their dependants all join the unemployed. Five years later, when the donated nets are torn, there is nothing to replace them. We can do without this kind of good-deed giving.

Handing out money to poor people to meet their basic needs will certainly assist in a crisis, but will not, in the long term, solve the pernicious problem of poverty. More is required. What we need is trade instead of more aid; we need investment in the training and transfer of skills, and we need our local industries to be supported. We also need a reduction of the barriers that nations in the south face on the global market. This would do more to reduce poverty than giving aid. It is very difficult for those who live in the south to compete with powerful economies that subsidise their agricultural sectors. Millions of peasant farmers in West Africa support their families by producing cotton more cheaply and in a more ecologically sustainable way than the twenty-five thousand highly mechanised cotton growers in the United States who are subsidised by some three billion dollars a year. I do, however, welcome certain kinds of aid as a form of sharing wealth, provided there are strict controls on where and how the money is spent, and a long-term vision that will empower the needy to be self-sufficient.

I have wondered whether the early Christian community in Acts (2:44-45) who "were together and had all things in common" and who sold their possessions and goods and distributed the proceeds to all "as any had need" has something to say to us today? Their sharing appears to have enhanced their communal relationships for "[t]hey devoted themselves to the apostles' teaching and fellowship (*koinonia*), to the breaking of bread and the prayers" (Acts 2:42). The early Jesus movement had to find a different way of being a community. Not all the early Christians were poor. The early urban communities were a mixture of different classes of people and yet they were willing to share their resources. Did this kind of sharing continue beyond the time of these early communities of believers? Probably not. It is true that collecting funds for the poor in Jerusalem plays a significant part in Paul's letters. In fact, he gives pretty clear instructions about such collecting. In his first letter to the church in Corinth (16:1-4), he suggests they give regularly. However, the ideal of a sustained community of sharing seems to have been short-lived and virtually impossible to reproduce.

I have also learnt that "having" is not necessarily a condition for sharing. Years ago, I spent the weekend with a small community of Korean Christians who lived outside Seoul on the largest garbage mountain in the world. I stayed with the pastor and his family in his two-roomed shack. Sleeping on a straw mat on the floor proved that garbage is an efficient form of central heating! After the Sunday service at which I preached, the congregation all left the church quite hurriedly. I wondered what had gone wrong. But soon they returned, each carrying a dish of food which was spread out on the floor of the little corrugated-iron building. All were invited to participate. They shared what they had with generosity and care. I have had similar experiences in my country. The capacity of the poor to share what they have shames those of us who "have".

Peter Singer's provocatively entitled work *The Life you can Share* is an exercise in practical ethics. He writes out of a deep concern for the plight of the poor. He too asks: "What ought I to be doing to help?" Rightly, he proceeds from the golden rule and finds that it is common to all world religions: "Do unto others as you would have done unto yourself." Addressing Americans, he proposes that those who are financially comfortable give five per cent of their income (and "rather more for the rich") to combat poverty. Christians are expected to tithe. The condition of "having" calls for continuous self-examination in order to share and share more.

The reason I have tried to wrestle with present economic realities in writing about this blessing is an attempt to understand how to share the bounty I have been given. Our contexts are forever changing: the structures in which we live and give change, and the needs, though ever-present, are also dictated by circumstance. In all this, discernment is at the nub of practical moral wisdom in the Christian life – how to bring the commitment to follow the man who borrowed a donkey into the stuff of everyday events, relationships and the use of what we have.

How can I share? I cannot answer for anyone other than myself. The short answer is "share more". Every day I think about what "enough" means. I am continuously caught between what I can do without and what is acceptable to have. I do have a growing need for simplicity, for having less and giving more, but I know that I will never find the whole answer to this question. Knowing when enough is enough is a work in progress. However, it is one I dare not avoid and one I can never lay to rest. For the time being, the mandate of my faith is clear: I must continue to explore how to share that which has been given to me. Not to do so is an act of disobedience, even idolatry. If, as I have written elsewhere, to live with gratitude is a blessing, then gratitude for what I have is expressed in sharing.

I have no neat recipes for this sharing. Circumstances change – today it may well be relief for starving Somalians, tomorrow for fire victims in one of our townships. I feel I should give locally, while at the same time I cannot turn my back on the plight of those far away. "Doing unto others" has no national boundaries. Sharing resources requires that I familiarise myself with the nature and scope of organi-sations involved in relief work. In addition, giving and sharing are not only about material resources. Every minute of our existence is also God-given. I know I must give of my time to others to the extent that I am able, bearing in mind my age and energy. Sometimes this is more costly than making a quick donation. I believe we also share with those closest to us. Giving to our children and helping them in their need is part of being a parent. However, I have learnt that giving to those closest to me may not divert me from the immense need that surrounds us. Whatever the need, the question that never leaves me is: When is enough enough – for me?

In his engaging work on economics and the Christian life, *Being Con-sumed*, William Cavanaugh explores the relationship between scarcity and abundance. For him it is two overlapping stories of hunger and consumption, exchanges and gifts. He points out, though, that the Eucharist does not begin with scarcity, but with the promise of abun-dant life, and cautions that it would be easy to assimilate the consum-ing of the Eucharist into a spirituality of consumption. But he adds that the practice of the Eucharist resists such appropriation because by consuming the Eucharist we are taken up into a larger body, the Body of Christ. We not only take Christ into ourselves but we are taken up by Christ himself. Jesus says: "Those who eat my flesh and drink my blood abide in me, and I in them" (Jn 6:56). This, says Cavanaugh, turns the act of consumption on its head: instead of consuming the elements of the Eucharist, we are consumed by Christ. As we are taken up into the Body of Christ, we become food for others.

Being a member of the Body of Christ, Cavanaugh continues, "has a dramatic effect on the communicability of pain from one person to another, for individuals are now united in one body, connected by one nervous system". If any one part of the body suffers, all suf-fer. If one member is honoured, all are honoured. No wonder Paul tells the Corinthians to take special care of the weakest members of the Body (1 Cor 12:22-25). He knows that the Body can only be as strong as its weakest members. Being an intrinsic part of this one Body underscores our obligation to feed the hungry and care for the suffering. Jesus is intent that his followers should understand how those in need are central to his ministry and how much he identifies with them. In his teaching on the last judgment, at the end of the Gospel of Matthew (25:31-46), feeding the hungry, welcoming the stranger and visiting the prisoner are blessed. "Truly I tell you, just as you did to one of the least of these who are members of my family, you did it to me," says Jesus (Mt 25:40). Ignoring the plight of those who are hungry, thirsty, naked, sick and imprisoned is condemned: "Truly I tell you, just as you did not do it to one of the least of these, you did not do it to me" (Mt 25:45). There is no dodging the truth that Jesus identifies with the poor and the needy. This is more than a guideline for us who "have"; it is a direct call from the one we follow. "The pain of the hungry person is the pain of Christ," Cavanaugh reminds us. Mercifully, in the Eucharist, "Christ is gift, giver, and recipient; we are simultaneously fed and become food for others".

According to Cavanaugh: "the body and blood of Christ are not scarce commodities …" Consuming the Eucharist is not appropriating goods for my private use – it is becoming part of the larger Body of Christ. My individual desires and needs are incorporated into this Body and I become one with others and share their fate. This is a different kind of sharing. Paul asks the Corinthians: "The bread that we break, is it not a sharing in the body of Christ?" (1 Cor 10:16). He answers his own question: "Because there is one bread, we who are many, are one body, for we all partake of the one bread" (1 Cor 10:17). We cannot share bread and wine and not share the pain, need, hunger and want of other members of the Body. If we are truly one body, we will feel the other's pain.

The man on the borrowed donkey is at the centre of the Eucharist, as both the gift and the giver. Every time we take Communion we are not merely acting as a part of a greater whole, as if Christ is divided into pieces. As a Eucharistic community we are, in the words of Cavanaugh, a "mini-cosmos in which the cosmic Christ is wholly present". Christ is the true concrete universal, the fullness of God, poured out in the Eucharist. Finally, in Cavanaugh's words: "To consume the Eucharist is an act of anti-consumption for here to consume is to be consumed, to be taken up into participation in something larger than the self, yet in a way in which the identity of the self is paradoxically secured." The Eucharist is God's bounty shared for us and thus a blessing that loosens the ties of all that binds us to stuff, and allows us not only to know when enough is enough, but to share our bounty with the hungry, deprived and suffering.

I have said that knowing when enough is enough is a blessing, for then we shall know how to share freely with others. Looking back on what I have written, I see that I have said little about the joy of sharing. Buddha said: "Set your heart on doing good. Do it over and over again, and you will be filled with joy." Socrates and Plato pointed out that the just person is happy. According to Peter Singer, the American Red Cross has a similar view. It tells its donors: "Helping others feel good helps you feel good about yourself!" However, one cannot be a happy giver with an attitude of giving so that one will be happy. Happiness comes from the dawning awareness that nothing we have is ours, so we sit lightly on our possessions. "Having" then becomes the source for sharing. I suspect that I have received much in order to give more and more. "Easy for you to give," I can hear some mutter, "when you are a person who has enough." Fair comment. I am caught in the vice of contradiction and paradox. Yet I am learning that there is happiness in sharing.

In 2010 I visited a remote region in the eastern basin of northern Tanzania, a part of the Rift Valley system. Some one thousand Hadza people live here, probably the last true hunter-gatherers left in Africa. They speak a language unrelated to any other known language, and they live entirely off what they can hunt with their bows and arrows and gather, such as roots, wild honey, berries and baobab fruit. Spending a couple of days with these people left me with vivid impressions of a life that defies the baggage of modernity. They are remarkably free of jealousy, resentment and elitism. Their scant structures are egalitarian. The women are feisty and equal to the men. Rape is unknown. As I mulled over my short time with these singular people, I asked myself why they are so remarkably free from the oppressive restraints that beleaguer life today. Then I realised – they share what they hunt and gather in order to survive, and they have no concept of private property! Enough is enough for them for the day. Is it conceivable that our ancestors, whom we now know probably all came from East Africa, lived in this way too? Is our concept of ownership (calling things "mine") responsible for our avariciousness and never knowing when enough is truly enough?

Dorcas and I are both members of God's household. So are the garbage pickers of Seoul and the Hadza people. Living together in a household signals interdependence, relationship, belonging and the common desire to keep the household sustainable, both socially and economically. Theologian Sallie McFague, seeking an ecological model to live by, claims that housemates abide by three rules: "take only your share, clean up after yourselves, and keep the house in good repair for future occupants." I knew from the beginning that there would be no easy answers to the "enough" question. More sharing, more cleaning up and more responsible stewardship is enough of a challenge for a lifetime. My share has given me more than a decent life. To be Dorcas's relative means to find ways of preparing a room for her in our household and to do so generously, unendingly and ungrudgingly so that we can both share in God's bounty.

NOTES

The National Poverty Hearings are a follow-up on poverty hearings held ten years ago when the South African National NGO Coalition facilitated a process of nationwide hearings that provided a platform for people living in poverty to speak about their experiences. A further valuable source of information on the issue of poverty and its many effects is African Monitor (African Voices for Africa's Development) founded by Archbishop Emeritus Njongonkulu Ndungane, who is its current president. African Monitor highlights issues that affect the lives of grass-roots people such as rural

poverty, health care, education, water and adequate sanitation, unemploy- .
ment, women's marginalisation and land restitution. It also monitors the
flow of aid money and invests significant resources into understanding and
countering these challenges so as to promote conditions in which people can
live with dignity.

The Gini Coefficient is a summary statistic of income disparity. It varies
from 0 (perfect equality of income) to 100 (total inequality of income). According to a UN Human Development Report (UNDP) 2005, South Africa's
coefficient stood at just over seventy-two. As the formal economy shrinks,
South Africa's official unemployment figure is around twenty-five per cent,
yet indications are that the informal sector of the economy appears to be
growing. South African Revenue Services' Report 2008 states that the total
tax collected was almost five hundred and seventy-three billion rand.

The African Religious Health Assets Programme (ARHAP) based at the
University of Cape Town conducts impressive research into the potential
role of faith-based organisations in combating HIV and AIDS. See, for
example, their Masangane Case Study conducted in the Eastern Cape and
published by them in 2006.

According to the World Bank (WB), in 2011 five hundred and ninety-seven
million people were living on approximately one dollar and twenty-five cents
per day in sub-Saharan Africa. Over all, roughly almost one and a half billion
people fall into this category. In contrast, roughly one billion people live at a
level of affluence never previously known. Before the 2008 economic crash,
there were more than one thousand one hundred billionaires in the world
with a combined wealth of close to four and a half trillion dollars.

The "sub-prime mortgage" system is a fancy name employed in the United
States for a pyramid scheme that most people did not grasp and that led to
the world economic crisis of 2008–2009. In essence, some large financial
institutions peddled mortgages to people who could not possibly pay the
monthly rates due on them, and then sold these debts to other institutions
and hedge funds that thought they were worth something.

For a discussion of the implications of globalisation for southern African economies and for women in particular, see Denise M. Ackermann, "Interrupting Global Speak: A feminist theological response to globalization from southern Africa" in *Oxford Handbook of Feminist Theology* (Oxford: Oxford University Press, 2011). See also *Highlights of the 8th International Forum on Women's Rights in Development*, Guadalajara, Mexico, 3-6 October, 2002, published by the Association of Women's Rights in Development (AWID).

The World Bank (WB) and the International Monetary Fund (IMF) perform different tasks that are often confused. Established at Bretton Woods in 1944, the World Bank is responsible for eradicating poverty, while the task of the International Monetary Fund is to maintain global economic stability. The World Bank tries to have a number of representatives in different countries, while the International Monetary Fund usually has only one representative and its programmes are dictated from Washington. When attempting to understand the economic implications of globalisation, it is important to know that in these institutions voting power is related to money: the more money a country contributes, the more votes it has. In assessing the contribution of the two Bretton Woods institutions, it is clear that they have largely failed in their purposes. There are more poor people in the world today than ever before and the earth is in dire straits.

Boerewors is a South African sausage made from beef and pork and heavily spiced with roasted coriander. It is an essential menu item of a *braaivleis* (barbecue).

Spaza shops are informal convenience businesses usually run from homes in the townships of South Africa. It is estimated that there are at least one hundred thousand such shops and, when combined with hawkers and shebeens (places where liquor is sold, often without licence), these informal markets account for sales of roughly thirty billion rand per year.

The Kant quotation is taken from "Groundwork of the Metaphysics of Morals", [AK 4:429], in Mary J. Gregor, *Practical Philosophy* (Cambridge: Cambridge University Press, 1999).

The word "ecology" was first used by a German biologist called Ernst Haeckel (1834–1919). It includes two Greek words: *oikos* that means house and *logos* that means word or study. According to Haeckel "Ecology is the study of the interdependence and interaction of living organisms (animals and plants) and their environment (inanimate matter)."

See the September 2011 issue of *Scientific American* on "Better Cities" for a number of articles of interest regarding urbanisation. According to the editors, the world's centre of gravity has shifted. For thousands of years people lived in the countryside and worked the land for a living. However, in the twentieth century cities grew more than ten-fold, from housing two hundred and fifty million people to nearly three billion. By 2050 urban dwellers are predicted to surpass six billion. One in seven people on our planet lives in squatter communities or shanty towns – often places of surprising innovation – and since 2000, two hundred and twenty-seven million people have moved out of slums.

Kirstenbosch is one of the world's great botanical gardens situated on the slopes of Table Mountain in Cape Town.

For a stinging critique of African capitalism, see *Architects of Poverty: Why African Capitalism Needs Changing* (Johannesburg: Picador Africa, 2009) by Moeletsi Mbeki (brother of former president Thabo Mbeki). He argues that instead of developing local industries, African capitalists are selling off the continent's assets in terms of raw materials. In the process they enrich a small elite and de-industrialise the continent's economies. In so doing, African nationalists are reproducing the patterns of colonial times and increasing inequality among Africans.

One example of the profligacy of some African leaders is President Teodoro Obiang of oil-rich Equatorial Africa, a country of five hundred thousand inhabitants. His official salary is a modest sixty thousand dollars, yet he owns six private jets, a thirty-five million dollar home in Malibu, homes in Maryland and Cape Town, and a fleet of Lamborghinis, Ferraris and Bentleys. Most of his people live in extreme poverty with a life expectancy of forty-nine years. The country has an infant mortality of eighty-seven per one thousand babies. Aid dependency is another complicating factor. For twenty-nine years Paul Biya has ruled Cameroon, a country that enjoys oil revenues, yet has received a total of thirty-five billion dollars in foreign aid. Closer to home, King Mswati III, the absolute ruler of neighbouring Swaziland, is infamous for his contribution to the shrinking coffers of his country. A recent International Monetary Fund Report affirms that Swaziland's economy has been in decline for many years. Two-thirds of this country's inhabitants live in dire poverty on less than a dollar a day, while the king buys luxury cars for his twelve wives, and is the owner of one of the world's most expensive cars, the Maybach. Photographing the royal garages is forbidden.

At a conference in San Francisco in the 1980s, I met a man whose name is synonymous with micro-financing. Muhummad Yunus, an economist, academic and winner of the Nobel Peace Prize in 2006, related the story of his entry into micro-financing. While doing research into rural poverty in 1976, he visited the village of Jobra in Bangladesh on a field trip. He saw how women making furniture had to borrow money to buy the cane they needed from the local moneylenders, who charged them high interest rates. This practice trapped them in a cycle of poverty. Yunus took the equivalent of twenty-seven dollars from his pocket and lent it to a group of forty-two women from the village. This seemingly insignificant act enabled these women to begin making a profit and to live independently and eventually to repay the loan. In his words: "First I lent money to replace the loan sharks. Then I went to the local bank to request them to lend money to the poor. They refused. After months of deadlock I persuaded them by offering myself as a guarantor. This is how micro-credit was born in 1976." The concept worked and it led to the founding of the Grameen Bank in 1982. Today that bank has more than a million customers in Bangladesh and has lent more than six billion dollars with a repayment rate of ninety-seven per cent.

In March 2011 Yunus was dismissed from his position in the bank by the Bangladeshi state because his tenure had exceeded the statutory retirement age. A recent report in the *Sunday Times Business* (13.03.2011) criticises micro-financing: the industry has grown too rapidly for its own good and there has been a breakdown in lending discipline with borrowers becoming overextended. Recently fifty-one cases of suicide in India have been linked to coercive behaviour by micro-financing institutions. It is also alleged that vested political interests do not take kindly to micro-financing as the poor are a valuable constituency to which the state prefers to act as lender. However, since that day in San Francisco I have wondered whether well-run micro-financing is not an appropriate means of empowering the poor, particularly poor women in South Africa. Locally, the Small Enterprises Foundation (SEF) began operating in 1992 with the aim of alleviating poverty through micro-financing. Located in Limpopo Province, where sixty per cent of households live below the poverty line, it uses the same methods as the Grameen Bank. By 2010 it had helped nearly seventy thousand clients of whom ninety-nine per cent were women. The average loan is two thousand rand to women organised in groups that are responsible for mutual accountability. The bad debt rate is between point three and point six per cent.

The Millennium Development Goals (MDG) agreed to by the leaders of all the world's nations in 2000 set out a broad base for solving world poverty. These targets are to be reached by 2015. So far the funds needed for these targets have not been forthcoming, but the goals remain a good start towards dealing with the problem. In his foreword to the 2010 progress report, United Nations Secretary General, Ban Ki-moon, writes: "It is clear that improvements in the lives of the poor have been unacceptably slow, and some hard-won gains are being eroded by the climate, food and economic crises." Natural disasters, the impact of climate change and ever-escalating food prices have all had a negative impact on the achievement of the MDG. The MDG aim at:

- reducing by half the world's extreme poverty
- reducing by half the proportion of people who suffer from hunger
- ensuring that children everywhere are able to take a full course of primary schooling
- ending disparity in education
- reducing by two-thirds the mortality rate among children under five

- reducing by three-quarters the rate of maternal mortality
- combating HIV and AIDS, malaria and other major diseases
- reducing by half the proportion of people without sustainable access to safe drinking water.

WORKS CONSULTED

Ackermann, Denise M. "Interrupting Global Speak: A feminist theological response to globalization from southern Africa". *Oxford Handbook of Feminist Theology*. Oxford: Oxford University Press, 2011.

Atwood, Margaret. *Payback: Debt and the Shadow Side of Wealth*. Toronto: Anansi Press, 2008.

Berry, Thomas. *The Dream of the Earth*. San Francisco: Sierra Club Books, 1988.

Boesak, Allan, Johann Weusmann and Charles Amjad-Ali, eds. *Dreaming a Different World: Globalization, and Justice for Humanity and the Earth*. Stellenbosch: The Globalisation Project, 2010.

Boff, Leonardo. *Ecology and Liberation: A New Paradigm*. Maryknoll: Orbis Books, 1995.

Brubaker, Pamela K. *Globalization at What Price? Economic Change and Daily Life*. Cleveland: The Pilgrim Press, 2001.

Cavanaugh, William T. *Being Consumed: Economics and Christian Desire*. Grand Rapids: Eerdmans, 2008.

Childs, James M. Jr. *Greed: Economics and Ethics in Conflict*. Minneapolis: Fortress Press, 2000.

Conradie, Ernst. *Christianity and a Critique of Consumerism: A Survey of Six Points of Entry*. Wellington: Bible Media. E-books, 2009. http://www.kalahari.com/Digital-Downloads/Christianity-and-a-critique-of-consumerism_p_46289864

Day, Dorothy. *Selected Writings*. Edited by R. Ellsberg. Maryknoll: Orbis Books, 1992.

De Gruchy, Steve. "Give Us This Day Our Daily Bread: Four Theological Theses on Food and Hunger." (paper presented at a workshop hosted by Pietermaritzburg Agency for Christian Social Awareness (PACSA), Pietermaritzburg, 2003).

Dillard, Annie. *For the Time Being*. New York: First Vintage Books, 1999.

Dower, Nigel. "World Poverty." In *A Companion to Ethics*, edited by Peter Singer, 273–283. Oxford: Blackwell, 1993.

Easterly, William. "Foreign Aid for Scoundrels." *New York Review of Books*, vol. LVII, no. 18 (2010).

Foster, Richard. *Celebration of Discipline*. London: Hodder and Stoughton, 1978.

Friedman, Thomas L. *Hot, Flat and Crowded: Why the World needs a Green Revolution and How We Can Renew Our Global Future*. London: Penguin Books, 2009.

González, Justo L. *Faith and Wealth: A History of Early Christian Ideas on the Origin, Significance, and Use of Money*. Eugene, OR: Wipf and Stock Publishers, 1990.

Green, Laurie. *The Impact of the Global: An Urban Theology*. London: The Urban Theology Unit of the Church of England, 2001.

Gregor, Mary J. *Practical Philosophy*. Cambridge: Cambridge University Press, 1999.

Grewal, David Singh. *Network Power: The Social Dynamics of Globalization*. New Haven: Yale University Press, 2008.

Grey, Mary. *Sacred Longings: Ecofeminist Theology and Globalization*. London: SCM Press, 2003.

Haddad, Beverly. "Theologising Development: A Gendered Analysis of

Poverty, Survival and Faith." *Journal of Theology for Southern Africa,* 110 (2001): 5-19.

Hammarskjöld, Dag. *Markings.* Translated by L.S. Sjöberg and W.H. Auden. New York: Ballantine Books, 1993.

Heslam, Peter, ed. *Globalization and the Good.* Grand Rapids: Eerdmans, 2004.

Irenaeus of Lyons. *Against Heresies.* Edited by A. Roberts, J. Donaldson and A. Coxe. Raleigh, NC: Ex Fontibus, 2010.

Jarl, Ann-Cathrin. *Women and Economic Justice: Ethics in Feminist Liberation Theology and Feminist Economics.* Uppsala Studies in Social Ethics 25. Uppsala: Acta University, 2000.

Johnson, Luke T. *Sharing Possessions: Mandate and Symbol of Faith.* Philadelphia: Fortress Press, 1981.

Landry, Charles. *The Art of City-making.* London: Earthscan, 2006.

Marx, Karl and Friedrich Engels. *The Communist Manifesto.* Reading: Merlin Press, 1998.

Mbeki, Moeletsi. *Architects of Poverty: Why African Capitalism Needs Changing.* Johannesburg: Picador Africa, 2009.

McCloskey, Deirdre N. *The Bourgeois Virtues: Ethics for an Age of Commerce.* Chicago: University of Chicago Press, 2006.

McFague, Sallie. *Life Abundant: Rethinking Theology and Economy for a Planet in Peril.* Minneapolis: Fortress Press, 2001.

Meeks, Wayne. *The Moral World of the First Christians.* Philadelphia: Westminster Press, 1986.

Miller, Vincent J. *Consuming Religion: Christian Faith and Practice in a Consumer Culture.* New York: Continuum, 2005.

Moyo, Dambisa. *Dead Aid: Why Aid is not Working and How There is Another Way for Africa.* London: Allen Lane, 2009.

Orr, Liesl. "Women's Work and Globalisation Trends: The South African Picture." *Agenda*, 48 (2001): 31-37.

Rasmussen, Larry. *Earth Community and Earth Ethics*. Maryknoll: Orbis Books, 1996.

Rohr, Richard. *Simplicity: The Art of Living*. New York: Crossroad, 1992.

Rosner, Brian S. *Greed as Idolatry: The Origin and Meaning of a Pauline Metaphor*. Grand Rapids: Eerdmans, 2007.

Royte, Elisabeth. *How Water Went on Sale and Why We Bought It*. New York: Bloomsbury, 2008.

Schweiker, William and Charles Matthews, eds. *Having: Property and Possession in Religious and Social Life*. Grand Rapids: Eerdmans, 2004.

Singer, Peter. *The Life You Can Save: Acting Now to End World Poverty*. New York: Random House, 2009.

Spohn, William C. *Go and Do Likewise: Jesus and Ethics*. New York: Continuum, 2000.

Stiglitz, Joseph. *Globalization and its Discontents*. London: Penguin Books, 2002.

Tanner, Kathryn. "Is Capitalism a Belief System?" *Anglican Theological Review*, vol. 92, no. 4 (Fall 2010): 617-636.

Wheeler, Sondra Ely. *Wealth as Peril and Obligation: The New Testament on Possessions*. Grand Rapids: Eerdmans, 1995.

Williams, Rowan. "Theology and Economics: Two Different Worlds?" *Anglican Theological Review*, vol. 92, no. 4 (Fall 2010): 201.

CHAPTER EIGHT

Blessed are those who can chuckle at the incongruities of life, for they will be able to laugh at themselves

When I was younger I was less inclined to be quietly amused at the inconsistencies and contradictions of life, and more likely to object, or rage, or be vehemently critical. Yes, I can still rant, but with age I am more able to chuckle at my own foolishness, at the folly of some of my actions, and at the fatuousness of self-importance. Incongruity and paradox sail in the same boat. The challenge is either to climb on board and enjoy a ride filled with surprises, unexpected turns and a fair amount of fun, or to remain on the shore, clinging to unexamined assumptions about life and ourselves.

Injustice, corruption and suffering surround us. There is little to find amusing in these grim realities. Yet, throughout the years I have known him (including "the years that the locusts have eaten"), Desmond Tutu (the Arch) has been able to laugh – in fact, he is famous for his laugh. He has known the searing injustice of racial discrimination, personal anguish, loss, sickness, and rejection by his own people. He has lived through the horrors of apartheid. He weeps when moved, and can grow volubly angry at injustice. He also loves a joke. He can laugh with much more enjoyment at his own follies than at those of others. He is free of self-importance, tolerant of the vagaries of life and a friend to those who fall. "We may be surprised at the people we find in heaven. God has a soft spot for sinners. His standards are quite low," he has said. He also knows the inevitability of human suffering: "Dear child of God, I am sorry to say that suffering is not optional." Despite his experiences of oppression and injustice, humour has not deserted him. The Arch is still laughing – sometimes gently, at other times raucously. Laughing with him is a blessing. To be amused at the incongruities of life is not to be blind to its pain. Rather, it is acknowledging the relief of seeing just how incongruous we are as human beings before the power of a loving God whose nature is always to have mercy. Self-importance is simply daft and being able to chuckle at it is a blessing.

Of course not all people agree about what is funny. Theologians writing about the comic in life are out on a limb as they are not traditionally known for their interest in levity. I cannot help wondering why this is so. Does God not laugh? Does God disapprove of a good chuckle? This cannot be. Conceiving of our Maker disapproving of laughter is tantamount to contemplating life without laughter. Nearly a hundred years ago, William Austin Smith shrewdly suggested:

> Every Divinity School might well have in its senior year, along with courses in systematic divinity and homiletics, a course in the great masters of comedy; and, to arouse our sluggish wits and keep us on our guard, it might not be amiss to carve upon our pulpits, side by side with the lean Gothic saints, the figure of Aristophanes or Molière with warning finger.

Sadly his advice has not been followed. Western philosophical and religious traditions have generally had a low view of the comic. But more about this later.

What does it mean to chuckle at the incongruous? To acknowledge incongruity is to see what is contradictory, often inappropriate, and certainly unsuitable in a given situation. There is contrariness in incongruity, something that is out of place, off-beat, laced with paradox. Incongruity fleetingly conjures up a different world in which different rules exist. Incongruity is not necessarily funny. There is nothing amusing about the incongruity of plastic-roofed shanties on the way to Cape Town's airport where tourists arrive to enjoy the "good life" the Cape has to offer. What I have in mind is the inherent contradictoriness of the human condition – that which punctures our self-importance, enables us to laugh at ourselves and gives momentary relief.

American sociologist Peter Berger writes: "Man is incongruent in himself." On the one hand, we live with bodies driven by primal instincts, while on the other hand, we can stand outside ourselves and judge our behaviour. We are both in control of our bodies and not. We can be in the middle of a serious conversation when our bodies do something quite uncontrollable. We are capable of standing outside ourselves and judging our behaviour, but we cannot prevent the body's need to hiccup, or burp, or throw up. A sense of humour helps us to see the ridiculousness of our place in the world and to temper our self-importance. We can land on the moon, but when we peer through a telescope at the night sky we are pulled up short – we are barely a speck in the enormity of the universe! As Berger says, our incongruity is "endearingly human". Chortling at what is incongruent is simply acknowledging that we are intrinsically incongruent within ourselves. We are essentially a tangle of contradiction and paradox. It is truly a gift to be able to laugh at how seriously we take ourselves!

Writing about what is amusing is a poor substitute for a good laugh, and trying to describe what is funny is, in German Catholic scholar Karl-Josef Kuschel's words, "like dancing on a volcano". As soon as one feels that one's description of what is funny is on safe ground, it veers off and the very attempt to write cogently about laughter becomes in itself laughable. Thank heavens there is no one universal theory of laughter or else my attempts to write about this blessing would be doomed. While I am able to remember the joy of being amused, I cannot explain what I find funny; I have trouble remembering jokes and inevitably forget the proper punchline.

Mirth can sneak up on us unexpectedly and evaporate almost immediately. Despite efforts to capture the quiddity of laughter, it remains elusive. We have never really been able to categorise or control laughter – which makes my effort to write about it rather comical in itself! Attempting to capture the essence of laughter is like trying to put the Cape's south-easterly wind into a test tube or attempting to blow away the cloth of cloud with which it covers Table Mountain. So why write about this blessing? Quite simply because I am finding that being able to chuckle at the contradictions and inconsistencies in myself tempers any tendency to self-importance, and enables me to laugh at myself. This is a blessing to relish and to share.

There are many kinds of laughter, and in different times, contexts and cultures people have found different things funny. We can laugh at what is good and at what is mean. Laughter can be playful, joyful, ecstatic, wry or contented; it can also be mocking, cynical, derisive, vulgar, even bitter or insane. Jokes can have a dual intent. A clean joke may elicit only a smile, while an off-colour joke may cause us to bellow. Laughter knows no limits. We are tempted to laugh at what is morally reprehensible. What does this say about us? We can laugh in moments of pure ecstasy as easily as we can be amused at an arrogant man slipping on a banana skin. Laughter and ethical self-restraint are connected. It is better not to laugh at all than to laugh at the cost of another in a way that is disrespectful of her or his human dignity. Yet we are endlessly tempted to do so.

Before her untimely death, philosopher Gillian Rose (1947–1995) explored the relationship between human sadness and divine comedy. For her there is an unavoidable discrepancy between our worthy intentions and our surprise at their outcomes. What we intend is often foiled by what we do. She postulates that there is no complete inner certainty, no "sureness of self" which is not basically "unsure" and we can only laugh at the mismatch between our aims and our achievements. This kind of laughter, says Rose, is not demonic or cynical, but holy. The simple ability to laugh even when we are sad and face failure is possible through the power of love. "Comedy is homeopathic: it cures folly by folly."

Is it common for us to find our incongruence good reason for a chuckle or are some of us totally devoid of humour, particularly when it involves ourselves? It is hard to know, though I can think of one or two for whom a hearty laugh appears to be a trial, and quite a few who are too important to laugh at themselves. Finding something amusing or odd can make us laugh exuberantly, or smile quietly – a necessary and momentary relief from self-centredness. Genuine amusement and laughter are not contrived and break through our self-imposed masks and defences.

Can we laugh at the absurdities of the human predicament in our world and at ourselves? Is it not preferable to laugh at rather than to mock or deride persistent human follies, and to be rescued by humour from any tendencies to presumptuousness or conceit? This kind of laughter finds the inconsistent or incongruent funny. It is qualified by tolerance and motivated by sympathy. It restores and liberates, rather than sneers or ridicules. It is an antidote to what is repressive and deprives us of our freedom; it is a way of releasing feelings, resisting fear and dealing with the contrariness of life. When we acknowledge the idiocies in life, laughter can act as a counter to the destructiveness of suffering because it shows a refusal to be controlled or destroyed by it. We may laugh when we see through pretension, as this frees us from any attempts at being false. Laughter that is restorative transcends language and explanation; it is liberating and joyful, healthy for us and good for our relationships, and indeed indispensable for making life worth living. Laughter is a dimension of being human before our Creator. It is a profound human achievement. I cannot let go of my conviction that being able to be amused at the incongruities in life is a blessing and an expression of unquenchable hope.

⁓

When did human beings first laugh? This may be a silly question, for how can anyone ever know! More specifically, we do not know with any certainty where the idea of the comical originated. The root of the word "comic" comes from the Greek word meaning "to revel". It is not surprising therefore that some believe that the idea of the comic originated in Greek festive processions of drunken partygoers wearing exaggerated costumes and indulging in ribald (often obscene) jokes. We have no idea what the ancient people who lived long before the Greeks actually found funny, because we are reliant on what is written. What we do know about the comic is found in the earliest recorded myths, those traditional stories, either wholly or partially fictitious, that explain popular ideas about life, social relationships and the created world.

Peter Berger says that the history of Western philosophy begins with a joke. Slightly exaggerating this point, he quotes an anecdote from Plato's *Theaetetus*, where a joke is told at the expense of the natural philosopher Thales of Miletus. In his conversing with The-aetetus, Socrates tells of "the jest which the clever witty Thracian handmaid is said to have made about Thales, when he fell into a well as he was looking up at the stars. She said that he was so eager to know what was going on in heaven that he could not see what was before his feet." I like this rather weak joke. It is more than an early instance of slapstick. It warns (take note theologians!) against otherworldly pretentiousness at the expense of wrestling with the predicaments of daily life.

I relish humour that shows up our frailties and helps us to laugh at them. However, there is more to humour than using it to respond to the incongruities in the every day. Humour has a darker, often hidden side. In contrast to the pleasure evoked by benign humour, the humour found in satire or irony is uncomfortable, probing, even attacking, but may at times be salutary. Satire is an effective tool in the hands of some writers. "Fools are my theme, let satire be my song", wrote the poet Lord Byron (1788–1824). Whereas benign humour is mainly spontaneous, satire uses irony or ridicule in a studied way to expose human folly. Someone said that satire "makes people laugh, then makes them think". Parodying, ridiculing or exaggerating are all part of the satirist's armour, often used to score a point in support of the satirist's ethical, political or social agenda. Satire is found in many different forms: drama, poetry, novels, newspaper columns, essays, pamphlets, aphorisms, or epigrams.

"Satire is moral outrage transformed into comic art," says author Philip Roth. I am not sure that *Gulliver's Travels*, probably the great-est satire written in the English language, would rate as comic art. I cannot remember laughing when I read it, though its exaggerations and ridicule were amusing at times. Wielding the scalpel of satire, Irish clergyman Jonathan Swift (1667–1745) parodies human frailties in a seafarer's mock travelogue. Gulliver visits four different imaginary lands. I vividly remember being enthralled when he becomes both a giant in the land of Lilliput and a midget in Brobdingnag. In the end the reader is left in little doubt: human pride is our downfall and Swift does not spare his readers as he satirises the human condition. This kind of satire can evoke strong feelings. "A man is angry at a libel because it is false, but at satire because it is true," remarks English writer G.K. Chesterton (1874–1936).

Wit is akin to satire, but more difficult to define. Wit is more economical than satire and is often found in one-liners. It is usually inventive, quick and clever. A joke with an intentionally good punchline is witty. Shakespeare knew this:

Therefore since brevity is the soul of wit
and tediousness the limbs and outward flourishes,
I will be brief: – your son is mad.

> Polonius in *Hamlet* II.ii.

We all have our favourites. I cannot resist a few quotes from a couple of mine, beginning with the nineteenth-century writer, poet and famed wit, Oscar Wilde (1854–1900). Through his well-known quips runs an underlying seriousness. "God writes a lot of comedy," he said. "The trouble is, he's stuck with so many bad actors who don't know how to play funny." Some of his wit is self-deprecating. "I can resist anything except temptation." "What is a cynic?" he asks, and then answers: "A man who knows the price of everything and the value of nothing." And finally an insightful truth: "Always forgive your enemies, nothing annoys them so much."

Another favourite of mine is Dorothy Parker (1893–1967), the American poet and satirist. She is famous for her cutting one-liners: "Men seldom make passes at girls who wear glasses." And, "I don't care what is written about me so long as it isn't true." Parker's understanding of wit is pertinent here: "Wit has truth in it; wise-cracking is simply calisthenics with words." One of my favourites: "If you want to know what God thinks of money, just look at the people he gave it to." Finally, a truth for theologians: "You can't teach an old dogma new tricks." Wit and satire are expressions of resistance. The tart verve of both wit and satire refuses to compromise, to applaud mediocrity, bigotry, injustice or what is cute or trendy. Wit and satire cut through our self-importance like a newly sharpened blade.

Then there is the gentle wit of American humorist and storyteller Garrison Keilor. His weekly broadcast, *The News from Lake Wobegon*, enthralled me during stays in the United States. His humour is a vehicle for his sympathetic yet insightful disposition towards people. It is a humour that warms while it amuses. "I believe in looking reality straight in the eye and denying it", or "When in doubt look intelligent." Both strike familiar chords. "Anyone who thinks sitting in church can make you a Christian must also think that sitting in a garage can make you a car" needs no comment.

A brief example of a typical kind of benign English humour is that of the legendary English writer P.G. Wodehouse (1881–1975). The relationship between Bertie Wooster, a brainless member of the upper classes in England, and Jeeves, his "gentleman's gentleman," has, in Berger's words, "an inspired idiocy". The following is an example of Wodehouse's enduring "idiocy":

> "In the spring, Jeeves, a livelier iris gleams upon the burnished dove."
> "So I have been informed, sir."
> "Right-ho! Then bring me my whangee, my yellowed shoes, and the old, green Homburg. I'm going to the park to do pastoral dances."
> "Very good, sir".

The sheer inanity of this exchange makes me smile. A "burnished dove" and a "whangee" – what on earth is he talking about? Class and contextually bound, it nonetheless conjures up a picture that is so fatuous that it is comical. Benevolent and non-threatening, it takes us out of the ordinary for one brief droll moment.

In our bathroom there is a well-thumbed book of curmudgeonly humour. A curmudgeon, according to the Oxford Dictionary, is a person who is "churlish or miserly". Churlish yes, and miserly with words it is. Here are some random examples of curmudgeonly wit:

> Freud is the father of psychoanalysis. It has no mother. (Germaine Greer)
> Conscience is the inner voice that warns us that someone may be looking. (H. L. Mencken)
> Religion consists in a set of things which the average man thinks he believes and wishes he was certain. (Mark Twain)

Not surprisingly, people who have known discrimination and marginalisation use humour as a means of resistance. This is certainly true of the humour of the people of mixed racial origins from the Western Cape. Sadly, this humour does not translate well into English. Musician Abdullah Ibrahim describes the humour of his people in the Western Cape thus: "We laugh at apartheid because we never want to be contaminated. It [laughter] is a purge." Whatever the causes for the originality of this brand of humour, it has its own way of reflecting the incongruities in the history of the people who identify themselves as coloured.

> A newspaper vendor is selling the afternoon paper at a busy intersection in Cape Town when a truck with a Free State registration pulls up at the robot. The burly, deeply tanned farmer leans out of the cab window and calls to the paper vendor, "Hey midnight, bring 'n koerant (a newspaper)". "Midnight" sidles over. They exchange money and a newspaper. The vendor steps back, looks the driver in the eye and says: "Djy roep my midnight? Djy's nie so ver van quarter-to-twelve djouself nie (You call me Midnight? You are not so far from quarter-to-twelve yourself)."

The humour of the coloured people is peppered with jokes that are funny while being self-deprecating. Stand-up comedian Marc Lottering, with his wild Afro hairdo and prominent grey streak, is from the Cape and has a long list of reasons why coloured people would not be successful terrorists. Here are several:

> With free food and cool-drink on the plane, we'll forget why we're there.
> We talk with our hands, so we will continually be putting our weapons down.
> We would all line up to have our photo taken by one of the hostages.
> We would all have wanted to watch the in-flight movie first.
> We would have dressed like terrorists for our airport go-away clothes: balaclavas, jumpsuits, karate shoes, dark glasses and a heck of an attitude.
> Before we go into action, we would all have queued up at the toilet to gel our hair.

I love Jewish jokes for their remarkable (and quirky) insight about human failings. Perhaps it is the need to survive situations that have too often been harrowing and marginalising that have given Jewish and coloured people's humour their distinctive character. I cannot resist this Jewish joke from Berger's book:

> Mrs Shapiro from Brookline, Massachusetts, was traveling in the Himalayas, in search of a holy man who lived in one of the most inaccessible peaks of that mighty mountain chain. After many weeks of travel, enduring great hardships, she finally reached that place. A young disciple of the holy man received her and told her. "The holy man is very busy. Today is Tuesday. He can see you on Friday, at three in the morning. In the meantime you can stay here in this cave." Mrs Shapiro stayed in the cave from Tuesday evening until very early Friday morning. It was very cold, she had to sleep on the ground, and

there was nothing to eat except wild berries and churned yak milk. On Friday, just before three in the morning, the young disciple came to pick her up. He led her to another cave. And there sat the holy man. Mrs Shapiro went right up to him. She said, "Marvin, come home!"

A further favourite is the story of the reading of the will:

The Rabinowitz family and friends are gathered to hear the executor read Isaac's will: "To my wife Rebecca, one million dollars, my Cadillac car and our house; to my son Jacob, half a million dollars and the cancellation of his debts; to my daughter Rachel, half a million dollars and a paid up holiday to a health farm; to my brother Abie, a trip to Israel to work on a kibbutz – and to my cousin Louis, who said I would never remember him in my will, 'Hello Louis!'"

In the hands of a gifted cartoonist, such as our own Zapiro, cartoons are a powerful tool. They comment on our social and political foibles, they destabilise and subvert reigning ideologies, and rib leaders lost in their own self-importance. Zapiro has gained world acclaim (or notoriety, depending on one's ideological or religious views) as an acute commentator on life in South Africa. Over the years I have often been angry about the shenanigans of local politicians. A good Zapiro cartoon helps to interrupt my anger and relieve the disquiet of frustrated hope. I seldom miss going to hear Peter Dirk Uys cleverly cut his way through contemporary politics with no holds barred. His other self, the pretentious ex-ambassador to a former "homeland", Evita Bezuidenhout, is now a national institution and a national asset. Other firm South African favourites are Trevor Noah and Nic Rabinowitz for their incisive social and political commentary.

My interest is in laughter that unmasks our pretentiousness and absurdities, and looks the incongruities of life in the face, while not devaluing people. Facing up to our conceits with humour is more likely to equip us to deal with the vexations of the day than a defensive seriousness that is simply a mask for anxiety. For example, having to deal with sexist attitudes for as long as I can remember is hardly fun. While this is not a laughing matter, a wry smile at sexism's inner contradictions and witlessness fortifies my resistance and enables me to cope with its irritating and destructive persistence.

~

As I have already suggested above, the ability to see the funny side of life is scarce in the writing of philosophers and theologians. Religion and laughter have generally been thought to inhabit two different spheres in our lives. One is concerned with ultimate meaning, while the other is seen as a physical reaction to a specific moment. One is serious, the other decidedly not. Apparently they do not go well together.

Both Plato and Aristotle speculated about why people laugh. For Plato, laughing could be a sign of anxiety or pleasure. Ethically he thought it should be avoided as "[…] persons of worth, even if only mortal men, must not be […] overcome by laughter […]." He felt that the writers of comedies that ridicule people should be fined three hundred drachmas! The Delphic ideal was self-knowledge, and ridicule was simply hostile to this ideal. Aristotle acknowledged that "[…] of all living creatures only man is endowed with laughter". He distrusted uncontrolled laughter, yet did not disapprove of amusing innuendos. He stated that "[m]ost people delight more than they should in amusement and in jesting, and so even buffoons are called ready-witted because they are found attractive […] the well bred man's jesting differs from that of a vulgar man, and the joking of an educated man from that of an uneducated." Neither of these two philosophers embraced the human capacity for laughter with notable enthusiasm, and on the whole laughter did not get a good press in their writings. One may wonder why this is so. Perhaps both Plato and Aristotle were alert to laughter's ability to undermine existing social arrangements and to disrupt the social order of the day. Perhaps the uncontrollable in laughter did not sit easily with the need for order and the distinctive role of reason in the life of the "virtuous man".

French mathematician and philosopher René Descartes (1596–1650) thought laughter was a kind of physical malfunction – people laughed when they suffered a sudden flow of blood. Later Immanuel Kant had a kinder view of laughter. He wrote, somewhat ponderously: "In everything that is to provoke a lively, uproarious laughter, there must be something nonsensical [...]. Laughter is an affect resulting from the sudden transformation of a heightened expectation into nothing. This very transformation, which is certainly nothing enjoyable for the understanding, is nevertheless indirectly enjoyable and, for a moment, very lively." He approvingly quotes Voltaire (1694–1778) who says that we are given two things as a counterweight to the burdens of life – hope and sleep. "He could also have added laughter," says Kant. Clearly neither Voltaire nor Kant considered those plagued by insomnia!

With few exceptions, the idea that laughter is somehow suspect has persisted for a long time in the history of Christianity. Christians, particularly members of religious orders, were counselled to keep their faces serious and to behave with decorum that excluded laughing. Clement of Alexandria (born c.150–died c.215) demanded that the faithful should control any tendency to smile. "It is true that man is an animal who can laugh; but it is not true that he therefore should laugh at everything," he warned. Benedict, in his well-known *Rule*, urged the monks to "[p]refer moderation in speech and speak no foolish chatter, nothing just to provoke laughter, do not love immoderate or boisterous laughter". Perhaps Benedict had in mind a kind of loud, ribald laughter that intrudes on the dignity of another. The Cappadocian Basil the Great (born c.330–died c.379) maintained that the Christian "ought not to indulge in jesting; he ought not to laugh nor even to suffer laugh-makers".

The Bible is a wondrously truthful book about the human condition. It says it as it is. It does, however, say little about laughter, playfulness or jesting (and not a great deal about human sexuality). Undoubtedly Noah's building an ark in what may well have been a hot and dusty place is an incongruous tale, but is it funny? David "danced before the Lord with all his might [...]. Michal daughter of Saul looked out of the window, and saw King David leaping and dancing before the Lord; and she despised him in her heart" (2 Sam 6:14, 16). Then she chastises him. But David does not mind making a spectacle of himself and this story records a certain joyful playfulness. (Just a thought – to this day Jewish dancing is joyful, rhythmic and very different from some of the joyless, slow "spiritual dancing" that I have seen in some contemporary churches.)

There is something enigmatic and uncanny about recorded instances of God's laughter in the Old Testament. It is not playful and can even be derisive. When Israel's subject peoples conspire against a new king, "He who sits in the heavens laughs; the Lord has them in derision" (Ps 2:4; see also Ps 59:8). In a more measured way the writer of Ecclesiastes (3:4) reminds us that "there is time to weep, and a time to laugh", but an irksome view of laughter persists throughout the Old Testament. "Even in laughter the heart is sad, and the end of joy is grief", says the writer of Proverbs (14:13). People are recorded as laughing. When Abraham and Sarah are told that at their ripe age they will have a child, Abraham laughs in disbelief, (Gen17:15-21), and later so does Sarah (Gen 18). God does not hold their laughter against them. Their son is born and they named him Isaac (*Yizchak* – "he laughed" in Hebrew). Laughter in the Old Testament is essentially laughter *at* the foibles of human beings or, as in Abraham and Sarah's case, a sign of lack of faith in God.

The Old Testament does, however, have its own kind of humour expressed in puns. There are more than three hundred puns in the book of Isaiah alone! Sadly, though, they do not translate well from the original Hebrew into English.

The first Christian text that refers to laughter clearly assigns tears to this world and joy to the hereafter. "Blessed are you who weep now, for you will laugh […]. Woe to you who are laughing now, for you will mourn and weep" (Lk 6:21, 25). Human salvation is at stake. Laughter's rightful place in everyday life is displaced to the hereafter. Implicit in Luke's words is a criticism of laughter as frivolous and unsuited for serious first-century Christians. Nevertheless, derisory laughter continues in the Christian scriptures. When Jesus tells the crowd that the leader of the synagogue's daughter is not dead but sleeping, "[...] they laughed at him". However, their laughter soon turns to amazement (Mt 9:24).

Recorded attitudes to laughter in the early church are largely hostile. While the Gnostics embraced spiritual laughter and laughter was part of carnivals and festivals in medieval times, the early church was not known for its humour. Perhaps this was due to the fact that Western Christianity was deeply influenced by Hellenistic culture. The Greeks, who differentiated between body and soul, regarded the body as being of less value than the soul. It is likely that laughter, seen as essentially a bodily act, became relegated to the realm of matter with its dubious status. Christians certainly believed that the body was destined for salvation, but for it to be saved, it had to be guarded or reshaped. Asceticism was embraced. The life of a virgin or a monk was prized above all. The church became more preoccupied with virginity, the blood of martyrs and the cult of relics than with joyous laughter.

Laughter was thus seen as expressing a lack of faith, as frivolous and worldly. There were exceptions, however, such as the tradition known as *risus paschalis* (the laughter of Easter). This strange custom is thought to have originated in Bavaria in the fifteenth century. Preachers would tell jokes, encouraging congregations to indulge in long and joyous laughter as a way of rejoicing at the triumph of life over death. More often though, Christians were encouraged to weep over the misery of the world and such weeping was considered virtuous. No wonder Nietzsche quipped that he would believe their saviour if his disciples looked happier about their salvation. Consequently he called his anti-Christian philosophy "the cheerful science".

Fortunately there were exceptions. Martin Luther's writings show evidence of a rough and ready sense of humour. Berger recounts the following stories:

When Luther was asked how God occupied himself in eternity, he replied that God sat under a tree cutting branches into rods to use on people who ask stupid questions.

When a young pastor asked for advice on how to overcome

his stage fright when facing his congregation, Luther suggested that he should imagine them sitting there naked.

When Luther attacked the Archbishop of Mainz, who announced that he would exhibit annually his collection of relics, Luther said that a few new ones had just been added – such as three flames from the burning bush of Moses, a piece of the flag carried by Christ into hell, a wing of the archangel Gabriel, and five strings from David's harp.

Christianity does not have a clear basis in faith for laughter and humour. Sadly it has all too often resorted to humourless dogmatism that can lead to intolerance. Desmond Tutu's remark that "[r]eligion is like a knife: you can either use it to cut bread, or stick it into someone's back" really applies to certain eras in Christian history. To think that a good laugh is in some way or other evidence of something fleshly and profane is unhealthy and untrue. We are embodied people, not beings in whom body and spirit are split into different parts of ourselves. Suffice it to say that religious fanaticism, ideological dogmatism and political tyranny are all marked by a lack of humour.

Ignoring or stifling the comic impulse can be risky. Jesuit Gerry Hughes, writing about false repentance, finds that "[t]rue repentance shares God's laughter and frees the mind to see the humour of situations". Seeing the incongruity in our actions and repenting of what we have done should not only temper our sense of self-importance, but should be cause for a chuckle at just how daft we can be. I want to believe that the survival of what is good and decent about our world depends to a significant degree on our ability to laugh, because people who laugh together are less likely to kill one another. In 1897, novelist George Meredith (1828–1909) wrote in an essay on comedy: "One excellent test of the civilisation of a country […] I take to be the flourishing of the Comic idea and Comedy; and the test of true Comedy is that it should awaken thoughtful laughter."

Through these myriad views and attitudes runs one unavoidable question: why is there no record in the gospels of Jesus laughing? Why did the writers of the gospels not think it important enough to mention the surely indisputable fact that Jesus laughed? They recorded his tears, his anger, his teaching, and his acts of love and compassion. But, according to these writers, Jesus never felt unwell, had a headache, or laughed from his belly. Clearly they were intent on capturing the extraordinary events in his life, and recording his teaching for all who had ears to hear and hearts that were willing to follow his way. Laughter was not a serious matter and was therefore not on their agenda.

John Chrysostom (born c.347–died c.407) was probably the first to point out that Jesus never laughed. We presume that he meant that the gospels never record Jesus as laughing. He stressed the fact that Jesus wept twice, once when he saw Jerusalem and then at the death of Lazarus. Considering the state of the world, Chrysostom thought it more appropriate to mourn than to laugh – a persistent theme in his sermons. Laughter would undermine the foundations of the ascetic life and lead to spiritual laxity. So there is no record of Jesus laughing. The One who was like us in all ways except sin never laughed? This cannot be. Jesus was deeply aware of the incongruities of life. His teaching in parables and his life and death are examples of inescapable contradictions. Surely the joy of being a blessed person must include laughter? The gospels do not relate a tragedy. They are good news, cause for wonder and joy.

Despite this reticence about laughter, Christianity also draws on the idea of the foolishness of our faith and has a long history of the tradition of the "holy fool". "Foolishness" or "folly" acquired a spiritual meaning that included the rejection of worldly cares and the imitation of Christ who endured mockery and humiliation. Paul writes to the Corinthians that in following Christ "[w]e are fools for the sake of Christ, but you are wise in Christ. We are weak, but you are strong. You are held in honour, but we in disrepute" (1 Cor 4:10). Here honour and strength have nothing to do with the common social rules of the day. Weakness and foolishness are marks of honour.

This is because "[…] the wisdom of this world is foolishness with God. For it is written, 'He catches the wise in their craftiness', and again, 'The Lord knows the thoughts of the wise, and they are futile'" (1 Cor 3:19, 20). Inherent in the notion of "foolishness" is paradox. The foolishness of the cross is the greatest paradox of all – God dying a criminal's death on a cross. All human wisdom, knowledge and rationality are suspended. All we can say is: "God's foolishness is wiser than human wisdom, and God's weakness is stronger than human strength" (1 Cor 1:25).

In Paul's second letter to the church in Corinth he again deals with the theme of human weakness and folly and what it could mean to boast in our weakness. In 2 Corinthians 11:23-29 he describes a litany of hardships he has had to endure. He then writes movingly of his entreaties to God to remove the thorn in his flesh. His request is refused. "My grace is sufficient for you, for power is made perfect in weakness," God replies (2 Cor 12:9). Here Paul, the first missionary of the church, shares his discovery of the contradictions and paradoxes of the life of faith. "Therefore I am content with weaknesses, insults, hardships, persecutions and calamities for the sake of Christ; for whenever I am weak, then I am strong" (2 Cor 12:10). Allowing ourselves to be weak, to laugh at our frailty and our inconsistency as we struggle to live out our faith has greater potential for insight and maturity than thinking that we are worthy believers only when we are deadly serious at all times. "But God chose what is foolish in the world to shame the wise; God chose what is weak in the world to shame the strong; God chose what is low and despised in the world, things that are not, to reduce to nothing things that are, so that no one may boast in the presence of God", writes Paul (1 Cor 1:27-29). These words temper, if not sink, our proclivity to egocentricity. We are all holy fools in the making.

The tradition of the holy fool is also present in the Old Testament. When God wants Egypt to take Isaiah's prophecies of its approaching captivity seriously, Isaiah is ordered to walk naked and barefoot for three years (Is 20:2,3) as he predicts Egypt's downfall. Hosea's marriage to the prostitute Gomer – an utterly foolish act in the society of his day – symbolises Israel's infidelity to their God. The sole purpose of such radical actions by the prophets is to call the people of Israel to repentance. At the same time there are many verses in the Old Testament that caution against being an unholy fool: "Fools say in their hearts, 'There is no God' " (Ps 14:1); "Fools think their own way is right, but the wise listen to advice" (Prov 12:15); "It is the wisdom of the clever to understand where they go, but the folly of fools misleads" (Prov 14:8). Clearly there is foolishness that is life-enhancing and foolishness that is not.

The men and women who lived in the deserts of Upper Egypt, Sinai and Syria were often viewed as holy fools. Their behaviour was countercultural, their solitariness unusual, and at best they were considered odd people whose lives bore the fruits of holiness. The ascetic Simeon Stylites (born c.390–died c.459) lived on top of pillar near Aleppo in Syria for thirty-seven years. He was a holy fool, venerated for his prayers of intercession and his theological wisdom. When Francis of Assisi, the son of a wealthy father, decided to devote himself to prayer and service of the poor, he gave away his possessions and embraced poverty. His simple and unaffected faith and his love of nature drew many followers to him. They, like him, lived as "holy fools". He famously said: "Preach the Gospel at all times, and when necessary use words."

The holy fool tradition reached its zenith in Russian Orthodoxy between the fourteenth and seventeenth centuries when a number of holy fools were made saints. For the most part the holy fools of the Eastern tradition were wandering pilgrims, embracing humiliation in imitation of the humiliation of Christ. Often naked, and sometimes violating the norms of decency, they provoked vilification, which was exactly the outcome they sought. Removed from the awesome authority of the church, the fool is playful – with the innocence of a child – while her or his behaviour results in a subtle yet unthreatening resistance to the weightiness of the established church. I venture to think that in modern times both Desmond Tutu and the Dalai Lama would not mind being called holy fools. Both are deeply serious men of conviction. Both share a ribald sense of humour. They laugh easily, they appear not to take themselves too seriously, and they delight in playing the fool.

However, it is Jesus who can be seen as the prime example of the holy fool. This is not the exalted Jesus of church pomp and ceremony, but the man who borrowed a donkey to ride into Jerusalem for his final encounter with the powers of his day. Jesus, who turned the world on its head, taught that to be reviled is to be blessed, that turning the other cheek is preferable to resisting an evildoer, that enemies are to be loved, that treasures are not to be stored up on earth, and that worrying about what we eat, drink or wear is futile, for God will care for us. Jesus could not have been unaware of the incongruity of his actions and his teachings. They were so contrary to the Jews' expectations of the coming Messiah, that they cannot but raise a smile. Aspects of Jesus' life can be read within the tradition of the holy fool. Yet his life on earth was more complex. The wisdom of his teachings, the authority of his miracles, the resolve of his silence when confronted by the might of the Roman authorities, his extraordinary death on the cross and the power of his resurrection present us with the truth of the fullness of his humanity and his divinity.

The belief that Jesus was truly human, yet without sin cannot mean that Jesus lived a humourless existence. On the contrary, Jesus is the perfect example of what it means to be human. To be fully human is to have the ability to laugh at oneself and at the absurdities of life. Jesus must have been aware of what was amusing and incongruous around him. He surely knew the joy of reciprocated relationships in which joy is shared. His birth is announced as "good news of great joy" (Lk 2:10). I see a current of this joy in Jesus' life as he interacted with his followers, performed miracles and broke the barriers that separated people. His restoring of life, giving sight to the blind, reaching out to those on the margins of society, and breaking social and religious boundaries were all causes for celebration and joy. I cannot picture Jesus eating with his friends and followers, visiting their homes, taking part in festivals and ceremonies, without smiles and laughter. Incongruity occurs in Jesus' stories. Perhaps his audience smiled when he said that it was easier for a camel to go through the eye of a needle than for someone who is rich to enter the kingdom of heaven (Mk 10:25). This statement, though serious, is laced with incongruous irony.

I am not trying to make a case for Jesus as the witty, humorous teacher. I am merely saying that incongruity runs through Jesus' life and teaching: his birth in a stable, his friendship with women, sinners and tax collectors, and the unusual images in his parables. All this incongruity is not devoid of humour. I am also affirming the fullness of his humanity that certainly includes the ability to laugh. The ultimate source of Jesus' joy is vested in his relationship with God. His intimacy with God, his constant life of prayer, his unique kinship with God, his utter confidence in God's love and abundant mercy are surely all sources of profound joy. The joy of Jesus is in essence the same as God's joy in all creatures, a joy that allowed the man of Nazareth to break taboos and to liberate people in a way that was scandalous to the religious authorities of his day.

Christianity not only has a long tradition of the holy fool, but the foundation for foolishness lies in the "foolishness of God" so clearly revealed in the life and death of Jesus. The entire story of the death and resurrection of Jesus is one that is exposed to mockery and derision. The "foolishness of God" chooses to be incarnated in a carpenter's son, whose life is short, whose death is ignominious, and whose resurrection is mysterious. Jesus' life was one of powerlessness and power, of defeat and triumph, of resistance to his teaching and of the beginning of God's reign on earth. It is not surprising that Christians should therefore mistrust any laughter directed at those who are vulnerable or powerless. To know God and to embrace God's "foolishness" is what Christian discipleship is about. God's foolishness is a source of our laughter.

I also see this "foolishness of God" as a kind of godly humour in creation. Just as amusing as our behaviour can be, so is that of the animal world. An hour spent viewing a David Attenborough film on the world's insects, or the diversity of creatures living in the sea, or the extraordinary habits of some birds is to wonder at the incongruities in nature. I think God must have had fun anticipating over two thousand species of earwigs in the world. Who would think that crabs have teeth in their stomachs or that giant petrels throw up over intruders to scare them away? I shall never forget the comical sight of baboons wading through shallow water in the Okavango Delta, holding their forearms up high like elderly waders gingerly tiptoeing into an icy sea, or the look on the face of a vervet monkey that had just snatched my granddaughter's apple right out of her hand!

I have never doubted that God's intentions for us are threaded with humour. I only have to look back on my own life to see incongruities that defy reason. That I should spend the last ten years of my professional life teaching at Stellenbosch University's Faculty of Theology is itself an example of God's sense of humour. In the early 1950s I was a student at this university and never came near this faculty, disparagingly described by us at the time as "the angel factory". It represented a form of conservative, narrow Reformed theology that supported apartheid, a humourless place dominated by elderly white men. Today it strives to be ecumenical, and its student body is a mixture of race, gender and culture. Change has taken place and it is a welcoming place across differences. The fact that I, an Anglican, was entrusted with teaching the traditions of Christian spiritual practices, drawing on the insights of Benedict and Ignatius as well as Calvin and Luther, to a largely Reformed body of students is to wonder at God's hand in the incongruities of life!

Surely our ability to laugh is God-given. God knows that we need to be rescued from ideas, attitudes and teachings that snag our beliefs into self-important certainty. So God chuckles with us and, hopefully, we with God. If laughter is part of being created in the image of God, then both God and we must laugh. A covenantal relationship with God for the whole of our lives without laughter simply does not seem possible. We laugh at ourselves. Hopefully, we can laugh *with*, but not *at*, other people.

The Jesus story is a story of a reversal of existing human values that ultimately reveals the absurdity of the human predicament. Measured by all worldly standards Jesus was a failure. Yet it is precisely his "failure" that is our salvation. How absurd! To become what we are meant to be requires being a failure in terms of the codes of the world. How comical! There is no place here for conceit or pretentiousness about our ability to make the grade!

So I am saddened by the general lack of laughter in Christian practices. There is no room for laughter in our liturgies, and our teaching and preaching are too often devoid of humour. We fear that which may destabilise the existing order. We tend to preserve a humourless decorum that conceals the absurdity of our pretensions to being the custodians of revealed truth. Only by admitting that there is something profoundly incongruous between our human inadequacies and the perfection of the Divine can we laugh in a way that tempers and then counters our conceit, pretentiousness and self-importance. Pompous piety, the absurdity of religious utterances that purport to capture the true nature of God, and the silly posturing and power games of some clerics can be redeemed only by seeing just how amusing they are when faced with the awesomeness of a man, who is God, on a borrowed donkey.

At the heart of the Christian message lies an immense paradox. Jesus, the man who had no place to lay his head, whose followers were a ragtag band of people, and who was humiliated and put to death by crucifixion, is hugely at odds with the victorious Christ of Easter morning. To live by this paradox is essentially foolish, but it is to live by the foolishness that confounds the wisdom of the world. It is, in fact, incongruous for it is incompatible with the values and ways of the world. We can only smile at our efforts to embrace this paradox, so central to our faith. We are basically incongruent in ourselves, and thus we are endearingly human.

Being able to chuckle at incongruity enables us momentarily to transcend the ordinary. The comic intrudes into the dense, heavy, difficult and dominant reality, and brings an effervescent, liberating note. There is an old myth that the devil fears laughter. Salvific laughter is healing laughter and a powerful antidote to apathy and world weariness. Laughter punctures the small world of our inflated egos, our conceit and our greed, and allows a stream of life to relieve our inner drought, revive our spirits, and give us a taste of freedom. To chuckle at the incongruities of life is a blessing.

A final anecdote about an artist's understanding of Jesus which does not bear directly on seeing the comic in order to rescue us from self-importance, but which lifts my spirit because it adds something "other" to the story of the crucifixion. On a visit to Javier in northern Spain, I walked around the castle in which Francisco Xavier (1506–1552) was born. A large wooden crucifix stopped me in my tracks. On the lips of the Christ figure, strikingly carved in wood, shining with the patina of age, was a distinct smile. What was the artist thinking as he carved, filed and smoothed the face of Christ? Is this smile the culmination of a life that is utterly pleasing to God; when "[i]t is finished" means "[i]t is *well* finished"? Is this smile the smile of one who knew that this was not the end? On Golgotha, God has the last laugh when our efforts to destroy goodness are finally thwarted.

NOTES

The "years of the locusts" refers to the metaphor found in the book of Joel that was the theme throughout my book entitled *After the Locusts: Letters from a Landscape of Faith* (Grand Rapids: Eerdmans, 2001).

For quotation from William Austin Smith, see: http://books.google.co.za/books?id=2mxo0J8zf_0C&pg=PA71&lpg=PA71&dq=william+Austen+smith+on+comedy+in+divinity+school&source=bl&ots=exWppXjzmG&sig=rIFxwcDmbGQHRi4miT1qQzQ7VIo&hl=en&sa=X&ei=WI0eT_3DK8SfOsOWuKgO&sqi=2&ved=0CDsQ6AEwBA#v=onepage&q=william%20Austen%20smith%20on%20comedy%20in%20divinity%20school&f=false.

Ingvild Soelid Gilhus in *Laughing Gods Weeping Virgins* (London: Routledge, 2009) writes on the origins of humour, examining ancient myths and finding traces of humour in a number of them. It is true that the Greek gods laugh, but their laughter is derisory – they laugh *at* their subjects.

Derisive laughter usually has a victim. "In Homer's works, laughing gods are a stock in trade, laughter being one of the gods' prerogatives and a symbol of their immorality [...]. There are many comic elements in Homer, but the laughter in the *Iliad* and the *Odyssey* is never innocent, even the most comic situation is not without spite," says Gilhus. She concludes: "Divine laughter was hardly nice laughter."

The origins of both the tragic and the comic are obscure. Tragedy as an art form is derived from reflection on human suffering and is found in the theatres of Athens some two thousand five hundred years ago in the works of Aeschylus, Sophocles and Euripides. Aristophanes is thought to have written some forty comedies, of which only eleven survive, filled with bawdy ribald songs and recitations. William Shakespeare's ability to write both tragedies and comedies is surely a mark of his greatness as a playwright.

Recent research has found that laughter is not only a human phenomenon. According to Jaak Pauksepp, professor of bio-psychology, see *National Geographic*, March 31, 2005, "human laugher has robust roots in our animalian past". Apparently the circuits for laughter exist in very ancient regions of the human brain. Research on rats shows that when they are tickled they chirp, and chimpanzees, gorillas and orang-utans make laughter-like noises.

For the quotation from Philip Roth see www.readersfirst.com/hangups.html. See also http://www.quoteswave.com/text-quotes/4255.

I am indebted to Michael Weeder, Dean of the St George's Cathedral in Cape Town, for the examples of local humour.

Zapiro is the pseudonym for Jonathan Shapiro, a well-known syndicated cartoonist in South Africa. I have collected the quips from a number of sources over many years and referencing these would not only be a deadening exercise, but beyond my ageing memory.

Pieter-Dirk Uys, the well-known South African satirist, performer, author and social activist, whose *alter ego*, Evita Bezuidenhout (known as Tannie

Evita), is a white Afrikaner socialite with pretensions to political activism. She was invited by Nelson Mandela to attend his inauguration as State President. Formerly an apartheid government ambassador to a fictitious homeland called Bapetikosweti, Evita has enabled South Africans of all race groups and political persuasions to laugh at themselves. Uys himself is extraordinarily insightful when lampooning the absurdities of the South African political scene and has devoted himself in recent years to programmes for teaching awareness about HIV and AIDS.

The Gnostics were a religious movement that came to prominence in the second century (C.E.) and took their name from the Greek word *gnosis* (knowledge). Early Christianity was a complex phenomenon in which many different groups held beliefs that were often in tension with one another. The Gnostics flourished at the time when the Christian doctrine was not yet firmly established. They attached great importance to *gnosis*, the supposed revealed knowledge of God and of the origins and destiny of humankind. Gnostic writings originating from the fourth century were discovered in 1945 at Nag Hammadi in Upper Egypt and have aroused great interest among scholars.

Søren Kierkegaard (1813–1855), the eccentric and morally courageous Dane who described himself as "essentially a humorist", was a Christian thinker who employed satire. In one of his journal entries he wrote: "But humor is also the joy which has overcome the world." He spent his life seeking answers to one question: what does it mean to be a Christian? He felt that most Christian environments, far from inviting people to embrace Christianity, put obstacles in their way. He criticised the church in Denmark under different pseudonyms, among which was a character called Johannes Climacus who used irony deftly to get his views across.

In more recent times several Christian theologians have applauded humour. Shortly before his death in 1968, Karl Barth apparently said: "Good theology should always be done cheerfully and with a sense of humor." According to Protestant theologian Reinhold Niebuhr (1892–1971), true laughter is akin to playing: "The intimate relation between humor and faith is derived from the fact that both deal with the incongruities of our existence" (quoted from

Discerning the Signs of the Times (New York: Scribner, 1946, 111 ff.)). Catholic theologian Karl Rahner, drawing on the work of historian John Huizinga, introduced the idea of *Deus ludens*, "the playful God". He found the playful God in the words of Divine Wisdom (Prov 8:27-31), who delights in God, rather than in the derisive and mocking humour found elsewhere in the Old Testament. Helmut Thielicke is another rare contemporary theologian who has written an entire book on the comic.

In a delightful article entitled "Boundaries and humour: a case study from the ancient Near East", *Scriptura* 63, 199, South African Old Testament scholar Ferdinand Deist (1944–1997) gives examples of humour among the peoples of the ancient Near East. According to Deist, "[t]hey used humour to draw, underscore and solidify the boundaries of areas where commitment mattered for them, for example, in defining their identity as social, occupational, ethnic, or religious groups. They also employed humour when power relations needed to be challenged, or when hope had failed them."

George Meredith's "Essay on comedy" was first given as a lecture at the London Institution on 1 February 1877 and then published in *New Quarterly* in April 1877 under the title "On the idea of comedy and the abuses of the comic spirit".

Umberto Ecco's *Name of the Rose* (which appeared in 1980) deals with the topic of laughter through the old blind librarian of a Benedictine monastery, Jorge de Burgos. "Laughter shakes the body, distorts the features of the face, makes man similar to a monkey," he says. "Laughter is a sign of foolishness. He who laughs does not believe in what he laughs at, but neither does he hate it. Therefore, laughing at evil means not preparing one's self to combat it, and laughing at good means denying the power through which good is self-propagating." Finally, he declares: "John Chrysostom said that Christ never laughed." This old man's fight against laughter ultimately drives him to madness and makes him a murderer for God's sake.

A literary gem on the topic of the holy fool is Fyodor Dostoyevsky's *The Idiot*. The trials of Prince Myshkin are those of a man who is simply too good to survive in a conniving world where goodness is seen as idiocy.

An engrossing recent work on the folly of preaching and the foolishness of the gospel is Johan Celliers and Charles Campbell's *Jesus the Holy Fool* (Waco: Baylor University Press, 2012).

WORKS CONSULTED

Ackermann, Denise. *After the Locusts: Letters from a Landscape of Faith*. Grand Rapids: Eerdmans, 2001.

Aristotle. *The Nicomachean Ethics*. Translated by D. Ross, revised by J. L. Ackrill and J. O. Urmson. Oxford: Oxford University Press, 1998.

Basil of Caesarea. *Letters, Vol. 1: Letter 22: On the Perfection of the Life of Solitaries*. Edited and translated by R. J. Defferrari. Loeb Classical Library. London: Heinemann, 1926.

Berger, Peter L. *Redeeming Laughter: The Comic Dimension of Human Experience*. Berlin: Walter de Gruyter, 1997.

Bretall, Robert. *A Kierkegaard Anthology*. Princeton: Princeton University Press, 1946.

Brown, Raymond. *An Introduction to the New Testament*. New York: Doubleday, 1997.

Buechner, Frederick. *Telling the Truth: The Gospel as Tragedy, Comedy, and Fairy Tale*. New York: HarperCollins, 1977.

Celliers, John & Campbell', Charles. *Jesus the Holy Fool*. Waco: Baylor University Press, 2012.

Cox, Harvey. *The Feast of Fools: A Theological Essay on Festivity and Fantasy*. New York and London: Harper and Row, 1969.

Fry, T, ed. *The Rule of St Benedict*. Collegeville, MN: The Liturgical Press, 1982.

Gilhus, Ingvild Soelid. *Laughing Gods Weeping Virgins*. London: Routledge, 2009.

Hong, Howard and Edna Hong, eds. *Soren Kierkegaard's Journals and Papers, Vol. 2.* Bloomington: Indiana University Press, 1967.

Hughes, Gerry. *God of Surprises.* London: Darton, Longman and Todd, 1986.

Kant, Immanuel. *Critique of the Power of Judgment.* Edited by P. Guyer. Translated by P. Guyer and E. Matthews. Cambridge: Cambridge University Press, 2000.

Kierkegaard, Søren. *The Laughter Is on My Side – An Imaginative Introduction to Kierkegaard.* Edited by R. Poole and H. Stangerup. Princeton: Princeton University Press, 1989.

Kierkegaard, Søren. *A Kierkegaard Anthology.* Edited by R. Bretall. Princeton: Princeton University Press, 1946.

Kierkegaard, Søren. *The Journals of Kierkegaard 1834–1854.* Edited and translated by A. Dru. London: Fontana Books, 1958.

Kuschel, Karl-Joseph. *Laughter: A Theological Essay.* New York: Continuum, 1994.

Lorenz, Konrad. *On Aggression.* Translated by M.K. Wilson. New York: Harcourt Brace Jovanovich, 1966.

Merton, Thomas. *Thoughts in Solitude.* New York: Farrar, Straus and Giroux, 1958.

Moltmann, Jürgen. *Theology and Joy.* London: SCM, 1975.

Niebuhr, Reinhold. *Discerning the Signs of the Times.* New York: Scribner, 1946, 111 ff.

Nolan, Albert. *Jesus Before Christianity.* Maryknoll: Orbis Books, 1992.

Plato. *The Laws.* Translated by T. J. Saunders. London: Penguin Books, 1970.

Rahner, Karl. *Man at Play or Did You Ever Practice Eutrapelia?* London: Burns and Oates, 1965.

Rose, Gillian. *Love's Work.* New York: Schonken Books, 1995.

Winokur, Jon, ed. *The Portable Curmudgeon.* London: Penguin Books, 1987.

CHAPTER NINE

Postscript: The blessing of birds

As far back as I can remember I have dreamt of flying like a bird. Some of my dreams were nightmares when I collided with telegraph wires. In others, I flew over mountains and seas. I cannot remember the psychological significance of these dreams. What I can remember vividly is a sunny morning some nine years ago when I parachuted – in tandem – off a mountain above Queenstown on the south island of New Zealand. For one glorious minute I soared, caught in an up-draught, and then came down gently to drift over toy-like cabins and miniature trees, over an azure lake with mountains in the distance until we made a running landing on a school field in the town below some thirty minutes later. Momentarily I had tasted the freedom of flight. I could have become hooked, but fortunately my age has rescued me from any further follies of an Icarus-like complex. I do, however, have one item left on my bucket list – a trip in a glider. Why this fascination with flight? And how does this relate to my love of birds? And what has all this to do with being blessed?

Flight and birds are inseparable in my mind. Soaring, wheeling, diving – birds are the sovereigns of the air. Their freedom stirs me. They come and go at will, often just as I have one within my sights. They take off and they land. They change their calls, yet there is a rhythm to their patterns of flight and breeding that makes them at home in our world. As Tim Dee, author and bird watcher writes: "Birds begin and end beyond us, out of reach and outside our thought, and we see them doing things apparently without feeling or thinking, but – and because of this – they make us think and feel."

I am an amateur bird watcher. I am not as proficient as our grandson Seth, who takes groups birding for Birding Africa. My earliest memory of birds is lying in my bed as a four year old listening to the distinctive *kuk-kooorrr* of a Cape turtle dove in the early morning. I would tiptoe to the window and greet the dove that returned over and over again to its perch in our garden. Then one day it vanished and I felt the loss. I trace my nascent interest in birds to that moment. Although I knew little about the different birds, I "noticed" them and enjoyed watching them from my hideout at the bottom of our garden. My next bird memory is seeing a condor hovering above me at the foot of Aconcagua in the Andes Mountains. I was twelve and travelling with my family on the then perilous journey across the Andes from Buenos Aires to Santiago in Chile on a dirt track with genuine hairpin bends. The condor hovered in the air, the tips of its immense wings gently moving, just holding it almost still above our heads. I was riveted and my awareness of a Creator was born in that moment. Later my interest became more focused when I decided that I wanted to know more about the birds I saw on repeated visits to our game parks. My life as a bird watcher began in earnest then. I bought bird books, binoculars, kept lists, became a member of the local bird club – perhaps all signs of what Tim Dee calls "the arrested development of a bird watcher". I fell in love with birds – forever.

What has this to do with blessing? Being a bird watcher says something about a person. Earlier I quoted Emily Dickinson, who said: "Hope is the thing with feathers, that perches on the soul [...]." I wonder if she had a particular bird in mind as she wrote those lines? In Dickinson's wonderful metaphor I see longing and hope and a reaching out, clothed in mysterious feathers. I know there is a long mythological tradition of linking the human soul with birds. I have read that the mystic poet Rumi thought that the human spirit was expressed in a parrot, a nightingale or a white falcon! And I have often wondered at angels and even the Almighty (according to Psalm 91) having wings? What is it in the human spirit that harbours a need "to feather" unearthly beings? And why have I spent half a lifetime pursuing birds? The answer is simple – watching birds has been an immensely fulfilling experience of the bounty of creation and my place in what Mary Oliver calls "the family of things" in her poem *Wild Geese*.

> You do not have to be good.
> You do not have to walk on your knees
> for a hundred miles through the desert, repenting.
> You only have to let the soft animal of your body
>   love what it loves.
> Tell me about despair, yours, and I will tell you mine.
> Meanwhile the world goes on.
> Meanwhile the sun and the clear pebbles of the rain
> are moving across the landscapes,
> over the prairies and the deep trees,
> the mountains and the rivers.
> Meanwhile the wild geese, high in the clean blue air,
> are heading home again.
> Whoever you are, no matter how lonely,
> the world offers itself to your imagination,
> calls to you like the wild geese, harsh and exciting –
> over and over announcing your place
> in the family of things.

Being "in the family of things" ushers us into the wonder of the presence of birds. I cannot recall many bird-free days. Wherever we find ourselves there are always birds. Even a prison inmate can glimpse a bird. This is not surprising, for conservation biologist Thor Hanson in his wonderful book *Feathers* tells us: "On any given day up to four hundred billion individual birds may be found flying, soaring, swimming, hopping, or otherwise flitting about the earth. That's more than fifty birds for very human being, one thousand birds per dog, and at least half-million birds for every living elephant […]."

There are over ten thousand bird species in the world, of which approximately two thousand three hundred are found in Africa. Our pickings are rich for those who have eyes to see and a spirit to wonder. The variety of the bird world – the different colours, shapes, sizes, habitats, behaviours – is a source of amazement. The beauty of a black eagle in flight, the fierce mastery of the peregrine falcon's pursuit of a victim, the vivid colours of a southern carmine bee-eater, the curiosity of a wagtail – all so different, yet all a cause for wonder; all so sublimely indifferent to us, yet sharing our world. I count the abundance and variety of birds as one of nature's great gifts to marvel at with delight.

Birds confront us with a heightened consciousness of time, both past and future. Since the momentous discovery in 1861of *Archaeopteryx lithographica* in the limestone slabs of Bavaria near the village of Solnhofen, the scientific world has been abuzz. This astonishing small creature with the apt name – "ancient wing written in stone" – has bones, claws, delicate teeth and beautifully preserved feathers: a small feathered reptilian dinosaur! It is now believed that birds are, in fact, descended from theropods – two-legged carnivorous dinosaurs. Proof for this theory mounts as, among other things, Chinese paleontologist Xing Xu continues to unearth rich finds of feathered theropods in the ancient shales of the Yixian formation in north-eastern China which demonstrate different phases in the development of feathers on dinosaurs. The wonder of the evolutionary development of species confronts us, occurring across time, not in straight lines, but in networks spreading branch-like in different directions. The story of birds is part of the millions upon millions of years of evolving life on earth.

As interesting as their past is, birds are also a constant reminder of the future. Paleontologist David Raup reminds us that almost ninety-one per cent of all species that ever lived on earth are extinct. This includes birds. Today it is estimated that over twelve per cent of the world's birds are under threat. Loss of habitat and climate change are the main culprits in this unfolding story. South Africa has over eight hundred species of birds, of which three hundred and fifty inhabit our grasslands. As sixty-five per cent of our grasslands have been lost over the last decades, life for the wattled crane, the blue crane, the kori bustard, the secretary bird and other grassland birds has become fragile. My regular copy of *Birdlife Africa* reminds me constantly of how endangered our southern African birds are: Cape vultures, African penguins, Rudd's larks – new names appear every month. I grieve for what may vanish. We forget that ours is no more than a story of moments. We are hardly permanent and are enjoined for this day to do what we can to be preservers and not destroyers. This reminder of the transitory nature of life is indeed a necessary blessing.

A related blessing has to do with memory. I need pointers, tags, or clues to make associations when my memory fails me repeatedly. However, when it comes to birds, I am blessed with memories that associate specific birds with particular events, sightings and places. Guillemots, great skuas and puffins remind me of having my appendix out in the Orkney Islands. The sun on the barred ginger breast of a Pel's fishing-owl takes me straight into the Okavango Delta in Botswana, probably my most favourite place on earth. The noisy courtship of the wandering albatross reminds me of a cliff on an island in the Galapagos. I see hundreds and hundreds of white pelicans on branches of trees, which are drooping under their weight, on Lake Manyara in Tanzania. The rattling call of a Hartlaub's gull puts my feet on the cliff path in Hermanus on the Cape's southern coast. The sight of a colony of over three thousand King penguins on South Georgia will stay with me long after I can no longer see birds. My storehouse of bird memories then fleshes out into places, people, smells and colours, and I can relive experiences that I would otherwise have forgotten. For this I am grateful as time erodes my sight and the retrieve button of my memory increasingly eludes me.

Bird watching is both a solitary and a shared interest. Sharing a birding outing with an interested friend, comparing notes, sitting quietly together in a bird hide, and enjoying veld and forest together are pleasures that are hard to beat. Being alone with birds is also fun. I have written elsewhere about awareness and the need to be mindful of the moment. Bird watching is a quiet activity that sharpens awareness. Being quiet in the bush, watchful and conscious of the smallest movement, a flash of colour, a faint sound, deepens awareness of place, the time of day, the intricate patterns of plants and the immensity of the sky above. A tree in fruit, a hole in a mud bank, an eggshell on the ground are noted as clues to what might be found. Bird watching is a good school for learning to wait patiently and deal with frustration. Birds do not appear on command, even when enticed by expert bird callers. I have never seen a narina trogon despite repeated visits to its habitat!

To watch birds migrating is to witness one of nature's great mysteries. The rhythms and cycles of migrations show us the planet at work. Can a fledgling barn swallow know that it will be undertaking a hazardous journey across continents, that there is no turning back and that it may never return to its place of birth? What is it like to be in the company of millions upon millions of swallows flying north and then south every autumn and spring respectively? What is it like to navigate by the earth's magnetism, the sun and the stars? What mysterious instinct tells these birds to get ready to leave and prompts them to put on as much body weight as they can in the week prior to taking off? Migration routes have evolved over millions of years. Some birds follow landmarks such as rivers or coastlines, others migrate non-stop over vast open distances. The arctic tern flies almost continuously for eight months of the year. It nests in the Arctic and winters in the Antarctic, sees two summers and travels over seventy thousand kilometres each year. No sooner has it finished nesting when it takes to the air again. Migration raises many questions, leaves us awed by the mysterious forces at work that dictate bird patterns, and compels us to embrace mystery.

Human beings have also migrated since the beginning of time: our ancestors moved with the sun, seeking food and shelter, spreading out across new landmasses, adapting to new climates and environments. Human beings have probably shared the exhaustion that birds know after a long journey, and, like them, we have needed to rest, feed, preen and breed. However, never have we known the freedom of the swallow; more often ours has been the experience of exile. The mysterious forces that keep birds moving according to the seasons remain a mystery at which to wonder.

Early one morning some years ago I sat on a mountain path above

Walker Bay on the southern Cape coast. Below me the long grassy slope was alive with birds. Thousands upon thousands of swallows clung to virtually every blade of grass, twittering and gently swaying in the breeze. Then, in obedience to some mysterious call, they took off simultaneously. I looked up. The sky was dark with birds. What I experienced that morning is aptly described by Tim Dee as he watched thousands of starlings take to the sky: "As they wheeled and gyred en masse, the sound of their wings turning swept like brushes dashed across a snare drum or a Spanish fan being clicked open." I was privy to a mysterious call that filled me with awe.

My bird watching days are over. My binoculars can no longer compensate for my diminishing eyesight. I am blessed with a plethora of memories, sights and shared pleasures. I can still hear the harsh *kerrrdik kek-kek* of the helmeted guinea fowl that come down our lane, the sweet whistle of the red-winged starling, the busy chattering of the white eyes and, when in the wild, the piercing call of the fish eagle. I have been blessed for decades by the wonder of creation and gratitude for the Creator's infinite imagination. And when I mull over why I am haunted by flight, I find truth in the words of pioneer aviator Wilbur Wright (1867–1912) from a speech to the Aéro-Club of France in 1908: "I sometimes think that the desire to fly after the fashion of the birds is an ideal handed down to us from our ancestors, who, in their grueling travels across trackless lands in prehistoric times, looked enviously on the birds soaring freely through space at full speed, above all obstacles, on the infinite highway of the air."

All theology is autobiography. The blessing of birds is part of my story of being "in the family of things" and "seeing" through "the felt life of the mind". Through birds I have seen the ongoing handiwork of the Creator. When I look at "the birds of the air; they neither sow nor reap nor gather into barns", and yet are fed by the hand that made them (Mt 6:26), I take courage that all of life is held in that hand, that despite suffering and our inhumanity to one another, we are not alone. Now worrying can be put aside, says the man on the borrowed donkey. Strive for God's reign to come on the earth, "and all things will be given to you" (Mt 6:33), he promises us. I will take my chance on the truth of his words for I have found that doing so makes life worth living.

NOTES

A Greek myth tells the story of Daedalus, a master craftsman, who made his son Icarus wings of feathers and wax so that he could fly. Ignoring warnings, Icarus flew too close to the sun, the wax on his wings melted and he fell to his death.

I think I recall that Jung and Freud could not agree on the symbolism of flight dreams. Was it a case of transcendence versus sex?

Tim Dee is a BBC radio producer and lifelong bird watcher, whose bird memoir, *The Running Sky: A Birdwatching Life* (London: Vintage Books, 2009), is one of the very best books on the love of birds that I have read.

The Andean condor, a large black bird with a white ruff, is a member of the vulture family and at some three plus metres has the biggest wingspan of any land bird. It is a national symbol in Argentina, Chile, Peru, Ecuador, Bolivia and Colombia, and plays an important role in Andean folklore.

Mary Oliver's poem is taken from *Dream work* (New York: The Atlantic Monthly Press, 1986).

In a supremely interesting book entitled *Feathers: The Evolution of a Natural Miracle* (New York: Basic Books, 2011), author Thor Hanson tells the story of John Buxton, a British soldier captured by the Germans in 1940. He was a poet and a bird watcher. He spent five years in German prisoner-of-war camps. During that time he studied redstarts and in 1950 published a monograph based on his wartime studies of that bird. The quote from Wilbur Wright also comes from Hanson's *Feathers.*

Some scientists speculate that the Hoatzin bird (also known as the Stink bird), which I was fortunate to see in the Ecuadorian Amazon, may be linked to *Archaeopteryx* because the chicks have claws on two of their wing digits. This bird has had more data analysed about it than any other bird and yet no distant relatives have been found. No satisfactory hypothesis exists as to its species and where to locate it in the avian family.

For a moving chronicle of the extinction of six American birds, see Christopher Colinos, *Hope is the Thing with Feathers: A Personal Chronicle of Vanished Birds* (New York: Warner Books, 2000).

The narina trogon is a brightly coloured, furtive inhabitant of forests on the eastern side of southern Africa.

WORKS CONSULTED

Colinos, Christopher. *Hope is the Thing with Feathers: A Personal Chronicle of Vanished Birds.* New York: Warner Books, 2000.

Dee, Tim. *The Running Sky: A Birdwatching Life.* London: Vintage Books, 2009.

Hanson, Thor. *Feathers: The Evolution of a Natural Miracle.* New York: Basic Books, 2011.

Oliver, Mary. *Dream Work.* New York: The Atlantic Monthly Press, 1986.